Moon on the Tides:
a Student Guide to the AQA GCSE
Poetry Anthology

Moon on the Tides:
a Student Guide to the AQA GCSE
Poetry Anthology

Dog's Tail Books

By David Wheeler

To Philippa with much love

*This book would not have been possible without the help of my
mother who proof-read various drafts; and my daughters,
Philippa and Flora, who were always willing to discuss ideas
and individual poems. Any deficiencies are mine alone.*

Table of Contents

Who or what is this book for?

Perhaps you missed that crucial lesson on one particular poem that you find hard to understand? Good lessons are better than this book, because through different activities and through careful questioning and probing, your teacher will help you to arrive at an understanding, an appreciation of the poem that you work out for yourself – and that process is invaluable – it's a process of thinking and exploring as a group, in a pair perhaps, and as an individual, and, no matter how good the notes that your class-mates made, those notes are no substitute for having been there and gone through the process of the lesson. So, maybe, through absence you feel a little out of touch with some of the poems: this book will help you.

You may be using some of these poems for Controlled Assessments and you want to read about ideas which you have not encountered in class. You may have the sort of teacher who allows you to respond in your own way to the poems; that is a completely valid and worthwhile approach, of course, but it does not suit every student: some students like to have clear guidelines about the meaning of what they read and to have various interpretations suggested to them so that they are at least aware of the overall gist of the poem. It still leaves you free to make up your own mind and have your own ideas, but it does provide a starting point – this book will give you that starting point. You may even be using these poems to practise for the unseen poem in the exam or to stimulate your own creative writing.

You may be trying to revise the poems in the final days and weeks before the exam and want a quick refresher on poems that you first studied in class a long time ago; maybe it was a Friday afternoon and you weren't paying complete attention; maybe you were late for the lesson and never quite 'got' what the poem is about; maybe you were distracted by something more interesting happening outside and spent the lesson gazing out of the window. This book will help you get to grips with those poems.

It is very unlikely, but you may be reading these poems on your own for the very first time – this book will help you too, because I have assumed that you know nothing about the poem or about poetry, and the commentary on each poem is written so that you can start from scratch. Of course, some of you might find this a tiny bit condescending – and I apologize for that. I should also apologize if there are ideas in this book which are different from ones you have encountered before in class. There are as many different ways to read a poem as there are readers, and each reader might have a slightly different view of a particular poem – as we shall see. For example, most readers (pupils, teachers, professional critics) would agree that 'Sonnet 116' by William Shakespeare is about the nature of love – but how you define exactly what Shakespeare is saying about the nature of love is very much up to the individual reader. And William Blake's 'London' is a bitter attack on the London that he lived in, but quite what the final verse means is open to a variety of interpretations!

So... if you want a book that tells you what each poem means; comments on features of style and structure; suggests the tone or the overall impact of each poem; gives you the necessary background knowledge to understand each poem – then this is it. At the end you will find a glossary of poetic terms and specific advice on how to answer exam questions, but after this introduction, there is a commentary on each poem – each commentary is self-contained and can be read on its own. Throughout the book I have used the words that I would use if I were teaching a lesson on these poems – if I use words you don't know or haven't heard, then look them up. Part of education, part of writing well about Literature is the way you yourself write, so to expand your vocabulary is a good thing.

Help Yourself!

I hope you find this book helpful in some ways, perhaps many ways. It deliberately does not include very detailed information about the authors for two reasons. Firstly, it would be a waste of space. Secondly, the internet is a rich source of information about writers and their work – an internet search on any of your studied poets or poems will throw up all sorts of interesting resources, including student chat boards, online revision chat-rooms as well as more obvious sources of information like Wikipedia or web sites associated with a particular author. Where there is detailed biographical information here, it is because it is vital to an understanding of the poem.

But do be warned – all the information you can possibly find about a particular poet may help to clarify something you already sensed about the poem, but it is no substitute for engagement with the poem itself. And in the examination the examiner does not want to read a potted biography of the poet whose poem you have chosen to write about. Besides - generalizing from what we know about a writer or his/her era is a dangerous thing: for example, it is important to be aware of William Blake's political beliefs and to be aware that he wrote 'London' during the years of the French Revolution – some might say that without such an awareness the poem cannot be fully appreciated and understood – BUT that will not help you explain the impact of individual words and lines and images at all, nor will it help you write well in the examination or for your Controlled Assessment. Very often I have started my commentary on a poem with necessary information to help you understand it, but you don't need to reproduce all that information in the exam - it is there to help you fully understand significant details about the poem; to try to reproduce the process of discovery that a good lesson will guide you through. But it probably has little place in the examination.

You may be the sort of student who is doing English Language or English Literature because it is compulsory at your school. But it may also be that as you progress through the course you come to feel that English is a subject that you like and are good at; you may even be intrigued or fascinated with some of the poems in the anthology. If that happens, then do not rely on this book. Look on the internet for resources that will further your interest. For example, if one poet makes a special impact on you – read some of their other work; you will find a lot of it available on-line. Many of the poets in the Literary Heritage sections are now out of copyright – their work is freely available on-line. Many of the contemporary poets have their own websites which can be a fascinating source of extra information and contain links to other poems or biographical information. So there are many ways in which you can help yourself: it's a good habit to get into, especially if you start thinking about the possibility of doing English at A level.

But please remember this is no substitute for a close engagement with the poems themselves. And just as importantly – this book is no substitute for a good lesson which allows you to think about the poem's language and ideas, and then slowly come to an understanding of it. After understanding it (and that is an emotional as much as a logical understanding of it) you may come to appreciate it. What does that mean? Well, as you go through the course and read more and more poems then you may find that you prefer some to others. The next step is to identify why you prefer some poems to others: in this there are no right answers, but there are answers which are clearer and better expressed than others. And preference must be based on reasons to do with the way the poem is written or its overall emotional impact:

it's your job to put what you think and feel into words – I cannot help you do that. I can merely point out some of the important features and meanings of the poems. As you grow in confidence and perhaps read other writing on these poems or listen to your teacher or your classmates, then you will start to formulate your own opinions – stealing an idea from one person, a thought from somewhere else and combining all these different things into your own view of the poem. And that is appreciation. As soon as you say you prefer one poem to another you are engaging in a critical reaction to what you have read – in exactly the same way that people prefer one film to another or one song or performer to another.

Contemporary Poetry & the Literary Heritage

You will probably have noticed that the poems within each section or cluster of your anthology are divided into two. Why? Contemporary poetry consists of poems written in the very recent past by living poets and they are here because as you study English or English Literature, it is felt to be important that you realize that poetry is not dead and poetry is not written only by dead, white Englishmen: it is alive and it is being written now all over the English-speaking world by men and by women from a wide variety of backgrounds. So the contemporary poems are there to remind you that poetry is alive and well and thriving. Indeed, as I have already mentioned, many of the contemporary poets have their own websites or perform poetry readings which you may be lucky enough to attend during your course.

The poems in the Literary Heritage sections are generally by dead, white Englishmen, although there are some poems by women and some by poets from Scotland, Wales and Ireland. That sounds dismissive (dead, white Englishmen), but it's not meant to be. They are in the anthology to remind you that writers have been writing poetry in English for hundreds of years and that what happens over those centuries is that an agreement emerges about which poems are some of the greatest or most significant ever written in the English Language. How does such agreement emerge? Well, mainly through people continuing to read the poems, respond to them and enjoy them; another concrete way is for the poems to appear in anthologies – which ensures them an even wider audience. The point you need to grasp is that English poetry has been written for hundreds of years and what has been written in the past influences what is written now.

Many contemporary poets will have read the poems that you will read in the Literary Heritage sections. So when you read, for example, 'Sonnet 116' by William Shakespeare for the first time, you will be joining the millions of English-speaking people all over the world who have read and enjoyed that sonnet. Organizations like the BBC have also run public surveys where members of the public can vote for their favourite poem – another way that we know which poems are popular. Such poems then become part of the canon. That is not to say, however, that all the poems in the Literary Heritage section are from the distant past: some like those by Philip Larkin, Ted Hughes and Vernon Scannell are from the closing decades of the 20th century; they are included in the Literary Heritage sections because already there is widespread agreement that these poets are important and influential and that their poems are rewarding to read, study and enjoy.

So part of our heritage, part of the culture of speaking English, whether you speak English in Delhi or London or Manchester or Lahore or Trinidad or Liverpool or Auckland or Toronto or Cape Town or Chicago, is centuries of English poetry and a continuing poetic culture which is rich and vibrant, and includes voices from all over the English-speaking world.

The Secret of Poetry

The secret of poetry, of course, is that there is no secret. Nonetheless, I have come across lots of students who find poetry challenging or off-putting or who don't like it for some reason. I find this attitude bizarre for all sorts of reasons. But some students are very wary of poetry or turned off by it. If you are – rest assured: you shouldn't be!

Poetry is all around us: in proverbial sayings, in popular music, in the nursery rhymes we listen to or sing as children, in playground skipping chants, even in the chanting heard at football matches. All these things use the basic elements of poetry: rhythm and rhyming and very often the techniques of poetry – alliteration, repetition, word play. Advertisements and newspaper headlines also use these techniques to make what they say memorable. Ordinary everyday speech is full of poetry: if you say that something is 'as cheap as chips' you are using alliteration and a simile; if you think someone is 'two sandwiches short of a picnic', if someone is 'a pain in the arse', then you are using metaphors – the only difference is that when poets use similes and metaphors they try to use ones that are fresh and original – and memorable, in the same away that a nursery rhyme or your favourite song lyrics are memorable. Even brand names or shop names use some of the techniques of poetry: if you have a Kwik Fit exhaust supplier in your town you should note the word-play (the mis-spelling of Kwik) and the assonance – the repetition of the *i* sound. There must be several hundred ladies' hairdressers in the UK called 'Curl Up and Dye' – which is comic word-play. You may go to 'Fat Face' because you like what they sell, but I hope that when you go next time, you'll spare a thought for the alliteration and assonance in the shop's name.

Poets also play with words. So when students tell me they don't like poetry, I don't believe them – I feel they have simply not approached it in the right way. Or perhaps not seen the link between the poetry of everyday life and the poetry they have to study and analyse for GCSE.

Poetry has been around a very long time: the earliest surviving literature in Europe consists of poetry. As far as we can tell, poetry existed even before writing, and so poems were passed down by word of mouth for centuries before anyone bothered to write them down. If something is going to be passed down and remembered in this way, then it has to be memorable. And, as we shall see, poets use various techniques and tricks and patterns to make what they write easy to remember or striking in some way. Just as you may remember the words to your favourite song or to a nursery rhyme that was recited to you as a small child. Let us take one example. The opening sentence of Charles Dickens' novel *A Tale of Two Cities* is

It was the best of times; it was the worst of times.

It is not poetry, but it is very memorable, because Dickens uses simple repetition, parallelism and paradox to create a very memorable sentence. Parallelism because the two halves of the sentence are the same – except for one word; and paradox because the two words – *best* and *worst* – seem to contradict each other. Now look at this recent slogan from an advert for Jaguar cars:

Don't dream it. Drive it.

This uses the same techniques as Dickens: parallelism and paradox (or juxtaposition) and it also uses alliteration. It is all about manipulating words to give them greater impact – to make them memorable.

As I am sure I will repeat elsewhere, it is always vital to read a poem aloud: your teacher might do it very well, you might be lucky enough to hear one of the living poets in the Anthology read their poems aloud or you can access many recordings via the internet. The AQA's own website has a recording of every poem in the Anthology. I think reading a poem aloud is a good way to revise it: it has been claimed that when we read something aloud we are reading twenty times slower than when we read with our eyes – and that slowness is vital, because it allows the sound of the poem, the turn of each phrase and the rhythm of each poem to stand out. As we shall see, the way a poem sounds is absolutely crucial to its impact – for one thing, it helps you pick out techniques such as alliteration and assonance.

One of the things we will discover is that poetry is partly about pattern – patterns of sounds, of words, of rhythm; patterns of lay-out too, so that a poem and the way it is set out on the page - often separated into separate stanzas (don't call them verses) – is vital. If you quickly glance at a page from the Anthology, you would probably assume that what is on the page is a poem – because we have certain expectations of the way that poems look. So what? You have probably been aware for a long time that poets often organize what they write into stanzas. For me this an absolutely crucial part of poetry because as human beings we are in love with patterns, we are addicted to patterns – and that is one of the many reasons we love poetry or find it so appealing. Patterns dominate our lives. We may have patterns on our clothes, our furnishings, our curtains, our carpets. But patterns rule our lives more completely than that: seen from above even a housing estate has patterns – the street lights at regular intervals, the garages and gardens in the same relationship to the houses; a spider's web on a frosty morning; the unique patterns of snowflakes; a honeycomb; your school uniform perhaps; the rhythm of your day, of the timetable you follow at school, of your week, of the seasons and of the year – we are surrounded by patterns. And where patterns do not exist we like to invent them: the periodic table of elements (which you may be familiar with from Chemistry) does not exist as a table out there in nature – it's the human need to organize and give things a pattern which is responsible for the way it looks. Or look at a map of the world, criss-crossed by lines of longitude and latitude – and invented by the human mind as an aid for navigation.

What on earth has this to do with poetry? Well, poetry, especially from the past, likes to follow patterns and this structure that poets choose is something we instinctively like; it is also important when poets set up a pattern, only to break it to make whatever they are saying even more memorable because it breaks the pattern. We will see this happen in some of the poems in the anthology.

Let us look at it another way. Take the sonnet: if you choose to write a sonnet, you are committing yourself to trying to say what you want to say in 140 syllables, arranged in equal lines of 10 syllables each and fitted to a complex rhyming scheme. It is very hard to do, so why bother? Partly because it is a challenge – to force you to condense what you want to say into 140 syllables concentrates the mind and, more importantly, makes for language that can be very condensed and full of meaning. And, of course, the sonnet has been around for centuries so to choose to write one now means you are following (and hoping to bring something new and surprising) to a long-established form.

So what is poetry? *The Oxford Concise Dictionary of Literary Terms* defines it as:

Language sung, chanted, spoken, or written according to some pattern of recurrence that emphasises the relationships between words on the basis of sound as well as sense: this pattern is almost always a rhythm or metre, which may be supplemented by rhyme or alliteration or both. All cultures have their poetry, using it for various purposes from sacred ritual to obscene insult, but it is generally employed in those utterances and writings that call for heightened intensity of emotion, dignity of expression, or subtlety of meditation. Poetry is valued for combining pleasures of sound with freshness of ideas....

Remember some of these phrases as you read this book or as you read the poems in the Anthology – which poems have intensity of emotion? Are there some which have a freshness of ideas? Or do some make you think about things more deeply (subtlety of meditation)? Perhaps there are poems which make you do all three? What can I possibly add to the *Oxford Book of Literary Terms*? Think of your favourite song – whatever type of music you listen to. The song's lyrics will share many of the characteristics of poetry, but the words will be enhanced by the music and the delivery of the vocalist. Is it a song that makes you happy or sad? Angry or mellow? Whatever it makes you feel, a song takes you on an emotional journey – and that is what poems do too, except they lack musical accompaniment. So think of a poem as being like a song – designed to make you feel a particular emotion and think particular thoughts; like some songs, the emotions, the thoughts may be quite complex and hard to explain, but the similarity is there. And that is another reason why it is important to hear the poems read aloud – they are designed to be listened to, not simply read. Short poems like the ones in the Anthology are often called lyric poems – and that is because hundreds of years ago they would have been accompanied by music. Before 1066 Anglo-Saxon bards telling even long narrative poems used to accompany themselves on a lyre – a primitive type of guitar and up to Elizabethan times lyric poems were set to music and performed.

Using the Anthology

Your teacher may well have made decisions about how you are going to use the Anthology. What follows here is a simple list so you know what you may be asked to do with the Anthology.

1.   You will probably study and prepare all the poems in one Section of the Anthology in order to answer a question in the English Literature examination. Remember, there are four sections: Character and Voice; Place; Conflict; Relationships. The examination question will ask you to write about two connected poems from the same section, so you really need to know the poems in your chosen section very well indeed.

2.   You may be using the Anthology for a Controlled Assessment. For this you have to range over several poems from one of the sections (probably from a different section from the one you have prepared for the exam) or even range over the whole Anthology. The questions are provided by AQA and change regularly.

3.   Because you face a question in the exam on an unseen poem, your teacher may well use some of the poems in the Anthology as practice for the unseen – these will come from Sections that you have not read or studied in class.

Making Connections

As you can see from what is written above, a lot of the work in English on the Anthology is about making connections – the exam question will explicitly ask you to do this. As you study the Anthology or read this book you should try to make connections for yourself. Free your mind and make unusual connections. For example, there are poems by Simon Armitage in every section of the Anthology; other poets have more than one poem in it; certain types of poems (like sonnets) recur frequently in the Anthology; you might feel that some poems take you on a similar emotional journey; some poems might use metaphor or personification in a similar way; some poems were written at the same time as others and are connected by their context.

If you can connect poems because of their written style or something like structure or technique, then that will impress the examiner more than if you simply connect them by subject matter. The poems are already connected by simply being in the Anthology, and then placed into the four different sections, so to start an answer, for example, by stating that two poems are about 'Conflict' is a waste of words. This book will make connections for you at the end of each section, but you should try to do some thinking for yourself – because it is a good habit to get into and helps prepare you mentally for the exam.

Do you have a favourite word? If you do, you might like to think about why you like it so much. It may well have something to do with the meaning, but it might also have something to do with the sound. Of course, some words are clearly onomatopoeic like *smash*, *bang* and *crack*. But other words have sound qualities too which alter the way we react to them – and they are not obviously onomatopoeic. For example, the word *blister* sounds quite harsh because the letter *b* and the combination of *st* sound a little unpleasant; and, of course, we know what a *blister* is and it is not a pleasant thing. On the other hand, words like *fearful* or *gentle* or *lightly* have a lighter, more delicate sound because of the letters from which they are made. Words like *glitter* and *glisten* cannot be onomatopoeic: onomatopoeia is all about imitating the sound that something makes and *glitter* and *glisten* refer to visual phenomena, but the *gl* at the start and the *st* and *tt* in the middle of the words make them sound entirely appropriate, just right, don't they?

Think of it another way: just reflect on the number of swear words or derogatory terms in English which start with *b* or *p*: *bloody*, *bugger*, *bastard*, *plonker*, *pratt*, *prick*, *prawn* – the list goes on and on. The hard *c* sound in a word like *cackle* is also unpleasant to the ear. So what? Well, as you read poems try to be aware of this, because poets often choose light, gentle sounds to create a gentle atmosphere: listen to the sounds. Of course, the meaning of the word is the dominant element that we respond to, but listen to the sound as well.

You don't need to know anything about the history of the English language to get a good grade at GCSE. However, where our language comes from makes English unique. English was not spoken in the British Isles until about 450 CE when tribes from what is now Holland invaded as the Roman Empire gradually collapsed. The language these tribes spoke is now known as Old English – if you were to see some it would look very foreign to your eyes, but it is where our basic vocabulary comes from. A survey once picked out the hundred words that are most used in written English: ninety-nine of them had their roots in Old English; the other one was derived from French. The French the Normans spoke had developed from Latin and so when we look at English vocabulary – all the words that are in the dictionary – we can make a simple distinction between words that come from Old English and words that come from Latin – either directly from Latin or from Latin through French. (I am ignoring for the moment all the hundreds of thousands of words English has adopted from other languages around the world.)

So what? I hear you think. Well, just as the sounds of words have different qualities, so do the words derived from Old English and from Latin. Words that are Old English in origin are short, blunt and down-to-earth; words derived from Latin or from Latin through French are longer and sound more formal. Take a simple example: house, residence, domicile. *House* comes from Old English; *residence* from Latin through French and *domicile* direct from Latin. Of course, if you invited your friends round to your *residence*, they would probably think you were sounding rather fancy – but that is the whole point. We associate words of Latinate origin with formality and elegance and sometimes poets might use words conscious of the power and associations that they have. Where a poet has used largely Latinate vocabulary it creates a special effect and there are poems in the Anthology where I have pointed out this feature.

Alliteration is a technique that is easy to recognize and is used by many poets and writers to foreground their work. It can exist, of course, in any language. However, it seems to have appealed to writers in English for many centuries. Before 1066 when the Normans invaded and introduced French customs and culture, poetry was widely written in a language we now call Old English, or Anglo Saxon. Old

English poetry did not rhyme. How was it patterned then? Each line had roughly the same number of syllables, but what was more important was that each line had three or four words that alliterated. Alliterative poetry continued to be written in English until the 14th century and if you look at these phrases drawn from everyday English speech I think you can see that it has a power even today: busy as a bee, cool as a cucumber, good as gold, right as rain, cheap as chips, dead as a doornail, kith and kin, hearth and home, spick and span, hale and hearty. Alliteration can also be found in invented names. Shops: Coffee Corner, Sushi Station, Caribou Coffee, Circuit City. Fictional characters: Peter Pan, Severus Snape, Donald Duck, Mickey Mouse, Nicholas Nickleby, Humbert Humbert, King Kong, Peppa Pig. The titles of films and novels: *Pride and Prejudice, Sense and Sensibility, Debbie Does Dallas, House on Haunted Hill, Gilmour Girls, V for Vendetta, A Christmas Carol, As Good as it Gets, The Witches of Whitby.*

So what? Well, as you read the poems and see alliteration being used, I think it is helpful to bear in mind that alliteration is not some specialized poetic technique, but is part of the fabric of everyday English too and it is used in everyday English for the same reasons that it is used by poets – to make the words more memorable.

An Approach

This next bit may only be relevant if you are studying the poems for the first time and it is an approach that I use in the classroom. It works well and helps students get their bearings when they first encounter a poem. These are the Five Ws. They are not my idea, but I use them in the classroom all the time. They are simply five questions which are a starting point, a way of getting into the poem and a method of approaching an understanding of it. With some poems some of the answers to the questions are more important than others; with some poems these questions and our answers to them will not get us very far at all – but it is where we will start. I will follow this model with each commentary. They are also a good way to approach the unseen poem. The five questions to ask of each poem you read are:

- Who?
- When?
- Where?

- What?
- Why?

WHO? This is the first and most basic question. In many poems the poets speak as themselves, but sometimes they are ventriloquists – they pretend to be someone else. So first of all we must identify the voice of the poem. We must ask ourselves to whom the poem is addressed. It isn't always right to say – the reader; some poems are addressed to a particular individual. And, of course, there may well be other people mentioned in the poem itself. Some poetry is quite cryptic, so who 'you' and 'they' are in a poem make a crucial difference to the way we interpret it. Why are poems 'cryptic'? Well, one reason is that they use language in a very compressed way – compressed perhaps because of the length of each line or the decision to use rhyme.

WHEN? This is where context is important. We know our context: we are reading the poem now, but when the poem was written and when the poem is set (not always the same, by any means) is crucial to the way we interpret it. The gender or background of the poet might be important, the society they were living in, the circumstances which led them to write the poem – all these things can be crucial to how we interpret the poem.

WHERE? With some poems this question is irrelevant; with others it is absolutely vital – it all depends on the poem. In the Anthology you will find some poems which depend on some understanding of where they are set for them to work (clearly all the poems in the section called 'Place' are like this); you will find other poems where the location is not specified or is irrelevant or generalized – again it depends on the poem.

WHAT? This means what happens in a poem. Some poems describe a place; some describe a particular moment in time; some tell a story; some have a story buried beneath their surface; some make statements. They are all potentially different, but what happens is something very basic and should be grasped before you can move on to really appreciate a poem. Very often I have kept this section really short, because it is only when you start to look closely at language that you fully understand what is going on.

WHY? This is the hardest question of all and the one with a variety of possible answers, depending on your exact view of the poem in question. I like to think of it as asking ourselves 'Why did the poet write this poem?' Or what is the overall message or emotional impact of this poem? To answer it with every poem, we need to look at all the other questions, the way the poet uses language and its effect on us, and try to put into words the tone of the voice of the poem. Students in the classroom often seem puzzled by my asking them to discuss the poem's tone. But it boils down to this - if you were reading the poem out loud, what tone of voice would you use? What is the mood or atmosphere of the poem? Does the poet, or whoever the poet is pretending to be, have a particular attitude to what he or she is writing about? Answering these questions helps us to discuss the tone of the poem. But you may not agree with everybody else about this and this is good: through disagreement and discussion, our understanding of what we read is sharpened. In the commentaries on each poem in this Anthology this question 'Why?' is answered at the very end of each commentary, because it is only after looking closely at the poet's use of language, form and structure that we can begin to answer it. If you feel you know the poem well enough, you might just use the section 'Why?' for each poem as a quick reminder of what its main message is. For all the poems the 'Why?' section consists of a series of bullet points which attempt to give you the words to express what the poem's main point is.

A Word of Warning

This book and the commentaries on individual poems that follow are full of words to do with literature – the technical devices such as metaphor, simile, oxymoron. These are the vocabulary to do with writing and it is important that you understand them and can use them with confidence. It is the same as using the word *osmosis* in Biology or *isosceles* in Maths. However, in the examination or in your writing in controlled conditions, it is absolutely pointless to pick out a technique unless you can write something vaguely intelligent about its effect – the effect is vital! The examiner will know when a poet is using alliteration and does not need you to point it out; the sort of writing about poetry that consists of picking out technical devices and saying nothing about their effect is worthless. I will suggest, in each commentary, what the effect might be, but we can generalize and say that all techniques with words are about making the poem memorable in some away – and this 'making something memorable' is also about foregrounding language. Language that is foregrounded means that it is different from normal everyday language and that it draws attention to itself by being different – it would be as if we all went round every day and tried to use a metaphor and alliteration in everything we said, or if we tried speaking in rhyme all day – people would notice!

Warming Up

Before we look at any of the poems from the Anthology, I want to briefly examine two poems to give you a taste of the approach that will be followed throughout the rest of the book. So we will start by looking at two completely different poems. I am not going to subject either to a full analysis, but I will demonstrate with both poems some crucial ways of reading poetry and give you some general guidance which will stand you in good stead when we deal with the poems in the anthology itself. This is not meant to confuse you, but to help. I cannot stress enough that these two poems are NOT ones that you will be assessed on. They are my choice – and I would use the same method in the classroom – introducing a class very slowly to poetry and 'warming up' for the Anthology by practising the sorts of reading skills which will help with any poem. Besides, you may find the method valuable in your preparation for answering on the unseen poem in the exam.

The Cathedral Builders

They climbed on sketchy ladders towards God,
with winch and pulley hoisted hewn rock into heaven,
inhabited the sky with hammers, defied gravity,
deified stone, took up God's house to meet him,

and came down to their suppers and small beer,   5
every night slept, lay with their smelly wives,
quarrelled and cuffed the children,
lied, spat, sang, were happy or unhappy,

and every day took to the ladders again,
impeded the rights of way of a another summer's swallows,   10
grew greyer, shakier, became less inclined

to fix a neighbour's roof of a fine evening,

saw naves sprout arches, clerestories soar,
cursed the loud fancy glaziers for their luck,
somehow escaped the plague, got rheumatism,   15
decided it was time to give it up,

to leave the spire to others, stood
in the crowd well back from the vestments
at the consecration, envied the fat bishop his warm boots,
cocked a squint eye aloft, and said, 'I bloody did that.'   20

This is the first. It is called 'The Cathedral Builders' and it was published by John Ormond in the 1960s. I don't think the poet's biography or nationality (he's Welsh) shed any light on this poem at all. However, the cathedrals he is talking about are those built throughout Europe in the Middle Ages, some eight centuries ago at least. Medieval cathedrals are astonishing buildings. You don't have to be a Christian to appreciate their beauty and the amazing accomplishment it was to build them in an age where there were no machines. Salisbury Cathedral is 123 metres high and took 38 years to build: it was started in 1220 and the main building was finished in 1258; the spire (the highest part of the building) was not completed until 1320. They are also renowned for the beauty of their stained glass windows.

winch and pulley – you should remember that every stone in every cathedral had to be hauled to enormous heights through human muscle power alone. The Middle Ages had very limited technology and no machines to replace human effort.

deified – to worship as a God.

small beer – low alcohol beer, produced because the process of fermentation helped to make the water safe to drink.

naves – the main part of a church or cathedral.

clerestories – the upper storey of a church or cathedral.

glaziers – the workers in glass who created the stained glass windows.

vestments – an item of clothing worn in religious ceremonies.

consecration – the act of devoting a building to a holy use.

aloft – up above.

Now let's apply the first four of the Ws to the poem.

Who? The cathedral builders – 'They' of the title are the subject of every verb in the poem; they have wives and children and neighbours; there are also the 'loud fancy glaziers'; and the 'fat bishop' in the final stanza. The voice of the poem is that of the modern poet, but an individual cathedral builder finally speaks in the final line. The poem is written in the past tense.

When? The poem is modern, but its setting is seven or eight centuries ago. The events of the poem last the entire lives of the builders – the length of time it took to complete the cathedral.

Where? Ormond does not mention a specific cathedral by name.

What? The cathedral builders are the men who hoisted huge and heavy rock which had been shaped and worked on by the stonemasons; the cathedral builders actually built the building to such incredible heights. But they live ordinary lives when they are not working on the cathedral. As the poem progresses the builders get older and greyer, but finally, in the last verse they live to see the cathedral consecrated and feel a sense of enormous pride in their achievement.

Students often find it difficult to talk about the structure of the poem, but you should notice that the poem consists of one long sentence – which is surely to suggest the length of time it took to build the cathedral: it must have seemed never-ending – just like the sentence of which the poem consists. But Ormond chooses to arrange the poem into four-line stanzas: this strict pattern perhaps suggesting the overall plan and design of the cathedral – not that it looks anything like a cathedral, but it does have a clear visual structure of roughly equal length lines divided into four. The sentence drives onwards towards the final line when the cathedral builders are given a voice by the poet.

The first stanza concentrates on the work that the cathedral builders did:

They climbed on sketchy ladders towards God.

The first stanza is held together by alliteration. You should note the alliteration on *h* in

hoisted hewn rock into heaven.

Ormond continues to alliterate on *h*: *inhabited, hammers, house, him*. It is much easier in spoken English to drop the letter *h* and you have to make an effort to say them clearly – this works because what it describes takes a tremendous effort – lifting lumps of rock hundreds of feet into the air. So alliteration doesn't just sound good and create patterns – sometimes it can even imitate something and starts becoming almost onomatopoeic. There is clever word-play on *defied* and *deified* and this opening stanza conveys a strong sense of the physical effort involved for the builders.

Because the poem is one long sentence, Ormond uses enjambment several times, but the transition from the first stanza to the second is very effective. The builders, having spent the day on ladders, come down at night to eat and drink and sleep. When we read the poem our eyes move from the fourth line down to the fifth

> *and came down to their suppers*

and our eyes move down to the fifth line just as the builders move down the ladders – so our act of reading mirrors the sense of the poem and this is all made clearer by the use of enjambment. What the builders come down to is a contrast to their working day because unlike their work – which is extraordinary – their lives are very mundane, very human. Ormond uses alliteration in this stanza too – mainly on *s*, largely it seems so that it is a contrast to the first stanza.

Having established this essential difference between their working lives and their home lives in the first two stanzas, Ormond continues to juxtapose the two in stanzas three and four – but this time using the first two lines of the stanza to describe their working life, followed by two lines which describe their lives as ordinary men. The cathedral builders get older

> *grew greyer, shakier*

but the cathedral gets bigger: the men see

> *naves sprout arches, clerestories soar.*

They

> *cursed the loud fancy glaziers their luck*

is an interesting line. The glaziers are lucky because they don't have to work at the heights of the ordinary builders. They also get all the attention, because stained glass windows are very attractive and eye-catching. But there is more to it than that. The words Ormond uses shows the contempt the ordinary builders have for the glaziers: they are *loud* and *fancy* and he uses *fancy glaziers* with its assonance on *a* to make sure we feel the disdain the ordinary builders have for the makers of stained-glass windows.

And finally in the fifth stanza the cathedral is consecrated. The cathedral builders are modest – they stand

in the crowd well back.

But they are also excluded because of their class. *Vestments* is interesting: it means all the priests who would have been present at the consecration and Ormond uses it perhaps to suggest the immense gap between the ordinary builders and the priests; the builders do not know these men – they just see their brightly coloured priestly robes. So the word suggests that the men who actually built the cathedral are excluded. It is also an example of synecdoche – which sounds difficult, but is a technique we will encounter again and which is used in everyday speech too. The sense of their social exclusion is increased by mention of the *fat bishop* (obviously well-fed!) and his *warm boots*.

And then finally Ormond gives the cathedral builders a voice:

'I bloody did that.'

And those four words are, for me, the most important part of the poem. The statement is full of pride at their achievement and Ormond ends the poem in this way because he wants to draw attention to the ordinary men who are now forgotten, but who achieved an extraordinary thing.

Why?

- Ormond wants to celebrate human achievement in building the cathedral, but in particular the achievement of the forgotten, ordinary people of history whose names we do not know and who are not famous.

- This is a poem that celebrates ordinary people.

- It also contrasts their very ordinary lives with the sacred act of building a cathedral to the glory of God.

- The poem also uses structure simply but very effectively – one long sentence with the builders finally given a voice in the final four words.

Here is the second poem that we will look at as an unseen:

The Sick Rose

O rose, thou art sick!
  The invisible worm,
That flies in the night,
  In the howling storm,

Has found out thy bed   5
  Of crimson joy,
And his dark secret love
  Does thy life destroy

thou – you.

thy – your.

Who? The voice of the poet, the invisible worm, a rose.

When? In the night during a storm.

Where? Hard to say... in the bed of the rose.

What? Just using what we know from the poem, we can say that an invisible worm discovers the dark secret love of the rose and destroys it during a storm.

It is obvious that this method will not get us very far with this type of poem or, at least, will not get us beyond a superficial interpretation of what it means. Before you read any further, please read my comments below about William Blake's poem 'London', because Blake is also the author of 'The Sick Rose'.

What can we say with any certainty about this poem? Its mood is sinister. It is night-time and there is a howling storm. An invisible worm has found out where the rose has its bed and is coming to take its life. *Found out* suggest that the bed needs to be hidden. Paradoxically, although the worm is going to destroy the life of the rose, the worm has a *dark secret love* for the rose: this is now especially disturbing – a love which is dark and secret and which is destructive of life. Not only is it night and, therefore, dark, but the love of the worm is also dark and secret and destructive. We expect love to be a positive emotion which brings good things to our lives.

When faced with this poem many readers want to interpret the poem symbolically – otherwise it becomes a poem about horticulture. The poem is full of words that we associate with love - *rose, bed, joy, love*. In addition, in our culture sending someone roses, especially red roses, is a token of love. But this is a love which has gone wrong and is destructive. Many readers also find the shape of the worm rather phallic – suggestive of the penis. Think of all the types of love which might be considered 'wrong' or destructive. This is the list I came up with, but I am sure you can think of many others:

- Love for someone who does not love you back.

- Love for someone who is already married or in a relationship.

- Love which cannot be expressed.

- Love that transmits disease through unprotected sex.

- Love between two people from different religions.

- Love which is against the law.

- Love which is unwanted by the person you love.

- Love between two people of different class backgrounds.

- Love between two people of the same gender.

- Love or sexual expressions of love which are condemned by the church.

- Love which is possessive and selfish.

The point of this list is really to show that Blake's power of compression suggests a love that has gone wrong and leaves us to interpret it. To say that 'The Sick Rose' is about any one of the situations listed above would be totally wrong; to say that it suggests them all and encompasses them all, suggests the power of Blake's writing.

Furthermore, if you have read 'London' and its section later in this book, and if you remember that the rose is the national symbol of England, then this poem becomes even more than a poem about love gone wrong – it becomes a poem about the state of England and a warning that it will soon be destroyed. You don't have to identify exactly what or who the worm is – the poem does that for you: the worm is destructive and capable of killing – it is a symbol of ALL the things Blake hated in his society. Blake's point is that the rose is sick and is about to be destroyed by sinister, invisible powers.

Finally, if you need any proof of Blake's power to compress meaning, just look at how many words I have used in an attempt to give meaning to his words: Blake uses (including the title) only thirty-seven! This is part of the poem's power and art – that it uses powerful words and imagery from which we can extract a multitude of meanings.

Why? This astonishingly compressed and darkly evocative poem is

- a protest about the England that Blake lived in.

- a protest about the way the church and society saw certain types of love as wrong.

- a warning that love – or what we call love - can be destructive if it is not fulfilled.

Endings

This may seem like an obvious point, one hardly worth drawing attention to, but you have seen from the poems discussed above that the endings of poem are absolutely vital and crucial to their overall effect. In 'The Cathedral Builders' the builder is finally given a voice in the final line; in 'The Sick Rose' the final word – *destroy* – carries threat and menace. You will find in many of the poems in the Anthology the ending – the final stanza, the final line, the final sentence, even sometimes the final word – changes what has gone before and forces us to see things differently. So be aware of this as you read and as you revise. When you are writing about poems, the way they end and the emotional conclusion they achieve is a simple way to compare and contrast them. It may not be easy to express what it is exactly that they do achieve, but make sure you write something about the endings, because the endings are often the key to the whole poem. Remember – a poem, like a song, is an emotional journey and the destination, the ending, is part of the overall message, probably its most important part.

The Lay-out of the Book

What now follows is a series of commentaries, like the ones above on 'The Cathedral Builders' and 'The Sick Rose', on all the poems in the Anthology. They are dealt with in the same order as they appear in your Anthology and are divided into the same four clusters or sections: Character and Voice, Place, Conflict and Relationships. After the final poem in each section there is advice on how to link poems from that section - with the examination question in mind, and with suggested answers to the specimen questions that AQA have produced. Finally there is a section on the Unseen Poem and a Glossary; the model answer to the unseen poem I have used for practice appears at the very end after the Glossary.

Character and Voice

In many of the poems in this section poets act as ventriloquists and adopt a persona to tell a story or describe a situation; in others the poets focus on an individual, but use their own voice to describe that person.

Contemporary Poetry

The Clown Punk – Simon Armitage

Context

Simon Armitage was born in 1963 in the village of Marsden in West Yorkshire and has spent most of his life in that area. He is a very successful and highly-regarded poet, celebrated for his down-to-earth language and subject matter. Several of his poems are in the Anthology. His poetry often (but not always) deals with the ordinary incidents and events of modern life and appear to be based on personal experience. 'The Clown Punk' comes from a book called *Tyrannosaurus Rex Versus the Corduroy Kid,* which, as the title implies, contains examples of poetry describing conflicts in a somewhat tongue-in-cheek manner.

punk – a follower of punk rock. However, this word has been around in English for centuries and its meaning used to be a worthless person.

shonky – dirty and derelict.

slathers – to smear.

mush – mouth, face.

Who? The narrator of the poem, the *town clown* and the narrator's children – the *kids in the back seat.* The poem is written in the present tense, but looks forward to the future in thirty years' time.

When? The present.

Where? In the *shonky* part of town at some traffic lights.

What? The clown punk pushes his face against Armitage's windscreen while his car is stopped at traffic lights. According to Armitage, this poem was based on a real incident.

Commentary

Unusually this poem is a sonnet – unusually because sonnets are more traditionally used for different subject matter than the one we find here. Armitage uses a mixture of full rhyme, internal rhyme and half rhyme, and there are no capitals (except at the start of sentences) which add to the unconventional feel given to this most traditional of forms.

The first quatrain seems addressed to the reader or a fellow resident of Armitage's home town and tells us that quite often, on the rough side of town, you will see the town clown. There is a marvellous simile to describe his untidy appearance

like a basket of washing that got up

and walked.

He does not have a dog lead, but just a rope – the assonance (*towing a dog on a rope*) adding to the comic picture and the slightly derisive tone. The sense that the poem is light-hearted up to this point is emphasized by Armitage's earlier use of slang – *shonky* – and the casual contraction of *you'll*.

However, the second quatrain reminds us – *don't laugh*. The punk is covered with tattoos which will never fade (*indelible ink*) and at the end of the quatrain Armitage urges us to

think what he'll look like in thirty years' time.

And the third quatrain reminds us of the ageing that will come to all of us – *the deflated face and shrunken scalp. Daubed* in line 10 suggests that the tattoos have been done poorly and *sad tattoos* suggests that they will, in thirty years' time, look merely pathetic. In line 11 Armitage's children are addressed: they *wince and scream* as the punk slathers his face against the windscreen: the assonance in *slathers... daft* and the slang word *mush*, suggest contempt and derision towards the punk.

In the final couplet the poet warns his children to remember the *clown punk with his dyed brain.*

Does *dyed brain* suggest that he is mentally trapped by his outlandish appearance, his out-of-date rebellion? It certainly connects the tattoos with his brain. What are we to make of the final line? Armitage urges his children to

picture windscreen wipers, and let it rain.

It seems rather dismissive of the punk – as if a bit of rain will wash away the memory of his face squashed against the windscreen, frightening the poet's children. Or perhaps we can detect some sympathy – for all his outlandish appearance and the tattoos which are a sign of his past-rebellion, the punk will grow old and become not a frightening figure who makes children scream, but an irrelevance, as easily wiped from our memories as rain from a car's windscreen. The punk's rebellion, expressed through his appearance and clothes, which was intended to be intimidating, has become simply comic. Armitage and his children are protected in their car and seem to symbolize a normal, conventional life which the punk has refused.

Why?

This interesting modern sonnet deals with:

- the effects of ageing and time.
- the position of the marginalized outsider.
- the inevitable end of youthful rebellion.
- it uses colloquial language and slang perfectly suited to its subject matter.

Checking Out Me History – John Agard

Context

John Agard was born in the former British colony of Guyana in 1949 and he has written many books for children and adults. He moved to Britain in 1977 and lives in Sussex with his partner Grace Nichols – who is also a poet. There are other poems by Agard and Nichols in the Anthology. Agard is well-known as a skilled and adept performer of his own poems and you may get the chance to see him perform his poems during your course. You should check out his performance of the poem 'Half- Caste' on YouTube, because his performance helps to bring the poem alive. In many of his poems he uses Caribbean accent and dialect to bring a Guyanese identity to his work, but he also uses Standard English in some poems – for example, in 'Flag' which is also in the Anthology.

This poem mentions certain historical figures and it is important to know who they are.

1066 is a crucial date in English history because it marked the start of the Norman/French takeover of English society.

Dick Whittington is a figure from English legend – a poor boy with nothing apart from a cat who became Lord Mayor of London and is the subject of fairy tales and pantomimes.

Toussaint L'Ouverture (1743 – 1803) was the black leader of the Haitian revolution against French colonial rule. He abolished slavery in Haiti and turned it into an independent republic.

Nanny de Maroon – *Maroon* is a general term used to describe black slaves brought to European colonies in the West Indies and South America who escaped from slavery and then lived in remote areas of the jungle in the colonies to which they had been transported. Nanny de Maroon (1700 – 1740) is the only woman who has been proclaimed a heroine of Jamaican history. She was a real historical figure who led the maroons on Jamaica in a rebellion against British rule. She organized many slave escapes, led the Maroons to victory in various battles against British troops and finally won improvements in the way slaves were treated in the plantations on the island.

Lord Horatio Nelson was a famous English admiral who inflicted a massive defeat on the French navy at the sea battle of Trafalgar in 1805. Although Nelson was killed in the course of the battle, he became a national hero and his destruction of the French navy resulted in the strengthening and extension of the British Empire.

The Battle of Waterloo in 1815 was the final defeat of the French army led by Napoleon. It confirmed Britain's status as the world's first super-power.

Shaka (1787 – 1828) was an influential leader of the Zulu nation. He united the Zulu people against other tribes and the increasing presence of white settlers, and made important innovations in battle tactics and new weaponry.

Caribs and Arawaks were the original inhabitants of the West Indies at the time that Columbus 'discovered' the islands. They were killed off either by war or through exposure to European diseases to which they had no immunity. 'Discovered' is in inverted commas there, because he only discovered it for Europeans; the islands and their inhabitants were already there!

Florence Nightingale (1820 – 1910) was a famous British nurse. She became legendary for her work in the Crimean War and for her innovations in hygiene and in post-operative care of patients.

Robin Hood was a legendary English hero, famed for fighting unjust authority (represented by the Sheriff of Nottingham) and for stealing money from the rich and giving it to the poor.

Mary Seacole (1805 – 1881) was a Jamaican woman who travelled to the Crimea to tend to wounded British soldiers in the same way as Florence Nightingale did. In her lifetime Seacole was as well-known as Nightingale, but she gradually faded from public memory. More recently, however, through writers such as Agard, she has been remembered as an example of a heroic black woman who made a unique contribution to our history.

The Crimean War (1854 – 56) was fought between the Russian Empire on one side and Britain, France and the Ottoman Empire on the other. Most of the fighting took place on the Crimean Peninsula (which is now in the Ukraine). The concentration of large numbers of troops in a relatively small area led to outbreaks of diseases such as cholera and, combined with poor supplies of food, resulted in many unnecessary deaths. At the start of the war the hospital facilities were inadequate and very unclean – a situation which Florence Nightingale did much to improve.

Agard also makes allusions to various well-known English nursery rhymes: 'The Cow Jumped Over the Moon' and 'Old King Cole'.

Dem – they.

me – my.

bout – about.

dat – that.

lick back – defeated.

de – of.

see-far woman – a woman who had a vision of how escaped slaves might live more freely.

Who? Agard speaks as himself protesting about the way black culture and history have been ignored or marginalized.

When? The poem is set in the present day, but looks back at the education system in Guyana and in the UK.

Where? There is no specific location.

What? Throughout the poem we alternate between lines full of references to white Europeans and their culture with different stanzas celebrating the achievements of black men and women.

Commentary

Agard was born in Guyana and this poem explores the contrast between the history that everyone is taught in schools and is common or general knowledge, and the history that is not widely taught or known about. The 'official' versions of history are filled with white people because, Agard and many others would say, it has been written by white people and it deliberately excludes famous black men and women who have had a remarkable effect on history or who deserve to be more widely recognized.

In the first stanza Agard begins with simple repetition. The tone is accusatory and angry:

Dem tell me

Dem tell me

What dem want to tell me.

Those three words – *Dem tell me* – are going to be used at the start of all the four line stanzas that rhyme. The repetition serves to emphasize the control that white society has over history. If you control the knowledge of the past, then you can control how people think and, more importantly, how they think about themselves, their sense of self-esteem and pride. Agard presents this distortion of history as a deliberate act in lines 4 and 5:

Bandage up me eye with me own history

Blind me to me own identity.

The alliteration on *b* at the start of each line suggests that this distortion of history is destructive and deliberate. Agard's choice of language in this poem is significant. In other poems he uses standard English, but it is appropriate that he should use spelling which imitates the way he speaks in this poem. The poem is all about his true identity – as revealed in the forgotten but heroic black figures of history; his voice is also part of his identity, reflecting his culture and background.

Line 6 begins a quatrain which is repeated in form throughout the poem. In each quatrain Agard begins by mentioning famous white figures from British history and usually ends the quatrain with some mention of a a black historical figure who is left out of the historical accounts. But there is more going on than that. The style of the quatrains with their predictable rhymes emphasize the childishness of what he has been told about the past and, as well as mentioning white heroes from British history, he also mentions characters from nursery rhymes and myth. The effect of all this is to mock what he has been told about the past and the attitudes of those who seek to ignore or marginalize black achievements.

Interspersed with these quatrains are longer verses which concentrate, in turn, on someone famous and remarkable from black history: Toussaint L'Ouverture, Nanny de Maroon and Mary Seacole. What is really important though is the way these verses are written: they lack the tone of mockery of the quatrains; they are italicized so that they stand out visually; the lines are shorter; they are written in free verse which is appropriate because Agard is using an unconventional form to introduce unconventional ideas. Agard does use some rhyme but not in the highly regular way he does in the quatrains, so the language does not feel predictable. Also they are filled with metaphor and positive imagery to convince us of the extraordinary nature of the figures that Agard chooses to write about. Here is the verse about Nanny de Maroon:

Nanny

see-far woman

of mountain dream

fire-woman struggle

hopeful stream

to freedom river

This uses language in unusual and original ways – *see-far, fire-woman* – because Agard is introducing unusual people whom we may not have heard of and his use of ellipsis makes her achievements sound extraordinary. In a similar way, the metaphor used to describe Mary Seacole is full of hope and promise –

a yellow sunrise

to the dying.

You might note too that nowhere in the poem does Agard use any punctuation – it is as if the rules of punctuation – like the white version of history – is something he chooses to reject, because it threatens his identity and imposes someone else's rules on him.

In the final stanza he angrily points out again that

Dem tell me wha dem want to tell me

but now he knows about Toussaint, Nanny de Maroon and Mary Seacole he is able to carve out his own identity and reclaim his pride.

Why?

This cleverly constructed poem

- uses a distinctive voice to reclaim black identity from the official white versions of history.

- makes the reader aware of our own assumptions about British history.

- introduces us to famous black men and women who achieved extraordinary things and acts as a memorial to them.

- rehabilitates the memory of black men and women who made extraordinary contributions to human history.

- reminds us that whoever controls the past controls the present.

- cleverly uses two types of stanza in order to underline the differences between the official version of history and the alternative view of the past.

- demonstrates that without a history and without a distinctive voice we may have no identity.

Horse Whisperer – **Andrew Forster**

Context

Andrew Forster was born in 1964 in South Yorkshire and, having lived in Scotland for twenty years, is now based in Cumbria. His first collection of poems, *Fear of Thunder*, was published in 2007 and 'Horse Whisperer' appeared in that collection. Apparently Forster read about horse whisperers in a book owned by a friend at a time when he was 'exploring writing in different voices and this seemed like an interesting subject to explore'. Forster has been acclaimed for his powers of narration and his physical descriptions: this poem adopts the voice of a horse whisperer and tells a carefully constructed story as well as giving us a strong visual sense of the horses – this will become clearer in the commentary below.

Horse whispering is the art of training or calming down horses which were violent and uncontrollable. You can find out more about it through an internet search, but it was and is cloaked in some mystery because the men who were horse-whisperers often kept their techniques secret. Why? Well, they could earn good money from being able to pacify and control dangerous horses and so the secrets of their craft tended to remain hidden. Horses can cost a lot of money and before the age of cars, the infrastructure of even the most civilized countries relied very heavily on horses. Successful horse-whisperers could demand huge fees for taming horses. The term 'horse-whisperer' came about because people who watched these men at work saw the horse-whisperer going up to the horse, looking it in the face and speaking to it – whispering so that no-one could hear what was being said. Of course, with the invention of the car and tractors, the economic importance of horses faded and so did demand for the services of horse whisperers. There is still uncertainty and a certain mystique surrounding what horse whisperers actually did.

rosemary, cinnamon – sweet-smelling herbs.

legacy – whatever you leave behind you.

pulpits – the raised part of a church from which the priest delivers his sermon.

hex – a spell which brings bad luck.

Shire, Clydesdale, Suffolk – breeds of huge, very powerful horses which were used to pull heavy loads.

Who? The poem is narrated by a horse whisperer in the past tense until a sudden switch to the present tense in line 31. 'They' are mentioned – these are the farmers who need his skills in calming horses and making them obedient.

When? Unclear, but his skills become irrelevant because of the development of new technology – the tractor. So we can speculate that this is in the early part of the 20th century.

Where? There is a generalized rural setting in a country which the horse whisperer leaves in the fourth verse.

What? The narrator describes how his skills were very much in demand until the arrival of the tractor and how he is no longer needed by the farming community. He goes into exile.

Commentary

In the first stanza the narrator tells us that *They* shouted for him when they needed his services and he describes his methods. The second stanza is very like the first. It repeats the opening line, gives us a sense of panicking horses and some detail of the horse whisperer's art. In the third stanza the tractor arrives and his skills are now seen as dangerous, superstitious nonsense: he is denounced in churches as a demon and a witch. In the fourth stanza the narrator takes his revenge on the community who no longer need him by putting a curse above a stable door so that the horses will start to behave badly. Then he emigrates – an outcast from the society that once needed his skills so much. The final stanza sees a change to the present tense and the narrator pays tribute to the power and magnificence of the horses he used to tame. The poem ends with a strong sense of nostalgia for the past and pride in himself and in the horses – this is emphasized through simple repetition

the pride,

most of all the pride.

This summary does not do justice to the poem at all. How are the horses presented in this poem? They have physical strength: *shimmering muscles, stately heads, searing breath, glistening veins, a steady tread* and, most importantly, *pride*. They are tender giants. The presentation of the horses is overwhelmingly positive and full of respect and affection. The horse whisperer himself is perfectly in harmony with these powerful beasts: he whispers – the farmers shout. In his hands the horses become like helpless children. By contrast the owners of the horses are almost wholly anonymous – they shout for the whisperer when they need him and then reject him cruelly when he and the horses are replaced by the tractor.

The arts of the horse whisperer are presented as esoteric and arcane with a whiff of magic and secret arts attached to them. He used a *spongy tissue* scented with herbs to pacify the horses; *a frog's wishbone* to fight the fear the horses have of fire. I find this detail very exotic and quaint. This poem has a very interesting structure. Each stanza is shorter than the preceding stanza: this reflects how the horse whisperer and his influence fade over the course of time as he is replaced by modern technology.

Why? This poem is

- a lament for the past.

- a celebration of the power of horses which exudes a sense of deep regret that their numbers have declined with the coming of modern technology.

- a celebration of the skills of the horse whisperer, for whom we are encouraged to feel empathy.

- an evocation of a lost world of mystery and magic.

- a reflection on what we sometimes lose for the price of technological progress.

Medusa – Carol Ann Duffy

Context

Carol Ann Duffy is one of the UK's most successful and best-known living poets. Her poems have a very wide appeal. On May 1st 2009 she became the nation's Poet Laureate – the first woman ever to hold the position. There are several poems by Duffy in this Anthology and her poems are often set for study by the examination boards – because they are thought of very highly and because many of them are very accessible. Her poems often use very modern and everyday language, but in fresh, funny and witty ways. She uses traditional forms like the sonnet and the dramatic monologue, but succeeds in breathing new life into these old forms by the modernity of her writing and subject matter. The accessibility of many of her poems may obscure the fact that she is highly skilled at a very intricate and ingenious manipulation of language.

'Medusa' comes from her 1999 collection – *The World's Wife* – which is a collection of dramatic monologues written from the point of view of women ignored by history in favour of their more famous male husbands – Anne Hathaway (Shakespeare's wife), Elvis Presley's sister, Mrs Darwin.

The story of Medusa which comes to us from Greek myth is very famous, and artists and writers have been inspired by it over many centuries. According to myth, Medusa was a beautiful priestess at the temple of Athena. She was seduced by Poseidon, the god of the Sea, and became pregnant by him. Athena was so angry at this act of betrayal that she turned Medusa's hair into serpents and made her face so ugly that if any man looked at her he would be turned to stone. Still motivated by revenge, Athena sent the hero Perseus to kill Medusa by cutting off her head. In order that he would not have to look at her directly, Athena gave Perseus a mirrored shield so that he could see Medusa but not look at her directly and thus avoid being turned into stone. Perseus succeeded in his mission.

Throughout the centuries artists and sculptors have returned to the Medusa myth and, forgetting her original beauty (which is why Poseidon seduced her) she has become a symbol of female evil and malevolence. However, feminists have re-interpreted the myth and Medusa's horrific appearance as symbolizing female rage against all the abuse and exploitation committed by men. There is a strong element of this in the poem as we shall see in the commentary.

Gorgon – originally from Greek myth, it has come to mean a very ugly or formidable woman.

Who? Medusa laments her fate and appears to address Perseus in the final stanza who has come with a shield for a heart. The poem is written in the past tense except for the imperative in the final line.

When? The poem has no specific historical setting – which is part of its power.

Where? No specific location – it could be anywhere.

What? The speaker re-tells the story of the Medusa myth, but by mentioning no names manages to transform the myth into a different story with a psychological drama – the speaker's feelings of betrayal – at its heart.

Commentary

This poem can be read as being simply about the Medusa myth as it has come down to us from the Ancient Greeks; on the other hand, because of the way Duffy re-works the myth, it can be read as the dramatic monologue of any woman in any age who has been betrayed by her male lover or who is worried that she will lose her man because of her fading looks. Duffy takes this centuries-old myth and turns it into an extended metaphor for all women.

The first stanza details the moment that Medusa's hair turned into snakes. In this version of the story it is the speaker's own feelings that have resulted in this transformation:

A suspicion, a doubt, a jealousy

grew in my mind,

which turned the hairs on my head to filthy snakes.

The suspicion, from the rest of the poem, seems to be about her lover and his faithfulness. Duffy's genius is to take the old myth and create a psychological reason for the hair turning into snakes. As the speaker says, it's as though her thoughts *hissed and spat on my scalp*. *Hissed* and *spat* are onomatopoeic and *spat* alliterates with *snakes* and *scalp* to make the stanza memorable.

The second stanza's first line is held together by continued sibilance – *soured, stank* – and given further harshness by the plosive alliteration of *bride's breath*. The sibilance is reminiscent of the way snakes really do hiss, so it has an onomatopoeic quality too. Half way through the stanza Duffy changes to the present tense to show that the psychological damage of the speaker's doubt is still present. The speaker claims she is *foul mouthed, foul tongued, yellow fanged*. She cries but with *bullet tears* – which hold an element of threat and violence. She then asks:

Are you terrified?

At this stage of the poem it is not clear who she is addressing.

The first line of stanza three answers this question with an imperative: *Be terrified*. The speaker goes on to explain the reason for him to be terrified – she loves him, but because her love is possessive and jealous, and because she fears that he will leave her, she would rather turn him to stone so that he will never be able to leave.

In the next three stanzas the speaker demonstrates her powers. In the fourth stanza she merely glances at things and they die: here a bee becomes *a dull grey pebble* and a singing bird *spattered* down to earth as *a handful of dusty gravel*. In the fifth stanza her power encompasses mammals: a cat is transformed into a house brick and a pig becomes

a boulder rolled

in a heap of shit.

Note how *shattered, snuffling* and *shit* all alliterate and *bowl/boulder/rolled* use assonance. The sixth stanza sees her powers growing: she has been transformed into a Gorgon and when she stares at a dragon he becomes a fire-spewing mountain. These three stanzas – the fourth, fifth and sixth – like the rest of the poem are written in almost free verse, but Duffy imposes a pattern on them. Think of each stanza as two halves each of three lines. The first line is broadly similar *I glanced* becomes *I looked* and then *I stared*; this is followed by whatever she saw and the second line is whatever that thing has been transformed into; the final line of each three line unit is then what happened to the now-transformed creature. Duffy also uses half-rhyme in the third and last lines of each of these three stanzas. As in many other poems, the half-rhyme seems to suggest that something is profoundly wrong with this situation.

The penultimate stanza addresses Perseus directly. He has come prepared not to be turned into stone. He has a shield for a heart and a sword for a tongue and he is accompanied by his female admirers, further evidence of male betrayal, especially as they are *girls* and therefore younger than Medusa. This prompts Medusa to ask

Wasn't I beautiful?

Wasn't I fragrant and young?

At this point the poem seems to depart from the myth and to become a universal lament for lost looks and fading beauty. The final line is isolated – as is the speaker – and contains an element of self-pity for her lost beauty:

Look at me now.

But, of course, if we do accept her invitation and look at her we will be turned into stone.

This poem is written in a series of short, simple and very direct sentences. Duffy mixes references to the myth with references to ordinary life (the cat, the pig) to explore the connections between the two. Yet none of the objects in the poem is especially modern (indeed, the dragon is a creature of myth and suggests the distant past) and this gives the poem an eternal, timeless quality suggesting that Medusa's plight is one shared by women across the centuries.

And what exactly is her plight? Having been betrayed by her lover, she thinks of herself as ugly and she is transformed physically, not by a God as she is in the myth, but by the accumulation of her suspicions and jealousy. As soon as she has become ugly and unwanted and unloved, her look kills other things and sucks the life out of them: in stanzas four, five and six all the things she turns into inanimate objects are living and moving – until she looks at them. Her ability to love has been destroyed by her betrayal and it affects her whole outlook on life.

The Perseus figure who is addressed in the penultimate stanza is partly a figure from myth – he has a shield and a sword. But these items – the shield and the sword – may be seen symbolically as things to defend himself with: so far from being just Perseus, he is a man who does not want to commit himself and who wants to protect himself from this woman whose love is essentially destructive – she has the ability to turn him to stone. In ordinary English we talk of someone having a heart of stone – lacking the ability to love unreservedly and whole-heartedly. Medusa in this poem can be seen like that. In turn, she affects the men who encounter her, so Perseus has a shield for a heart to protect himself from love.

This is what makes the poem so rich: the way Duffy has taken a centuries-old myth and not simply updated it, but shown its psychological depth. Betrayal and deceit lead to distrust, destruction and an inability to love. And beneath it all is the fear of being abandoned by your lover for a younger, more attractive partner. Do we live in a superficial society where women are judged by the way they look and their apparent youth? But then in the poem the speaker has been made to feel ugly by her lover's betrayal of her and, because of this, she will never trust another man again.

Why?

This modern re-telling of the Medusa myth:

- becomes a lament for all betrayed women and a cry for revenge on all unfaithful men.

- movingly shows the physical decay that comes with age.

- reveals the psychological reasons for Medusa's transformation.

- uses simple, clear language in new and startling ways.

Singh Song! – Daljit Nagra

Context

Daljit Nagra was born in 1966 to Punjabi Indian parents. He has been hailed as one of the most exciting poets of his generation. His first collection *Look We Have Coming to Dover!* is full of monologues which attempt to capture the experience in Britain of the Indian working classes. His poetry is preoccupied with what it is like to be an Asian growing up and living in Britain, so his work touches on issues of belonging, identity, racism, but also what it means to be British. It is a stereotype of Indian-ness that they run corner shops; when many Indians first arrived in the UK, it was certainly one quick and legitimate way for them to establish themselves in business, because they could buy a corner shop and run it as they chose without any barriers because of their race.

Who? The narrator is Singh, an Indian shopkeeper who runs one of his father's shops. There are references to his parents, to his new bride and to the customers of his shop.

When? Now – in the early 21st century. The poem describes a typical day for the narrator and ends in the evening when the moon is visible.

Where? In the narrator's father's shop and the flat upstairs where his new bride waits for him. The mention of Putney in line 9 suggests it might be set in south west London.

What? Singh describes his day in the shop and the time he spends with his wife upstairs in the flat.

Commentary

In this amusing yet ultimately tender poem Nagra adopts the voice of a young Indian man in the UK who runs one of his father's corner shops. This partly corresponds to a racial stereotype about Indians running corner shops in urban or suburban areas. Nagra embraces the stereotype and reveals a truth behind the image. Although the overall effect is deeply funny, the poem also raises serious questions about identity and culture.

The title of the poem is a pun. The narrator is a Sikh and Singh is a common Sikh surname; in addition, many people say that Indians speak English in a sing-song manner because of the rhythm in which they speak English. So it is the song of Singh and it also reflects the way he speaks: throughout the poem Nagra uses phonetic spelling to imitate Singh's accent and his use of half-rhyme and full rhyme increase the poem's song-like qualities.

The opening two stanzas tell us about the narrator's situation: he runs one of his father's shops and is expected to be open from nine in the morning until nine at night. But when there are no customers Singh shuts the shop and goes upstairs to make love to his wife.

The third stanza describes what happens when he returns downstairs to the shop. The lines in italics are the voices of his customers who pour out a litany of complaints about his shop, concluding that Singh's is

di worst Indian shop

on di whole Indian road.

The next three stanzas are devoted to his new wife and we can see that he is totally obsessed with her. Each stanza begins *my bride* – which suggests they have not been married for very long. He hears her high heels tapping above his head and imagines her flirting with other men on a Sikh dating website. Singh's wife seems to be Indian: she swears at his mother

she effing at my mum

in all di colours of Punjabi

but her *red crew cut* and the clothes she wears (*a Tartan sari*) suggest she has absorbed some parts of Western culture, while rejecting the work ethic of her husband's parents' generation. She mimics his father too – showing a lack of respect. We can imagine that Singh's father runs a very efficient shop which is clean and where the bread is not stale and the milk is not out of date.

The voices of the customers are heard again complaining about the products in the shop – Singh has neglected all this, because he would rather be upstairs making love to his wife. The poem repeats certain stanza structures which suggests that there is a monotonous daily routine to running the shop.

Line 43 begins a lovely romantic interlude. At midnight, Singh says, he and his wife come downstairs, sit together on the stool behind the counter and stare out of the shop's windows, beyond the shop window, beyond the community which criticizes Singh's abilities as a shopkeeper and they see

all di beaches ov di UK in de brightey moon.

They stare past

di half-price window signs

which suggests they do not care about them.

We then hear his wife speak for the first time in the poem. She asks him

How much do yoo charge for dat moon baby?

He tells her it is half the price of her and that in itself is priceless, so she must be doubly priceless. And so the poem ends on a note of intense romantic tenderness.

His wife's question is deliberately couched in financial terms: corner shops might have all sorts of offers – things that are half-price or on special offer or two for the price of three, but true love and passion cannot be bought and sold and have no price.

Singh does not care about running his shop efficiently; he only cares about his wife and her pleasure. This is a love poem and a poem about rebelling against the expectations of your parents and the community.

Why? This hilarious poem, full of tender, romantic love

- explores the cultural fusion of second generation British Indians.

- rejects the work ethic and materialism of older generations.

- shows a character rejecting the role picked out for him by his father.

- imitates accent to give us an authentic sense of character and culture.

Brendon Gallacher – Jackie Kay

Context

Jackie Kay was born in 1961: her mother was Scottish and her father Nigerian. She and her brother were adopted and brought up in Glasgow by adoptive parents who were heavily involved in left-wing politics. It is not surprising given her background that her poems should be very preoccupied with questions of identity – questions which have led Kay to explore black culture and history. Kay has said:

It's a huge freedom to be allowed to make things up in your head. I always loved that as a kid.

This quotation has clear relevance to this poem – as we shall see. Kay has written widely for adults and for children; she has published novels and short stories as well as poetry and has written for the theatre and for TV. She often draws on autobiographical material for her subject matter.

cat burglar – a burglar who performs nimble climbing feats.

wee – small, short.

burn – brook or stream.

Who? The narrator, the narrator's mother and Brendon Gallacher. The poem is in the past tense.

When? During the speaker's childhood at the age of 6.

Where? In the Glasgow of the poet's childhood.

What? The speaker tells us about her best friend, Brendon Gallacher.

Commentary

The opening stanza gives us some basic information about Brendon Gallacher. The phrase *My Brendon Gallacher* is used almost as a refrain at the end of lines 1, 2 and 5. The language is child-like, even though the poet is looking back and writing as an adult. Each line is a separate sentence and it sounds like a six year old breathlessly telling us about her best friend. We learn that Brendon's father is in prison and that he has six brothers. There seems to be a note of childish pride in this recitation of facts.

In the second stanza we learn more about Brendon. There is an element of childish romance: he holds the poet's hand and they walk by the river, while he tells her his plans for the future: his family is poor and he dreams of taking his mother out of Glasgow to a better life. In line 10 the speaker reveals that she would talk to her mother about Brendon.

In the third stanza the speaker's mother invites Brendon round for dinner, but the speaker makes excuses, saying she would prefer to meet him in the open air.

And then in line 15 (which leads into the following stanza) *one day after we'd been friends for two years* (one day is repeated in line 16 to warn the reader that something momentous is about to happen) the speaker's mother reveals that she has been asking around and discovered that the Gallacher family do not live where the speaker has told her they do – and it is at this point that it is revealed to the reader that Brendon is an imaginary friend.

As the speaker poignantly says

he died then, my Brendon Gallacher.

We are given vivid details of Brendon as the poem closes which show how the speaker had imagined him – he has *spiky hair*, an *impish grin* and *funny flapping ears* – and the final line with its exclamation at the start and the repetition of his name emphasises the sadness the speaker feels at his 'death':

O Brendon. Oh my Brendon Gallacher.

You might notice that Brendon is very different from the narrator: he comes from a big family and is Irish; his father is in prison and his mother drinks, while the narrator's father has a serious job in the world of politics. His desire to take his mother some place nice, some place far away, perhaps reflects the poet's desire for a better, more rewarding existence which is why she needs to invent Brendon in the first place.

Kay writes the poem in very straightforward English with some words specific to Scots English. The repetition in the poem mimics the way a child speaks and, until the end Brendon's name is always written in full; the repeated use of *he* and *his* shows a proud possessiveness on the part of the narrator: she is showing off about

Brendon and his family who lead a a more eventful and romantic life than the poet – from a child's perspective.

Why? This simple poem in simple language:

- evokes a strong sense of the reality of childhood dreams and fantasies.

- expresses sadness at the death of the fantasy in the final line.

- celebrates the imaginative powers of children.

- shows a tolerance for those from different backgrounds – Brendon is attractive because his family life is so different from the narrator's.

Give – Simon Armitage

Context

Simon Armitage was born in 1963 in the village of Marsden in West Yorkshire and has spent most of his life in that area. He is a very successful and highly-regarded poet, celebrated for his down-to-earth language and subject matter. Several of his poems are in the Anthology. His poetry often (but not always) deals with the ordinary incidents and events of modern life and appear to be based on personal experience. 'Give' comes from a collection called *The Dead Sea Poems* – an allusion to the Dead Sea Scrolls discovered in 1947. The collection as a whole features several poems – like this one – that give a voice to figures who are often marginalized by society.

frankincense – a sweet-smelling resin from Arabia.

myrrh – an aromatic gum extracted from plants.

Who? Armitage adopts the persona of a homeless person and addresses a passer-by and the reader.

When? No time is specified.

Where? The homeless person is in a doorway.

What? The homeless person pleads for change.

Commentary

What is your attitude to homeless people who beg on the streets? Do you give them money? Or do you never give them money? Do you look in their eyes? Or do you hurriedly pass by without making eye contact? If you give them money, why? If you don't give them money, why don't you?

The answers to these questions will not help you write well about this poem, but you should consider your own attitude to homeless people, because it might help you refine your response to this poem. I have friends who refuse to give to homeless beggars on the grounds that they must have done something to deserve their homeless state. I have other friends who always give on the grounds that no-one chooses to be homeless and to live on the streets and that every homeless person you see is someone's son or daughter. And that maybe one day, it could be you.

We are not given any details about the speaker and their background, how they have become homeless, why they are living on the streets. I think this is because it doesn't matter. The speaker can be seen as standing for all homeless people all over the world.

The poem is very simple. The title is an imperative, an order – *Give*. The poem opens with a neat couplet addressed to a fellow human being in whose doorway the speaker has been sleeping. *To make a scene* is a pun – it can mean to create a disturbance, but it also means to put on a show – which ties in with some of the things the speaker offers to do later in the poem. The second sentence begins with the same three words – *of all the*. The speaker has chosen this place and this doorway which perhaps implies that he/she has not chosen to be homeless: homelessness was not a choice. *Under the stars* makes the situation seem rather romantic.

The third stanza lists the things the speaker is prepared to do for money. For small bronze coins, he will sing or dance; for silver he will eat fire and swallow swords; for gold he will perform acts of escapology. The stanza is given structure by the repetitive start of each line.

The next short stanza mentions the gifts that the Wise Men brought Jesus when he was born. The speaker doesn't want those – he just wants gold. Perhaps we are meant to remember that Jesus (in Christian belief, the son of God) was homeless when he was born, which may stir our sympathy for the speaker. The speaker just wants change – another pun because *change* means small change, the coins you might happen to have in your pocket or in your purse, but the speaker might be implying that he wants a change in people's attitudes to the homeless or to the economic system that forces homelessness on some people.

The first ten lines of the poem have a jaunty tone, helped by the regular rhythm and Armitage's occasional use of rhyme. The final couplet changes the tone:

You give me tea. That's big of you.

I'm on my knees. I beg of you.

Here the heavy caesuras (heavy because they are full stops, not commas) disrupt the rhythm that Armitage has established earlier in the poem and, combined with the half rhyme of *big/beg* create a sense of pathos and sadness. How does this poem make you feel? Annoyed? Sympathetic? Compassionate?

Why? This short and simple poem

- highlights the plight of all homeless people.
- reminds us of Jesus and the gifts that were given to him at his birth.
- suggests that something about our attitude to the homeless must change.

Les Grands Seigneurs – Dorothy Molloy

Context

Dorothy Molloy (born in 1942; died in 2004) was an Irish poet who worked as a painter and journalist before starting to write poetry. This poem comes from her collection *Hare Soup* which was published in 2004, shortly after her death. Almost all the poems in the collection are written in the first person.

Les grands seigneurs – the great lords.

buttresses – a projecting support built on to the outside of a wall. A particularly common feature of castles.

castellated – having turrets and battlements like a castle.

bowers – a lady's private room.

cockatoos – large crested parrots from Australia.

ballast – heavy material used to weigh down and steady a ship.

hold – the interior of a ship used for storage or cargo.

hurdy-gurdy – a barrel organ.

courtly love – this was a medieval tradition that grew up in France in the 14th century. It imagined relationships between a man and a woman modelled on the feudal relationship between a lord and his servants. In the courtly love tradition men worshipped the woman from afar, writing poems in her honour, composing songs and performing acts of kindness and bravery for her sake. It imagined the male lover as the woman's slave who would do anything she asked him to do. The whole point of the courtly love tradition was that the love was never fulfilled and that women were unattainable and adored from afar, put on pedestals and worshipped. Its key influence was on Medieval and Renaissance literature, but you might feel it persists in modern times: the cards and roses we send on Valentine's Day can be seen as a diluted version of courtly love attitudes. Men still write songs and poems to women that they love, so you could argue that the courtly love tradition is alive and well. Or rather it is alive and well and, according to this poem, it is still souring relationships between the sexes!

troubadour – Medieval poets of courtly love.

damsel – a young unmarried woman. A slightly old-fashioned word now.

peach – this word can mean the very best of its kind. It has also been used in the past as a symbol for the female genitals.

Who? The poet adopts the persona of an unnamed woman.

When? Some readers feel very strongly that this poem is set in the Middle Ages and that the speaker is an aristocratic lady. I don't agree. The poem uses vocabulary and attitudes taken from the Middle Ages, but it also mentions very modern things such as bandstands and hurdy-gurdies. The language in the final stanza is modern and colloquial. As far as I am concerned, this poem is set now – in the 21st century and simply uses medieval references to sum up a mental attitude.

Where? In an imaginary setting.

What? The speaker describes her relationships with men before marriage and then afterwards.

Commentary

This is an interesting poem about the relationships between men and women and the stereotypes of women that men use in seduction and romance and then in marriage. The first 11 lines of the poem are packed with unusual and vivid metaphors, but these are replaced in the final sestet by expressions which are metaphorical but also idiomatic – that is to say, they are part of everyday language and Molloy uses them to show how love or romance fades and dies when people are married. The speaker in the poem is adored and idolized by men before she is married, but after marriage she finds herself trapped in male stereotypes of a submissive and subservient woman.

The opening sentence presents men in terms of safe places where the speaker is able to rest and the implication is that she feels safe and protected in these places. The second sentence alludes to the opening sentence of *A Tale of Two Cities* which we looked at in the introduction and then Molloy uses birds as metaphors to describe the different types of men that the speaker has known. The purpose of the men seems merely decorative and infinitely variable – they are able to transform themselves into anything they like. Cockatoos have a decorative crest which becomes erect during mating, so that image is full of sexual connotations; nightingales sing at night to attract a mate; while the strutting flamingos might remind you of men who are self-important and confident.

The second stanza continues this hyperbolic metaphorical description of what men were for the speaker. They were animals to entertain her – *dolphins* and *performing seals* – they were her *sailing-ships* and the *ballast in my hold*. All these metaphors imply that men only existed for her pleasure and that she commands them all. The idea of entertainment continues as we are told that men were her *rocking-horses*

prancing down the promenade, the bandstand

where the music played. My hurdy-gurdy monkey men.

The men she has known seem infinitely adaptable – as if they will do anything or be anything just to please her. They seem to exist solely for her protection and amusement. The sense that the men are slightly ridiculous is reinforced by the alliteration on *p* and the catchy rhythm of *hurdy-gurdy monkey men*. They sound faintly absurd. Barrel organs require no musical skill; you play a tune on them just by turning a handle and monkeys are associated with barrel organs.

The third stanza sums up her position – *I was their queen*. While she is *out of reach*, she is *enthroned* and treated with devotion and adoration. Molloy then refers to courtly love. The men play the role of the *troubadour*; she is the *damsel*; and she is the *peach* – the best of her kind, but this might also refer to her keeping her virginity by not sleeping with any of the men she has known.

The whole tone of the poem alters abruptly in line 12 and the change of tone is signalled by the word *But*. As soon as she has committed to a relationship – *wedded, bedded* (note the internal rhyme) – everything changes and she becomes the possession of one man. Overnight she becomes reduced to the demeaning roles of

a toy, a plaything, little woman,

wife, a bit of fluff.

Note how the word *wife* is just jumbled up with other words that imply a demeaning and derogatory attitude to her such as *little woman, plaything, a bit of fluff*. This shows that to be someone's wife, according to the speaker, is not a very special thing.

Looking back now at the title we can see that it is ironic – that men only pretend to be *les grands seigneurs* during courtship, but as soon as they have married the woman, their attitudes change completely. By the end of the poem the husband is in complete control:

My husband clicked

his fingers, called my bluff.

It is interesting in this poem that explores relationships between the sexes, that love – apart from the slightly unreal courtly love – is not mentioned. Relationships in this poem are seen in terms of control: in the first eleven lines the speaker is in control; as soon as she is married her husband is in control. Molloy uses the occasional rhyme – often within the line and called internal rhyme – to draw attention to the stereotypical attitudes she is satirizing: *reach/peach, wedded/bedded, fluff/bluff.*

Why? This highly original poem

- is packed with hyperbolic and extravagant metaphors.

- gives a disillusioned view of the relationships between men and women.

- sees what we call love as to do with power and control.

- uses imagery from an earlier age of chivalry and romance to underline the reality of how women are treated once they are married.

The Literary Heritage

Ozymandias – Percy Bysshe Shelley

Context

Percy Bysshe Shelley was born in 1792 and drowned in a boating accident just before his 30th birthday in 1822. He lived in turbulent times: the French Revolution had begun in 1789 and in Britain the Industrial Revolution was changing the country in deep and lasting ways. Shelley was quite a rebel – and was a political radical. He sympathized with the ideas behind the French Revolution and wanted to see greater change in Britain – more democracy, more freedom, less oppression. You should remember that although Britain was an enormously wealthy nation (because of the Industrial Revolution and the huge expanse of the British Empire), the majority of the population lived in appalling poverty and most of the population did not have the right to vote; the right to vote was limited to those who owned a certain amount of property and was, therefore, limited to a tiny minority of adult males. It was not until 1928 that all men (regardless of what they owned) were able to vote.

'Ozymandias' by Percy Shelley is one of his best-known poems, although, as we shall see, not very typical of his work. Shelley was a political radical which meant that he felt the England of his day was repressive and unfair and was in great need of political reform. He was very conscious of the massive gap between rich and poor, the lack of real democracy and the terrible conditions of the workers in the factories that had sprung up as a result of the Industrial Revolution. Britain was the first country in the world to have an industrial revolution and, with the British Empire also growing and expanding at the same time, Britain was an enormously rich and powerful country – the leading superpower of the day (especially after 1815 when the Duke of Wellington defeated Napoleon and the French at the Battle of Waterloo). However, this enormous wealth was concentrated in the hands of the rich and powerful. The mass of the population lived in conditions of great poverty. In most of his poems Shelley is very open and explicit about his feelings of hatred and anger towards the government of his day; in that sense, 'Ozymandias' is less typical because it takes a very long historical perspective and makes no mention of contemporary politics or political leaders.

Ozymandias is another name for Rameses II who was the king of Egypt in the 13th century BCE – over three thousand years ago. The king clearly commissioned a sculptor to carve a statue of him with the inscription 'Look on my works, ye Mighty, and despair'. Why would such a powerful ruler commission such a statue? So that his power and rule will be remembered forever. However, this has not happened. All that remains of the statue are *two vast and trunkless legs of stone*. Nearby *half-sunk* in the sand is part of his head, buried by the sands of time. The point of the poem is that for all Rameses' power and his arrogant assumption that he would be remembered because of this huge statue, the statue has been destroyed by time.

A little known fact is that, in a spirit of friendly rivalry, Shelley wrote 'Ozymandias' in an informal competition with another writer Horace Smith. Below is Smith's version. You will see that Smith's poem touches on the same themes as Shelley's, but is a little more chilling in its depiction of a future London through which a hunter wanders, trying to make sense of the ruins of what was once British civilization. Shelley's poem lacks that explicit warning for the political rulers of his day – although you could say it is implied. Interestingly, at the time, Smith's poem was considered better. You can judge for yourself. Here is Smith's poem, also called 'Ozymandias' originally.

In Egypt's sandy silence, all alone,

Stands a gigantic leg, which far off throws

The only shadow that the desert knows:

'I am the great Ozymandias,' saith the stone,

'The King of Kings, this mighty city shows

The wonders of my hand.' The City's gone –

Nought but the leg remaining to disclose

The site of this forgotten Babylon.

We wonder – and some hunter may express

Wonder like ours, when through the wilderness

Where London stood, holding the wolf in chase,

He meets some fragment huge, and stops to guess

What powerful but unrecorded race

Once dwelt in that annihilated place.

It is part of the mystery of the canon that Shelley's poem is so well-known, but that Smith's is hardly ever re-printed. Which do you prefer? I quite like the last line of Smith's because of his use of the word *annihilated* – it also brings home the point of both poems more forcefully, you might argue, because it stresses to the contemporary reader the idea that even British civilization may one day crumble and become a wilderness (think of what we know about Britain's status in the world at that time) and the British become an *unrecorded race*.

antique – ancient.

trunkless legs – the trunk is the main part of the body, containing the stomach and rib cage. It has disappeared – only the legs are left.

visage – face.

Who? The narrator of the poem meets a traveller who tells him what he has seen in the desert.

When? The poem was first published in 1818.

Where? London, but the antique traveller talks of ruins of a statue seen in Egypt.

What? The traveller tells the poet about some ruins he has seen in Egypt.

Commentary

'Ozymandias' is a Petrarchan sonnet named after Rameses II who died in 1234 BCE. The narrator of the poem recounts a conversation he has had with a traveller from an antique land. The final 13 lines of the poem quote what the traveller told Shelley. In the desert the traveller has found the remains of a statue of Rameses II. All that is left are

Two vast and trunkless legs of stone.

The head of the statue is lying nearby half-covered in sand. It is still possible to discern aspects of Rameses' face: the *frown*, the *sneer of cold command* which tell us he was an autocratic and authoritarian ruler. We are told that the sculptor understood those aspects of Rameses' character – the vanity and pride, the evil and unpleasant characteristics of a man used to complete power and total obedience from his subjects.

In the sestet Shelley explores the fate of such vanity and pride. Despite the often-quoted inscription

Look on my Works, ye Mighty, and despair,

nothing beside remains but ruin and devastation – a *colossal wreck*. There is a double irony: both Ozymandias and the unnamed sculptor share the same fate – neither the ruler nor the sculptor nor the statue remain in any shape to prove Ozymandias' boast of power and authority. Here, I think, we can see the point of telling the story second-hand. We are reading a poem written by a man who had a conversation with someone who had been to the desert and seen the ruins of the statue: this distancing serves to diminish Ozymandias still further. These are second-hand words reported to us by the poet. This distancing effect helps to stress Ozymandias' obscurity even more.

This sonnet is remarkable for the spare and stark imagery which the poet uses. There are lots of words which suggest solitude and decay – *trunkless, half-sunk, shattered, decay, wreck* – and so in the monotonous wastes of the desert – the traveller, the poet and then the reader encounter this ruined monument to earthly power and arrogance. We might be shocked by the ravages of time which the statue has suffered, but we end up mocking the presumptuous self-centredness and self-importance of Rameses II – and, by extension, of all autocratic rulers.

Shelley gives aural unity to the poem by the use of alliteration in the octave – *said, stone, stand, sand, sunk, shatter'd, sneer, sculptor, survive.* In line 8 he uses parallelism:

The hand that mocked them and the heart that fed.

Lines 10 and 11 are the words of Ozymandias which ring very hollow given the destruction of the statue and the decay of his civilization. Line 12 begins

Nothing beside remains.

and the strong caesura here emphasizes even more the fact that the statue is wrecked and Ozymandias' arrogant boast has come to nothing. Line 13 ends with memorable alliteration – *boundless and bare*, while the final line returns the whole sonnet to the power of nature:

The lone and level sands stretch far away.

An amazing line – the double alliteration *lone/level* and *sands/stretch* followed by the assonance on the long *a* sounds in *far away* not only make it memorable, but also remind us of the isolation and barrenness of the desert.

On the one hand, this sonnet was a message to the rulers of Britain in Shelley's time: he disagreed violently with the government's policies. On the other hand, it is a more timeless message for all humanity: civilizations fall and crumble, eroded by time and nature. It is interesting that the words of the inscription have survived: perhaps Shelley is stressing that words – the words of poets, for example – will outlive dictators and tyrants.

Why?

In this justly-famous sonnet Shelley wants to show

- that human beings will all be swept away by the power of time.

- that Ozymandias, the sculptor, the traveller and Shelley himself all face the inevitability of death –*the bare and boundless sands.*

- that the hubristic pride of rulers such as Ozymandias is wrong and will not survive.

- that there is a message in all of this to the autocratic rulers of England in Shelley's own era.

- words and language can survive the destructive power of time.

My Last Duchess – Robert Browning

Context

Robert Browning was born in 1812 and became one of the most famous English poets of the Victorian era. He was married to Elizabeth Barrett Browning who was a semi-invalid with an over-protective father. The couple were married in secret and then went to live in Italy. Browning's best work is often set in the past and he was a master of the dramatic monologue, in which the imagined speaker of the poem reveals their innermost thoughts and feelings, often going on to uncover uncomfortable truths about themselves.

This poem is based on real historical events. Duke Alfonso II of Modena and Ferrara (1559 – 1597) married Lucrezia de Doctors and she died four years after the wedding in mysterious circumstances. This is the starting point for Browning's poem. Victorian Britain was rather obsessed with the Italian Renaissance. Many of Browning's monologues are set in Renaissance Italy. The Renaissance, around the period 1450 – 1650, was a cultural and intellectual movement which happened all across western Europe and it involved the rediscovery of many of the skills that had been forgotten or ignored since the fall of the Roman Empire, especially in painting, art and sculpture. We can understand why the Renaissance began in Italy and the Italians felt themselves to be the heirs of the ancient Romans. In Italy the ruins and ancient buildings were a constant visual reminder of the arts of Rome. The artistic achievement of the Renaissance was helped by a system of patronage: wealthy dukes, merchants and princes commissioned great artists to create paintings and sculptures, just as in the poem the Duke of Ferrara has commissioned Fra Pandolf to paint the portrait of his first wife and Claus of Innsbruck has sculpted Neptune taming a sea-horse.

But the Renaissance, especially in Italy, had a sinister side to it. Many of the wealthy and powerful patrons of art were just as capable of paying to have an enemy assassinated or poisoned because the power and wealth they had allowed them to do so. What seems to have fascinated the Victorians was the co-existence in the Italian renaissance of art works of stunning beauty alongside moral and political corruption. As Victorian Britons they hoped to emulate the cultural achievements, but looked down upon (even as they were fascinated by) the moral corruption.

Fra Pandolf – an imaginary painter who supposedly painted the portrait of the Duchess.

a day – for many days.

countenance – face.

durst – dared.

mantle – a cloak.

favour – a thing (a jewelled brooch perhaps or a flower) worn as a token of love or affection.

officious – too forward in offering unwelcome or unwanted services.

nine-hundred-years-old name – this simply means that the title the Duke of Ferrara was first created nine-hundred years before the poem is set.

forsooth – truly.

the Count, your master – this phrase is important because it makes clear that the speaker of the poem is talking to a servant of the Count, who is visiting (it later becomes clear) to discuss the marriage of his daughter to the narrator.

munificence – generosity.

nay – no.

Neptune – the God of the Sea.

Claus of Innsbruck – an imaginary sculptor who has sculpted the statue of Neptune for the Duke.

Who? The Duke of Ferrara talks to the representative of an unnamed count who is there to arrange for his daughter to marry the Duke – she will be his next Duchess. The poem is written in the present tense.

When? In the 16th century, in the Duke's palace. This is very important because Browning and his fellow Victorians were fascinated by the Italian Renaissance period.

Where? In Ferrara in northern Italy.

What? The speaker tells the story of his first marriage by reference to a portrait of his first wife which hangs on the wall.

Commentary

'My Last Duchess' by Robert Browning is a very famous and much-anthologized poem. It is a dramatic monologue – that is to say the poet adopts the voice of someone else and speaks throughout as that person. It was first published in 1842 and is one of many dramatic monologues that Browning wrote.

The speaker in the poem is the Duke of Ferrara, an Italian nobleman from the 16th century. – we are told this from the note at the beginning. This immediately tells us the location of the poem (Italy) and the social background of the speaker – he is a powerful and wealthy aristocrat.

As the poem develops we come to understand that the Duke is talking to a representative of the family of his fiancée, his future wife, and that they are talking in the Duke of Ferrara's house. We can be even more precise and say that for most of the poem they are standing in front of a portrait of the Duke's former wife (now dead). The Duke talks about his dead wife and, in doing so, reveals a great deal about his character, the sort of man he is. We also learn the terrible fate of his first wife.

The opening sentence refers the reader to a painting hanging on the wall. The painting is so good that his previous wife is

Looking as if she were alive.

Browning establishes that the painter was skilled and produced a *wonder* – a masterpiece. The painter fussed over the portrait and over the duchess – *his hands worked busily a day.* In line 5 we realize for the first time that the duke is speaking not to the readers as such, but someone else; he invites him to sit and look at the portrait of his dead wife. He says he mentioned Fra Pandolf *by design* – perhaps to imply that he was an exceptionally well-known and highly sought-after painter (but remember that he has been made up by Browning).

The long sentence that begins on line 5 may be a little hard to follow. Note that in lines 9-10 the duke reveals that the painting is normally concealed by a curtain which only he is allowed to open; this suggests perhaps a man who is used to being obeyed, even in petty things like a curtain covering a painting. When people like the person he is talking to – *strangers like you* – see the painting, the duke says, they are always moved to ask him (he's always there because he controls the curtain!) what caused the *depth* and *passion* in the look on the duchess's face. You might note the phrase *its pictured countenance* – I know he is talking about a painted image, but it may strike you as unusual that he doesn't use the word *her* when talking about his dead wife. We might also note that the visitor hasn't asked about the *earnest glance* in the duchess's face – perhaps only the duke sees it. He seems to like the painting of her very much indeed and we will return to this idea later in this commentary.

The duke continues by saying that his visitor is not the first person to ask him why she looked so passionate in the portrait. The duke states

Sir, 'twas not

Her husband's presence only, called that spot

Of joy into the Duchess' cheek.

Her husband's presence – are we to assume that he was there in the room all the time while she had her portrait completed? I think we are – it fits with what we are starting to find out about his character. The duke seems to have been jealous when other men paid any attention to his wife – something she appears to have enjoyed since it brings *a spot of joy* to her face. He seems to have seen Fra Pandolf as some sort of rival and repeats things that the painter said to his wife in lines 16 – 19. You may feel that the duke really suspected that Fra Pandolf was his wife's secret lover or you may feel that the duke thought she was a little too easily impressed by male attention.

The duke then expands on his wife's faults. She was *too soon made glad*; she was *too easily impressed*; she could not discriminate:

she liked whate'er

She looked on and and her looks went everywhere.

She looked on everything with the same undiscriminating affection.

My favour at her breast – some precious brooch pinned on her breast and given her by the duke was given the same importance as the sunset or some cherries brought to her by a servant or riding a white mule along the terrace of the palace. You might feel that riding a white mule is a slightly eccentric thing to do – but she is the wife of a wealthy and very powerful man and she can do what she likes, whatever takes her fancy.

Line 33 reveals the duke's arrogance about his title and position. He talks about his nine-hundred-years-old name and clearly feels that his position and his title as Duke of Ferrara should have been given more respect by his wife. Note that he calls his name *My gift* – as though she should have been grateful that he married her.

In line 34 he starts to suggest that his attitude to all this was casual and relaxed. He calls her behaviour *trifling* and says he would not *stoop* to blame her. *Stoop* is an important word because it reminds us of his high social status and makes it clear that he regarded his wife as beneath him and inferior to him: it is a word that he repeats in the next few lines. And so it was that even though his wife's behaviour disgusted him, he never said a word.

Browning allows the duke to say he is not good at speaking and so may not have been able to explain his misgivings to his wife – but this is sheer nonsense: every line of this poem shows that the duke (as Browning has created him) is a clever manipulator of words. He says that she might have argued with him: *plainly set her wits* against his; and that even if he could have explained, it would have been degrading for him to have done so:

E'en then would be some stooping, and I choose

Never to stoop.

Once again we are reminded of his arrogance and superciliousness. It is interesting that he could not speak to his wife, but he takes 56 lines of the poem to talk to his visitor. She remained friendly to him – she smiled when she passed him, but she smiled at everyone and his sense of his own importance cannot allow that. And then we come to the heart, perhaps, of the poem:

I gave commands;

Then all smiles stopped together.

The duke gave some orders and had his wife murdered. This is quite clear. Browning said of the poem in an interview:

I meant that the commands were that she should be put to death....Or he might have had her shut up in a convent.

Now look back at line 19. It refers to the painter saying that he can never hope to reproduce in paint the flush *that dies along her throat* – that fades along her throat, but now we have read more of the poem and we know what the duke did to his wife, it is clear that Browning is preparing us verbally for the truth. Did she have her throat slashed? Or was she strangled? Either could be true. And his final sentence about his wife also suggests that she was murdered: *there she stands/As if alive.*

In line 47 he invites his visitor to stand and go downstairs with him to meet the company – the group of people who are waiting for them down below. Line 49 reveals that he has been talking to a servant of an unnamed Count (*your master*) whose *known munificence* means that he (the duke) expects a very large dowry. Having mentioned the dowry, the duke asserts that he doesn't really care about money – he is only interested in the count's daughter.

As they go down the stairs the duke points out a bronze statue, another of his pieces of art, sculpted by Claus of Innsbruck for him. The statue's subject matter is important: it shows the god of the sea, Neptune, taming a sea-horse. This demonstrates the relationship that the duke had with his first wife (he tamed her), with his servants and with his future wife – the daughter of the Count. Like Neptune ruling the sea, the duke likes to have power over people and beautiful objects like the painting of his wife and this statue. It is significant that the final word of this poem is *me* – because the duke's self-centredness has slowly been revealed the more we have read.

Browning writes in rhyming couplets of ten syllables, but his use of enjambment means that, because the lines are very rarely end-stopped, the poem drives onwards, just as the duke almost compulsively reveals what has happened to his wife. The enjambment also prevents the rhyming couplets from becoming too monotonous and make them sound more like real speech. The duke's hesitations and frequent interjections make him appear reasonable, although he is talking about the murder of his first wife. He has a very casual attitude to it all: he acquired a wife; she did not behave as he liked; he disposed of her. The naturalness of the sound of his speech, its casual, relaxed tone suggests that he does not see anything wrong in what he has done and expects his listener to find it normal too.

Although he claims he is not skilled in speaking, Browning ensures that the Duke gradually reveals the truth about what happened to his wife and the truth about his own character: he is possessive, jealous and likes the idea of controlling people. He is proud and arrogant about his aristocratic title and his family's history. He seems to prefer the painting of his dead wife to her living reality: he can control the painting, but he could not control his first wife. The poem ends on a note of dread – dread on behalf of his second wife who does not know what lies in store for her. He also seems to treat his wives like objects: objects are much easier to control than living human beings.

He seems more interested in being seen as a man of great taste than as a good husband. He draws the servant's attention to the painting and to the sculpture at the end. These objects are meant to demonstrate his taste and his wealth – he is connected to the great artists of his day. But his taste is limited to things he can control and totally possess – for example, he does not seem to be aware of the irony in the sculpture of Neptune and the fact that it might symbolize his relationships with other people, especially women.

Why?

This casual-sounding but deeply sinister poem

- shows the pride and arrogance of the aristocracy.

- is a portrait of the psychology of a murderer.

- shows that money and status and power can corrupt.

- shows the domination of men over women.

- raises questions about the relationship between art and life.

- is superbly written by Browning so that the reader must read between the lines as the terrible truth dawns upon us.

The River God – Stevie Smith

Context

Florence Margaret Smith (known as Stevie) was born in 1902 and died in 1971. She published three novels and nine collections of poetry. Her poetry is very quirky, individual and distinctive. Her poems often address questions of loneliness, war, religion and loss of faith. She can draw heavily on ideas of myth and fairy tales – as she does in this poem. As a child she was often separated from her mother because of illness and long periods in hospital and she suffered from depression for most of her adult life. In an interview with the BBC she said that she thought of death as a release from 'the pressure of despair' that she felt about life.

Rivers in human history and myth have always been seen as sacred. There are logical reasons for this: most early human settlements grew up near rivers because water was needed to wash, to drink, to water crops and to give to animals – so it is no wonder that they assumed enormous power in the minds of our distant ancestors. Prehistoric, pagan people did assume that rivers had gods, because water was so important in their lives. We see, perhaps, an echo of this in the way that even now people throw money and valuable objects into fountains and make a wish. Rivers have always had an ambivalent place in human culture: on the one hand, they provide drinking water and water to fertilize seeds, but they are also capable of great destruction when they flood. In ancient myths from a variety of cultures it is quite common for Gods to steal human women for their own pleasure. But there is a problem with this: the gods are immortal and do not understand death and mortality. Despite being stolen by a god, the humans always die.

weir – a dam across a river.

Who? Smith adopts the persona of the river god. The poem is written in the present tense.

When? Not specified. It could be at any point in human history because gods are immortal.

Where? The river god is very selfish. He sees only his point of view. Any 'action' takes place in the river.

What? The river god's monologue makes clear his attraction to women and his ability to trap them through death and keep them.

Commentary

This poem is written as one long stanza: ideas and thoughts and concepts flow into one another and this reflects the shape and nature of the river itself – one long continuous thing. Initially and for much of the poem, the tone is comic – this is helped by the colloquial language, the irregular line lengths and the use of rhyme, especially rhyme on two syllables : *swimming/women* and *drowning/clowning*.

The river has no illusions about his attractiveness:

I may be smelly and I may be old

But because he is a god he has great powers despite his unattractiveness. Smith writes cleverly throughout the poem. Note line two:

Rough in my pebbles, reedy in my pools.

Note the parallelism here and the alliteration on *r* and *p*. But despite the relentlessly jaunty tone, he is a dangerous river and has the power of life and death over human beings. And he seems to enjoy their suffering or at least be oblivious to it:

I throw them up and down in the spirit of clowning.

And just look at the high-spirited playfulness of the next two lines:

Hi yih, yippity-yap, merrily I flow,

O I may be an old foul river but I have plenty of go.

The poem then starts to focus on one woman in particular who has drowned. She drowned in an accident and the river god has brought her down to the river-bed. He seems insecure and worried:

Oh will she stay with me will she stay

This beautiful lady, or will she go away?

He seems aware that he is unattractive – *smelly and old* – and fears the loneliness of not having her. He is aware of her fear: he tries to

wash away the fear

She looks at me with.

But then he re-assures himself and says he will keep her because she has been forgotten by everyone on earth. The last four lines merit a close look:

They say I am a foolish old smelly river

But they do not know of my wide original bed

Where the lady waits, with her golden sleepy head.

If she wishes to go I will not forgive her.

Smith has abandoned the jokey rhyme and half-rhyme and so the tone of the poem becomes more sombre and dark. The river god's love is strong but very possessive and there is something awfully dangerous in *I will not forgive her*.

As a god he does not need to justify his actions. He gives the lady who has drowned no choice. He can certainly inspire fear, but he knows nothing of love because he is not mortal and cannot die. Therefore, he is condemned to be always lonely.

We might be tempted to interpret his strange and haunting poem symbolically. Does the river represent death? He certainly keeps the lady's corpse and she has drowned in it. The river will never give her up – just as we never return from death. Or is the river symbolic of all men and what they do to women in relationships? Men subdue the personality and the individuality of women and never let them go. They are attractive:

I like the people to bathe in me, especially women,

but possessive and getting involved with them might seem like a 'death' – of a woman's individuality and freedom. Perhaps Smith intends for him to represent not all men, but those whose love is selfish and possessive.

Why?

- This poem, like many of Smith's, has an eerie, dreamlike quality.

- Using the persona of the river lends a mythic, almost timeless quality to the poem.

- The tone changes from jaunty humour to something sinister at the end and this is achieved through the use of language.

- The symbolic nature of the river is open to debate.

The Hunchback in the Park – Dylan Thomas

Context

Dylan Thomas was born in 1914 and died in 1953, at the relatively young age of 39 after a lifetime of alcohol abuse. He was brought up in South Wales but spoke only English. His poetry quickly established his reputation, but he was also a successful and charismatic speaker, making over 200 broadcasts for the BBC and going on poetry-reading tours of America after the Second World War. Many would argue that his most successful work is *Under Milk Wood* which was a radio play about an obscure Welsh village.

The house where Thomas grew up in Swansea is very near Cwmdonkin Park and Thomas draws on his memories of the park in this poem about the day in the life of a hunchback.

Who? The poem centres on the hunchback and his day in the park. He is teased by boys playing truant and other people are mentioned like the park keeper. The poet appears in line 10 and, although this poem was written as an adult, the lack of punctuation and the long sentences give us the impression of seeing things through a child's eyes. In every other sense the poem is presented in the past tense by the poet as a detached observer of events.

When? One full day.

Where? In Cwmdonkin Park in Swansea.

What? The poet describes a day in the life of a hunchback spent in a park where he is teased by *truant boys from the town*.

Commentary

I don't think there is another poem quite like this in the Anthology. Thomas writes in long, impressionistic sentences and, apart from three full stops, uses no punctuation so we get a fast and whirling picture of what is happening. Adding to the sense of the confusion is the fact that the truant boys play games of fantasy and make-believe and the hunchback himself also fantasizes at one point. The first two stanzas are one sentence; the third and fourth stanzas are the second sentence; and the final three stanzas are the final sentence.

The hunchback seems lonely and is isolated from ordinary society by his unusual appearance and his habit of spending all day in the park. He is there as soon as the gate is unlocked in the morning and stays until the church bell signals that evening has arrived. He is associated with dogs – *he returns to his kennel in the dark* (line 42). He is teased by the boys: they shout at him and mock his appearance in line 21 by pretending to be hunchbacked like him. The boys are truanting from school and the hunchback would appear to be unemployed – which is why he can spend all day in the park. The hunchback represents an unorthodox way of living: he is on the margins of society:

Eating bread from a newspaper

Drinking water from the chained cup

which the children have filled with gravel and he

Slept at night in a dog kennel.

Yet, despite his eccentric life-style, he is capable of dreams and in stanza six he imagines

A woman figure without fault

Straight as a young elm

Straight and tall from his crooked bones.

The park is an important place in this poem: it appears as a place of freedom where truanting schoolboys can annoy hunchbacks and park keepers, and the hunchback can be alone. But it is more than that – it represents a dream of freedom and the boys can have daydreams and the hunchback can find find freedom in his thoughts of the woman figure he imagines. The park is a place where the imagination can be free.

The boys also have daydreams and fantasies. They

Make tigers jump out of their eyes.

They imagine they are in a zoo and they see sailors.

Throughout the poem Thomas contrasts the boys and the hunchback. They are loud; he is quiet. They are young; he is old. They are filled with movement and life; he is mainly still and static. The children are presented by Thomas as being full of energy and innocence, but they are also unthinkingly cruel to the hunchback.

The structure of the poem is very interesting. The stanzas are very ordered in terms of their line length, the number of lines in each stanza and the rhyme scheme – Thomas uses either rhyme or half-rhyme very consistently. This regularity suggests that what happens in this poem is a regular, everyday occurrence. But when we read the individual stanzas we have a different impression: everything happens in a quick blur of activity which may suggest the speed of events in the park or the haziness of Thomas's memory of it or, perhaps more convincingly, the magical quality of the park – a place where fantasies can float free. This speed also suggests the energy of the boys – the poem is energetic in the same way that the boys are.

What I have not mentioned yet is that this poem is rich with descriptions of nature: the trees, the lake, the grass are all personified. The act of personification brings these things alive and contributes to the sense of the park as a very special place. It is full of nature and is therefore different from the world of civilization. It represents a place where adults who are not part of conventional society can be free and where they and the truanting boys can indulge in a freedom of the imagination.

Why?

In this highly original poem Thomas

- uses sentence length, lack of punctuation and sentence structure to suggest the energy of childhood.
- celebrates the park as a place of freedom and the imagination.
- shows the appeal and power of the human imagination.
- presents outsiders in society in a sympathetic light.

The Ruined Maid – Thomas Hardy

Context

Thomas Hardy (1840 – 1928) is best known as a novelist. He wrote 15 novels, most of which are set largely in Dorset and the surrounding counties, and which deal with the ordinary lives of ordinary people in stories in which they struggle to find happiness and love – often battling against fate or their own circumstances. His final two novels *Tess of the D'Urbervilles* (1891) and *Jude the Obscure* (1895) both portray sex outside marriage in a sympathetic way and there was such a hysterical public outcry about the novels that Hardy stopped writing fiction and devoted the rest of his life to poetry. Although some of his poetry is intensely personal, this poem is also typical of his work in that it gives a voice to two ordinary women.

'Melia – a shortened form of Amelia, but cleverly chosen by Hardy: 'Melia is an ironic pun on the Latin word *melior* which means better.

this does everything crown – this is better than anything else.

garments – clothes.

tatters – rags.

spudding up docks – removing weeds (*docks*) with a short knife (*spud*).

barton – farmyard.

thee, thou – you.

thik oon – that one.

theas oon – this one.

t'other – the other.

ee – he.

hag-ridden – plagued by evil spirits.

sock – to suck, to take a sharp intake of breath – the opposite of a sigh.

megrims – migraines.

melancholy – sadness, depression.

Who? Two young women, who were once acquaintances, talk to each other.

When? Late Victorian Britain.

Where? In 'town' – 'Melia has moved to town while her acquaintance has continued to live and work in the countryside.

What? The poem consists of a dialogue between the two girls.

Commentary

This poem consists of six quatrains all of which (except the last) are organized in the same way. The first girl – whose name we never know and who lives and works in the countryside – addresses her friend in the first three lines of the quatrain; in the final line of each stanza, 'Melia, who used to work with her friend but who now lives in Town, answers. In her responses 'Melia always uses the word *ruin* or some version of it. *Town* seems to be the nearest large city in the farming area that the young women live in; it might even be London.

The opening stanza establishes that 'Melia has undergone a change of routine since they last met: her friend comments on her fair garments and her apparent prosperity. Note how Hardy prints *prosperi-ty*: he is gently mocking the friend's pronunciation of the word, so that we are forced to put the stress of the word, unnaturally, on the final syllable, and, of course, by stressing the final syllable he is emphasising its rhyme with the fourth line. This mis-pronunciation also occurs in lines 11, 15 and 19.

The second stanza gives us more detail about the life 'Melia used to live in the countryside. Her clothes were poor and she worked on the land, doing heavy manual labour. Now, however, her dress has improved: she has *gay bracelets* and wears three fine feathers in her hat.

In the third stanza the speaker draws attention to the way 'Melia's speech has changed. When she worked in the fields she used antiquated dialect forms of speech, but now her speech has changed and has given her some *polish*. She has changed her way of talking now she has left her old life behind.

The details in the fourth stanza give us a hint of the reality of hard manual labour on a farm. 'Melia's hands used to be *like paws* and her face was *blue and bleak* from working outside exposed to all the weather of every season. Living in town has softened her skin and her hands are like a lady's – not hardened and roughened by work.

'Melia's mood has changed too: she is no longer plagued by depression, sadness and migraines. 'Melia admits in the final line that now she is *pretty lively*.

The final stanza changes the pattern of the previous five. In this third stanza the unnamed friend from the country speaks the first two lines and 'Melia has a two line response. The friend wishes that she could live the same life as 'Melia, enjoy the same material comforts and strut about Town. But 'Melia points out that her friend cannot because she is not *ruined*. Note the use of the word *ain't* in the final line: this shows that 'Melia has not really acquired all the polish that her friend thinks she has. The word reveals that despite the superficial changes she has undergone, she is still using speech which is considered wrong and ungrammatical.

You should note that Hardy is a master of poetic techniques. Many lines are given added power by alliteration, assonance and consonance or the use of simple similes – *like paws*.

At the heart of this poem is the word *ruin*. This is actually a poem about prostitution in Victorian England. In public the Victorians were very straight-laced and uptight about sex, but in reality it has been estimated that 20% of the adult female population were prostitutes or someone's mistress. It is unclear whether 'Melia is a prostitute with numerous clients or whether she is mistress to one wealthy, married man, but what is clear is that all the changes in her life have come from selling her body. The bracelets and the three feathers are the signs of her trade.

To be 'ruined' in Victorian Britain meant to have lost your virginity before marriage. 'Melia is ruined in the sense that she will no longer be able to get married in a respectable way because of her occupation. The irony is that, despite the implications of the word, meaning to be spoilt forever, she is actually living a much better life than she did as a farm labourer. Hardy is exposing Victorian hypocrisy about sex in this poem. He is also attacking the class system of his day. 'Melia has no other way to become better off and live a materially better life than to sell her body. Victorian society kept women, especially working class women, in subservient positions. Women like 'Melia have no access to education or the professions and therefore the only alternative to being a farm labourer is to become a prostitute.

Through her acquaintance's words we get a vivid picture of how hard life as a farm labourer must have been and so it is natural that 'Melia's friend (who does not appear to understand exactly what 'Melia does in order to dress so well) envies 'Melia her new-found wealth – her improved speech, clothes, mood and complexion. So women had a limited choice: they could become morally ruined as 'Melia has done or they can remain financially and physically ruined by remaining as a farm worker.

'Melia's own attitude to her change of circumstances is hard to read. She seems proud of her new clothes and new ways of talking; she says that she lives a *lively life* and boasts that she does not have to work. However, you may detect in her final speech a sense of regret that in order to have a better standard of living she has had to sell her body.

Hardy's own attitude is also hard to discern, especially as he has no voice within the poem: he presents the dialogue without authorial comment. However, if you were to read his later novels I think you would be able to work out that Hardy sympathizes with both women. He is very sympathetic to Tess in *Tess of the D'Urbervilles* who loses her virginity through rape and then, when she is later married to another man, is condemned by him for not being a virgin! Hardy seems sympathetic to the acquaintance because of the back-breaking work she has to do as a farm worker, and he extends his sympathy to 'Melia too - who is condemned by society and seen as *ruined* when that is her only option to get a better life. This is hypocrisy because Victorian society condemns working class women to manual labour and also condemns 'Melia and women like her who become prostitutes – but prostitutes who are used by 'respectable' wealthy men. If society were fairer, Hardy seems to be saying, then women would have the chance to escape from manual labour without having to sell their bodies. It is interesting that the title does not make clear which of the two women is ruined – in a sense, they both are.

However, on the surface this is a casual, almost light-hearted poem which in a way reflects the fact that this is a conversation between two acquaintances – one of whom does not understand the true nature of the situation and the other who does not want to reveal fully the truth of what she does. As I have said above, it all hinges on the word *ruined*.

Why?

In this superficially straightforward poem written in largely everyday language, Hardy

- expresses sympathy for the plight of Victorian working class women.

- attacks Victorian attitudes to class and sex.

- reveals the hypocrisy at the heart of respectable society.

Casehistory: Alison (head injury) – U A Fanthorpe

Context

Born in 1929 Ursula Askham Fanthorpe (always published as U A Fanthorpe) was educated at Oxford and taught English for 16 years, before working as a clerk at a hospital in Bristol – in the neuropsychiatric unit which deals with disorders of the brain. This was when she first began writing and publishing poetry, and her first collection – *Side Effects*, published in 1978 – clearly shows the influence of where she worked. As she said of this first collection

At once I'd found the subject that I'd been looking for all my life: the strangeness of other people, particularly neurological patients, and how it felt to be them, and to use their words.

This poem is about someone who is suffering from brain damage and is not even sure who she is. Fanthorpe said of her poetry:

I'm particularly involved with people who have no voice: the dead, the dispossessed, or the inarticulate in various ways – people at the edge of things.

Fanthorpe published another eight collections of poetry, and she was widely recognized as an important and influential poet before her death in April 2009.

autocratic – an autocrat is someone who is a dictator and who rules by his own power. Her autocratic knee means that before her head injury she could control her physical movements.

A Degas dancer's – Degas was a 19th century French painter whose paintings of ballet dancers are amongst his most famous. In the paintings they are presented as slim, graceful and full of poise. This allusion in itself suggests that Alison, before the head injury, was educated and cultured. The image of the Degas dancer draws attention to how Alison was, but also makes clear that now she has to *lug* her body upstairs and her face is *broken*.

Who? Fanthorpe adopts the voice of Alison who has suffered a brain injury and is looking at a photograph of herself. She mentions her mother and father and a husband, but mostly she talks about her former self in the third person.

When? This is a modern poem, but no particular time is specified.

Where? No particular place is specified, but we can tell from what we know of Fanthorpe's life that Alison is a patient in a neuropsychiatric unit.

What? Alison's dramatic monologue focuses on the photograph of her when she was younger and a growing revelation of what she is like now.

Commentary

The title and the sub-heading of this poem are vital to note in order to get our bearings. Alison has suffered a head injury which has affected her brain, her ability to think and her memory. Her monologue is a reaction to a photograph of her younger self before whatever accident caused the damage to her brain.

Look at the opening stanza:

I would like to have known

My husband's wife, my mother's only daughter.

A bright girl she was.

She is talking about herself, but by putting this in the third person Fanthorpe ensures we are clear about the contrast between what she was and what she is now. She is aware that she was a bright girl, but the inversion (putting *she was* at the end) in line three sounds awkward, as if Alison is struggling to remember – the past and even her own identity.

Now that she is ill she is

Enmeshed in comforting

Fat.

But before her head injury she was a woman of *delicate angles* and looked like a dancer in a painting by Degas. Her *autocratic knee* is important – it suggests that now she can no longer control her own body. It is also significant that she wonders at her photograph – she can barely remember the person she used to be. Now she has put on weight her knee *lugs me upstairs* – but with great difficulty: Fanthorpe delays the most telling word until the next line which is the start of the next stanza – *hardly*. Her head injury has affected her memory, her ability to think and her ability to control her own body.

In the photograph she is smiling, but now Alison has forgotten why she was smiling –and everything else of importance. In the past her face was broken by *nothing sharper than smiles* – which suggests that now she is full of other emotions.

Stanza five talks about her father's death. It seems to have happened before her own injury and she got over it, because she detects in the smile in the photograph a sense that her younger, uninjured self had *digested mourning*.

The speaker's plight is made even more clear in the sixth stanza. She says she needs reminding every morning and she tells us that she will *never get over what/I do not remember*. We get the sense that she needs reminding every morning of who she is and what has happened to her. Unlike the death of her father – which she got over in the past before the photograph was taken – she will never get over the damage to her brain.

Stanza seven states boldly: *Consistency matters*. Perhaps this means that now she has to live a life that is highly structured and organized because she can no longer think for herself. She says she wants to *keep faith* with her younger self's *lack of faith* – which in itself is a contradiction, but it is irrelevant anyway, because Alison has forgotten her reasons for her earlier lack of faith. Faith is a word that is associated with religion. This stanza seems to suggest that before the injury Alison's younger self did not believe in God: she had a lack of faith. This is surely very appropriate to the subject matter of the poem: what has happened to Alison and the life she now leads is exactly the sort of thing that forces some people to question their belief in God.

The eighth stanza makes it clear that the speaker is aware of her former self's talent: she is proud of her achievements, her A levels – and this awareness makes her current situation even more sad and poignant. The speaker is aware of what she has lost.

Line 25 begins with an exclamation:

Poor clever girl!

And then the speaker, with terrible irony, points out that for all her cleverness she now knows one thing that her younger self did not:

I am her future.

She will never recover and will stay trapped like this forever. Note how both lines 24 and 27 end with the word *future*, but in a completely different sense – the future that Alison once looked forward to, and the future she now has after her head injury.

The final stanza consists of one line only and it is the third line of the first stanza. Here at the end of the poem it stands alone and isolated – just as Alison's past self with all her promise is isolated by being in the past and just as her present self is isolated by her brain damage. We now read it with an understanding of all that is wrong with Alison: its effect, therefore, is one of tremendous sadness and pity for the speaker.

This poem is written in stanzas of only three lines, most of which end with a full stop. This short, rather stilted style suggests the speaker's difficulty in saying more than a few words at a time, the difficulty she has in trying to express herself and articulate her thoughts. Her mental dysfunction is also conveyed by her speaking about her younger self in the third person – using *she* and *her*. The confusion is enhanced by Fanthorpe's use of tenses: Alison talks about her younger self in the photograph in the present tense and also uses the present tense to describe her current state. But she also refers to the future because she knows that there will be no improvement in her present condition. The title *Casehistory: Alison (head injury)* makes it sound like Alison's medical record, but the poem is a dramatic monologue in free verse and is written in largely everyday language: we get the truth about Alison in her own voice without any medical jargon. The title in itself is rather ironic since Alison cannot remember many details about the past.

Why? This moving poem

- gives a voice to someone with brain damage and this makes the poem immediate and moving.
- explores the problems of memory and thought through its short stanzas and muddling of tenses.
- constantly contrasts the woman Alison once was with the woman she now is.
- draws our attention to those whom we might otherwise ignore and provokes our pity.
- shows a character caught by her medical condition and unable to move on.

- uses a curiously unemotional tone to show that Alison could be talking about a different person and that her brain is not functioning properly.

On a Portrait of a Deaf Man – John Betjeman

Context

John Betjeman was born in 1906 and died in 1984. He wrote a lot of poetry and was made Poet Laureate in 1974. He was married and had two children, but in later life he and his wife grew apart over differences in their attitude to religion: she converted to Catholicism, while he became increasingly agnostic.

Betjeman is not often seen as an especially private poet, but we may come to the conclusion that this poem is partly about his father and at the same time partly about himself.

shroud – a large piece of cloth in which dead bodies were placed before coffins became more widespread.

London clay – the rock that London is built on is clay.

Highgate Hill – a cemetery in north London.

Carrara – a place in Italy famous for its marble quarries. The marble is used to make the headstones in cemeteries all over Europe.

Who? Betjeman addresses the deaf man named in the title of the poem.

When? After the deaf man's death.

Where? No particular location, but we do learn that the deaf man is buried in Highgate Cemetery in north London.

What? Betjeman remembers what the deaf man liked to do in life, but constantly reminds us that he is now dead.

Commentary

The opening stanza describes the clothes the deaf man used to wear, but the final line reveals that now he is dead, since he wears a closely fitting shroud; the second stanza starts to tell us what he liked, using the past tense, but the tense changes to the present to remind us that his mouth is open not to eat potatoes in their skin, but

to let

The London clay come in.

He is in the ground, buried. The poet then remembers what the man used to do with him: he knew every bird they saw, but could not identify their sound because he was deaf. It was for this reason too that the walks were long and silent. The fourth stanza returns to the fact that he is dead: he could not hear the poet, but now the poet is disturbed by the thought of maggots eating his eyes in the ground. The poet gives us more detail in the fifth stanza about what the man liked: the air of Cornwall, the smell of ploughed soil and painting.

There is a sudden switch in the sixth stanza to describe the place he disliked the most – Highgate Cemetery, filled with marble monuments to the dead. His death seems to have been sudden: the poet says he would have liked to say goodbye,

Shake hands with many friends,

but even that thought of shaking hands is used by Betjeman to remind us that he is dead and that now

his finger bones

Stick through his finger ends.

The final stanza changes direction and Betjeman addresses God who asks us to pray for the souls of the dead. Betjeman expresses his doubt about the existence of God and the resurrection:

You ask me to believe you

And I only see decay.

Although no detail in the title or the poem tells us, Betjeman wrote this poem shortly after his father died and all the details of what the deaf man liked are true of Betjeman's father. Betjeman shared many of his father's interests and passions, so we may also feel that the poet is describing himself and anticipating his own death. And it is important to note that there is no consolation found to the inevitability of death – the final word of the poem reminds us all of what we face: *decay*.

This poem is written in ballad form which is quite unusual for this very personal subject matter. Ballads are more often rather impersonal: perhaps the choice of form is Betjeman's way of distancing himself slightly from the grief and sadness that he feels. By 'distancing' here, I mean controlling it: the ballad form is highly structured and by conforming to its structure, Betjeman does not allow himself to get carried away with unrestrained, hysterical grief. In a similar way there is no specific word in the poem or its title that tells us this is about Betjeman's father. Although the poem is sad, inevitably because of its subject matter, there is no great outpouring of emotion: it is as if the emotions we feel when someone very close to us has died are held in check by the rigid structure of the ballad from; that, in itself, may suggest that the emotions are actually very strong – they have to be controlled by the form of the poem or Betjeman would break down completely. Almost every stanza includes some detail about Betjeman's father with some chilling detail of the reality of his dead body in the soil of north London – and so death and life are constantly before us in the poem. Betjeman presents his relationship with his father with affection and the details of his likes and dislikes are recalled fondly.

Why?

This is an interesting variation on the ballad form which shows:

- the love between a father and his son.

- the sadness and inevitability of death.

- a lack of faith in God and an after-life.

- the physical decay that awaits us in the ground.

- a fascination with, and affection for, the very ordinary things which make life worth living.

Character and Voice: Connecting the Poems

In this section I will be examining the specimen questions provided by AQA and going on to discuss other ways to connect the poems in this section. The difference between questions on Foundation Tier papers and Higher Tier papers is simple: the Foundation questions use bullet points to guide you in your response to the question.

These questions are for English Literature, Unit 2 entitled *Poetry across time*. You have one hour and 15 minutes to answer the paper. There are two questions on each section of the Anthology; you answer only one. There is also a question on an unseen poem. However, the question on the Anthology carries 36 marks and the advice on the paper is to spend 45 minutes on it. The unseen poem carries only 18 marks and you are advised to spend 30 minutes on it. I deal with the unseen poem at the end of this book. There is also general advice on answering questions in the examination at the end of the book. The questions that follow have been produced by AQA as specimen questions. My answers are simply suggestions.

Compare the ways that characters are presented in 'The Hunchback in the Park' and one other poem from 'Characters and voices'.

Remember to compare:

- **the characters in the poems.**
- **how the characters are presented.**

The hunchback in Dylan Thomas's 'The Hunchback in the Park' like the punk in Simon Armitage's 'The Clown Punk' are both marginalized figures in society, but they are presented in very different ways.

Armitage's punk is marginalized because of his appearance. His appearance is scruffy!

like a basket of washing that got up

and walked.

He is seen in the *shonky* part of town and is covered in *sad tattoos*: Armitage remarks that *every pixel* of his skin is *shot through with indelible ink*. He also behaves in an anti-social way. When Armitage stops in his car at traffic lights, the punk slathers his daft mush on the windscreen, making Armitage's children wince and scream in the back seat. Similarly, Thomas's hunchback is ostracized because of his appearance. Early in the poem, Thomas calls him a *solitary mister* and he appears to be homeless because he sleeps in a kennel. He eats bread from a newspaper and drinks the free water in the park. The truant schoolboys taunt and tease him without mercy. He seems to spend all day in the park, because he is unemployed and has nowhere else to go.

Despite these superficial similarities between the two characters, they are presented in very different ways by the poets. In Armitage's poem his punk is described as the *town clown* and the poet appears to show little sympathy towards him. The punk frightens the poet's children and Armitage reminds them and the reader to

think what he'll look like in thirty years' time

with his *deflated face* and *shrunken scalp*. The final lines suggest the encounter with the punk can be washed away by the car's windscreen wipers.

By contrast, Thomas is less critical of the hunchback. Like the schoolboys who allow their imaginations freedom in the park, the hunchback creates in his imagination a woman figure without fault – and this act of the imagination gives him validity and meaning.

The two poems are written very differently. Armitage's poem is colloquial, sounds like speech and has an adult voice; but Thomas uses long sprawling sentences and vivid metaphors to suggest that the park is a special place for everyone - the hunchback and the truant boys. The rhythm mirrors the energy and movement of the boys.

Both poems present outsiders who are marginalized. However, their presentation reveals different attitudes on the part of each poet. Thomas seems to feel that the hunchback's ability to dream of a woman redeems him; Armitage seems to suggest that the outward signs of youthful rebellion will become comic and grotesque with age.

Readers like some poems and dislike others. Compare your responses to 'Checking Out Me History' and one other poem from 'Characters and voices', saying whether you like or dislike the poems and why.

Remember to compare:

- **the characters or ideas in the poems.**

- **how the poems are written.**

John Agard's 'Checking Out Me History' is an interesting poem which forces us to re-assess our ideas about history and I liked it because in order to understand the poem I found out things I did not know before. Thomas Hardy's 'The Ruined Maid' would appear to be very different − a poem written nearly one hundred years before Agard's and, on the surface, with a completely different approach and subject matter, but there are striking similarities.

The idea of Agard's poem is straightforward: because white people have controlled the education system, famous black men and women have been ignored or forgotten by official versions of history. Throughout the poem Agard juxtaposes famous figures from white British history and popular culture with less well-known black figures who achieved as much and, Agard implies, deserve to be known about too. Agard seems to speak as himself, but his spelling represents his accent as a black Briton and the tone of the poem is one of anger, shown in the repeated use of *Dem tell me* − and what they have told him is a biased and whites-only version of history.

The idea of Hardy's poem is straightforward too. Hardy presents a dialogue between two rural working class women from the late 19th century who have not seen each other for quite a while. One of them − 'Melia − has had a change of life-style since she moved to town. The poem contrasts her material comfort with the hard working life that her friend still endures back in the countryside. 'Melia now wears *bracelets,* feathers, and *a fine sweeping gown*, and no longer suffers from *megrims or melancho-ly*; she left her home *in tatters* but now wears *fair garments*.

Agard's poem is written in an interesting way. In the stanzas describing the conventional version of history he uses rhyme and repetition and this sounds quite childish − like the narrow version of history he is attacking. But the stanzas describing famous black people from the past are visually different because they are italicized and he uses more metaphorical language: Nanny de Maroon is a *hopeful stream/to freedom river* and Mary Seacole is a *healing star* and *a yellow sunrise/to the dying*. In Hardy's poem 'Melia hardly speaks, but there is a reason for this: 'Melia does now have a better life, but only because she has become a prostitute – the word *ruined* tells us that she has lost her virginity and will never be able to have a respectable marriage. Her fine clothes are the social signs of her profession. Are we to see her silence as embarrassment or a reluctance to admit to her friend the truth of her position?

What I like about both poems is that they give a voice to groups of people who have been ignored by official histories and who are marginalized by conventional society. Both poems reveal important truths about the past and our history. Both poems give a voice to groups in our history who have been exploited.

Compare how a character's voice is created in 'The River God' and one other poem from 'Characters and Voices'.

Stevie Smith's 'The River God' and Robert Browning's 'My Last Duchess' create the voice of a character who is the narrator in very different ways, but with very similar effects. Both poems are dramatic monologues and the narrators reveal more of themselves as the poems proceed. In addition, Smith gives a voice in the poem to an ancient river god, while Browning, writing in the 19th century, gives a voice to an Italian Renaissance nobleman – in both cases the reader is likely to be intrigued by a figure we know little about.

Our first impressions of the river god are that he is a cheerful, humorous character. This is because of the way Smith writes. She uses colloquial language – *plenty of go*; rhymes on two syllables – *swimming/women*; lots of rhyme and half-rhyme; and playful high-spirited exclamations – *Hi yih, yippity-yap*. The irregular line lengths and the river god's disarming honesty:

I may be smelly and I may be old

create a figure that we might initially regard with affection.

The Duke of Ferrara in 'My Last Duchess' is an accomplished speaker. Browning is writing in rhyming couplets, but his skilful use of enjambment means that the rhyme words hardly ever intrude and the poem comes across as an intimate conversation with the servant of the Count, the father of his new bride-to-be. What can we tell about the Duke from what he says to the servant? He seems very proud of his works of art – the portrait of his last wife (which is covered by a curtain which he controls) and the statue of Neptune that he mentions at the end of the poem as they descend the staircase. He also likes to name drop – Fra Pandolf and Claus of Innsbruck are supposedly very famous artists whose work does not come cheap. He also seems very arrogant, very aware of his noble background – his *nine-hundred-years-old name*. His arrogance is such that although his first wife displeased him, he says he would not *stoop* to discuss her behaviour with her.

And so we have two very different male characters: one jaunty and cheerful, the other proud but interested in art and cultural artefacts. As each poem progresses, however, the truth is revealed about both men which completely undermines any other impression we have of their characters. They both mistreat women. In Smith's poem the river god keeps a woman on the river bed for his own pleasure and will not let her go. In 'My Last Duchess' the Duke reveals that he had his wife murdered because he disliked her flirtatious behaviour. Both characters – despite their glib and perhaps attractive way of speaking – hate women and have a possessive attitude to them.

Compare how a character is presented in 'Medusa' and one other poem in 'Characters and Voices'.

Carol Ann Duffy's 'Medusa' and Dorothy Molloy's 'Les Grands Seigneurs' both give a voice to women who have been manipulated by men, but their use of language and their presentation of character are radically different. The poems share another similarity. Duffy's is based on an ancient Greek myth which she interprets in an interesting psychological way; Molloy's is based on the clichés of the medieval courtly love tradition which she debunks at the end of the poem.

Duffy's poem consists of many short, direct statements which suggest that the speaker is focused on one thing – revenge. She does use metaphors at the beginning of the poem to suggest the reason why Medusa's appearance changed. Her *doubt* and *suspicion* about her lover's fidelity grew and her hair turned into *filthy snakes* and her thoughts, she says, *hissed and spat on my scalp*. The speaker's transformation is complete: her lover's betrayal of her has turned her ugly and so Duffy uses a lot of unpleasant words: her *bride's breath soured* and *stank*; her lungs are *grey bags*; she is *foul mouthed*, *foul tongued*. Her betrayal has made her hate life itself and in stanzas four, five and six she looks at living things and transforms them into inanimate objects. Her lover has betrayed her for a younger, more beautiful woman and this is clearly shown towards the end of the poem when the speaker asks

Wasn't I beautiful?

Wasn't I fragrant and young?

Psychologically the speaker has not been turned only into Medusa, the figure from Greek myth, but also into every embittered wife left for a younger, more attractive woman.

Molloy's poem also deals with stereotypes of women and male behaviour towards women. However, because the first eleven lines of the poem deal with the speaker's relationships with men before she is married, the tone is very different from 'Medusa'. Molloy uses hyperbolic, extravagant metaphors to describe what men were like before she was married: they were her *castellated towers, peacocks, cockatoos, my performing seals*. These lists all suggest that the speaker controlled the men and that they transformed themselves into anything in order to please her and win her attention. The speed of the lines also suggests that the speaker enjoyed the attention. The speaker's relationship with men is summed up in line 9:

I was their queen. I sat enthroned before them.

But in line 12 the tone and the vocabulary are transformed. As soon as she is *wedded, bedded* – the internal rhyme emphasizing the speed of the transformation – she becomes another tired cliché of a married woman and the extravagant metaphors and references to courtly love from earlier in the poem are replaced by the dismissive, derogatory terms used to degrade married women – *a plaything, little woman, bit of fluff*.

In both poems, therefore, the speaker is a woman who is presented as having been betrayed in some way by men: in 'Medusa' the betrayal is a literal one and she has been transformed into an ugly, revengeful Gorgon unable to trust any man; in 'Les Grands Seigneurs' which begins with such lively and hyperbolic metaphors, by the end of the poem, the woman has become under her husband's control – his *toy*.

Other thoughts

Of course, you cannot predict what questions will come up in the examination, but you can do some thinking before the exam and select poems that work well together for various reasons. You will still need to do some quick thinking in the exam AND you must answer the question that has been asked: you cannot simply write about two poems that in your preparation you have decided go well together. What follows now are some brief notes which give some examples of poems that work well together, depending on the question. These are not exclusive – I am sure you can make connections which I have not spotted or thought of.

'Clown Punk' and 'The Hunchback in the Park' would be an interesting pairing. Their written style is very different; they both deal with marginalized figures, but the poet's attitude is completely different to their subject matter. Armitage writes in very colloquial English; Thomas's poem is packed with imagination and fantasy and inventive figurative language.

Any two of 'Checking Out Me History', Singh Song!' and 'The Ruined Maid' would work as a pair because all three poems use dialect and also because all three poems deal with people who are not in the mainstream of society. Of course, Hardy's poem is very different because he is writing so long ago and because he is concerned with class, not race but that is something you would point out in your answer.

'Medusa', 'Les Grands Seigneurs', 'The Ruined Maid', 'My Last Duchess' and 'The River God' all present attitudes to women on the part of men. They are very different poems but that gives you more to write about.

'Ozymandias' and 'My Last Duchess' both write about powerful people and both implicitly criticize them, but their forms are very different. Browning's poem is a dramatic monologue in which the Duke slowly reveals the truth; Shelley's sonnet is much more concerned with revealing a general, universal truth about what happens to tyrants. Browning's poem is very intimate; Shelley's takes a broader global and historical stance. In addition, Ozymandias and the Duke place great importance on material things: the statue of Ozymandias and the painting of the Duke's dead wife.

'Medusa' and 'The River God' are both about mythical beings and they both deal, in a way, with the relationships between men and women. They both have threatening, dangerous elements but the tone of the speaker in each poem is very different.

'The Ruined Maid', My Last Duchess' and 'Les Grands Seigneurs' all deal with the male exploitation of women.

'Ozymandias' and 'On a Portrait of a Deaf Man' – although one is very political and the other is very personal – both deal with death and decay. And for the purposes of the exam, the fact that Shelley writes a sonnet and Betjeman a ballad gives you so much to write about concerning their differences in form.

'Ozymandias' and 'Checking Out Me History' can be seen as anti-authoritarian: Shelley attacks the tyranny of Ozymandias; Agard attacks the emphasis on white historical figures. But Shelley is writing in a very traditional form while Agard invents his own form and uses two different styles of verse structure. The tones of the poems are different too: Shelley is wistful and elegiac, Agard angry and bitter.

'Clown Punk', 'Give', 'Casehistory' and 'Horse Whisperer' all deal – in very different ways with people who have been rejected by mainstream society – either because of their class, their circumstances or because of the advent of new technology.

'Brendon Gallacher' and 'Hunchback in the Park' both present childhood as a time of fantasy but differ, because Kay uses the first person, whereas Thomas describes the truant schoolboys in his own voice. The way the poems are written is differently different too.

'On a Portrait of a Deaf Man' and 'Casehistory: Alison' both deal with outsiders – but outsiders because of some physical defect – Alison's head injury and Betjeman's father's deafness. They can be linked potentially with all the poems in this section with outsiders, people who are marginalized.

'Brendon Gallacher' deals with love and other poems do too – although in a more negative way such as 'Medusa' and 'Les Grands Seigneurs'.

'Checking Out Me History' and 'Singh Song!' can be linked because they are written by poets from non-white backgrounds.

Many of the poems in this section deal with change and time such as 'Horse Whisperer', 'Brendon Gallacher' (the change of growing up), 'Ozymandias', 'Medusa' and 'On a Portrait of a Deaf Man' – which would be a useful way to link them.

Place

What is your favourite place in the whole world? What is the place you dislike the most in the whole world? Is there a place or places that hold special memories for you or which you associate with some special event in your life? If so, then you will start to be in tune with many of the poems in this section. Almost all the poems in this section deal with a specific place that is important to the poet; many of them are set in the countryside, but there are some with urban settings; some of these places prompt happy memories, but others evoke a sense of sadness or other less positive emotions.

Contemporary Poetry

The Blackbird of Glanmore – Seamus Heaney

Context

Seamus Heaney is an Irish poet, widely recognized as one of the best poets writing in English today. He was born and brought up in Northern Ireland, but has lived in the Republic of Ireland since 1973. Heaney considers himself an Irish poet and has objected to being included in collections of 'British' poets. Northern Ireland has had a violent and troubled history, but Heaney's poems (even those which do address political concerns) are always deeply personal and rooted in everyday events and circumstances. This poem (first published in 2006 in the collection *District and Circle*) revisits the memory of the death of his brother at the age of four in a car accident; Heaney wrote the poem 'Mid-Term Break' in the 1960s about the same incident.

In cultures all over the world blackbirds are seen as birds of ill omen, usually foreshadowing death or some other terrible disaster. Heaney turns these associations on their head and takes a very different view of the blackbird in this poem.

Yon – that one.

Who? The poet speaks as himself in the present tense. He addresses the blackbird of the title. He remembers his younger brother and he reports the words of a neighbour, said after his brother's accident.

When? The present but the poet remembers the past and hints at the future at the end of the poem.

Where? Outside the poet's home in Ireland.

What? The poet arrives home and sees a blackbird which prompts memories of the past.

Commentary

The opening stanza sees Heaney arrive at his house to be greeted by the blackbird – but the blackbird is not identified until line 6. The blackbird is presented in a very positive light – *filling the stillness with life* – and it is

ready to scare off

At the very first wrong move.

Wrong move suggests that Heaney will have done something wrong if he scares the blackbird off. The blackbird is in the ivy when he leaves the house and it seems that he likes the familiarity of the blackbird – its presence whenever he leaves or arrives at his house. It is part of his life, his routine.

In line 6 – a single line stanza – is the first explicit address to the blackbird and Heaney reveals that he loves the bird.

In the third stanza Heaney gets out of the car – his actions imitated by the commas which punctuate his actions and given unity by the alliteration – *park, pause* – and assonance – *heed, breathe, breathe*. He stands completely still and remembers lines he once translated which evoke a sense of impending death:

I want away

To the house of death, to my father.

This memory leads to thoughts of his brother who is fondly recalled as a *little stillness dancer* and his brother's delight at Heaney's return home from boarding school after his first term.

This in turn leads to a memory of a neighbour who commented (long after the accident that killed his brother) that he knew something bad was going to happen to him because a blackbird had been sitting around on the roof of the house for weeks. This is the popular and worldwide folk superstition that blackbirds are birds of ill omen.

In line 25 Heaney locks the car – note the onomatopoeic assonance of *clunks shut* – and the blackbird is momentarily startled. For a split second Heaney sees himself as the blackbird sees him, in a line held together by assonance:

A shadow on raked gravel.

The final six lines are directly addressed to the blackbird or *Hedge-hop* as Heaney calls him. He loves the blackbird without reservation: his song, his nervousness, his timidity and the fact that he is always there:

On the grass when I arrive

In the ivy when I leave.

The poem ends with lines that the poet had already used in lines 1 and 6, but here brought together for the first time. In the classical world of ancient Greece and Rome ivy was presented in a crown and given to outstanding poets. It has for centuries symbolized life: think of the Christmas carol 'The Holly and the Ivy'. Heaney has spent the whole poem remembering a very tragic event from his past, while addressing a bird usually considered a symbol of ill omen. The poem has many arrivals and departures: the departure of his brother from life; his own arrival at his childhood home after his first term away at school; his own departure for boarding school all those years ago; his arrival and departure at his house; the blackbird 'departs' if there are sudden noises – Heaney, I would suggest, is, in the last two lines, paying tribute to the importance of routine, but also imagining his own future departure through death.

But the end of the poem is not gloomy or pessimistic; the tone is quiet and gentle and resigned. He celebrates the blackbird as a symbol of life and continuity, and, through the ivy, also acknowledges his own poetic achievements – which, like the blackbird and the ivy, will remain after he has gone away to the house of death. This is why the repetition of lines from the opening of the poem are so important: we arrive at the end of the poem to lines from which the poem had departed in the opening stanza. We might even see the single isolated lines which punctuate the poem as a way of reminding us that we face death alone.

Why?

This very personal poem

- remembers with sadness and affection the death of Heaney's younger brother.
- celebrates the virtues of routine and ritual.
- offers an unorthodox view of the blackbird.
- contemplates the poet's own death with calm equanimity.
- celebrates the continuity of life and the lasting power of poetry.

A Vision – Simon Armitage

Context

Simon Armitage was born in 1963 in the village of Marsden in West Yorkshire and has spent most of his life in that area. He is a very successful and highly-regarded poet, celebrated for his down-to-earth language and subject matter. Several of his poems are in the Anthology. His poetry often (but not always) deals with the ordinary incidents and events of modern life and appear to be based on personal experience.

Who? The poet speaks as himself in the present tense, sometimes switching to the past tense.

When? The poem looks into the past, but is set now in present-day Britain. It was first published in 1998 as part of the collection entitled *All Points North*.

Where? The final verse is at the local landfill site. Before that there is no specific location.

What? The poet recalls the plans that were made to rejuvenate and transform British towns and cities; he reflects on what happened to those dreams of the future; in the final stanza he finds the plans drawn up by architects and town planners thrown away at the local rubbish tip.

Commentary

The most important part of this poem is really the final stanza, and this allows you to make a good point about the structure of the poem. Armitage delays telling us the full context of this poem until the final four lines, and this creates impact and leads us to see what has gone before in a different light.

The poem opens with an intriguing, general statement which gives no clue about what will follow in the rest of the poem:

The future was a beautiful place, once.

This is intriguing because although he is writing about the future he uses the past tense – so his view or our view of the future was beautiful in the past, when we looked towards the future that was yet to come. That single word *once* implies that it is no longer beautiful and foreshadows the end of the poem.

The first stanza rapidly clarifies what he is writing about: the plans for a utopian future that consisted of sketches, artists' impressions and scale models of what a town centre or a housing estate might look like in the future. These were often displayed in public buildings like the Civic Hall for members of the public to look at and to be consulted about.

The next three stanzas describe what the full-blown balsa-wood town looked like. It is an idealized vision of the future. There is a strong emphasis on environmental issues: there is a bottle-bank; the cycle path encourages cycling; and the people drive electric cars. Some of the vocabulary is drawn from town planning and architecture: *blueprints, suburbs, modes of transportation, cantilevered.*

But this vocabulary is juxtaposed with other words that suggest the plans are unreal, just a dream. *Boulevard* is one example: it's a French word and to apply it to an English town or city hints at a hopeless romanticism, an unreal view of the future. All the other words that Armitage chooses are to do with games, models and toys, and this suggests that the vision of the future contained in the plans is rather childish and not to be taken seriously: *board-game, fairground rides, executive toys, fuzzy-felt grass.* These words suggest that the planners are not being wholly realistic about the future – that they are playing games.

The plans seemed genuine. Armitage describes them as *neat, true, legible.* However, they are written with the *left-hand.* Left-handed people are apparently statistically more likely to become architects, but, more importantly, throughout human history left-handed people have been treated with suspicion and mistrust. Perhaps this is a clue that the plans were always doomed to failure, that they presented a dishonest, unrealistic view of what the future might be like.

And then we read the final stanza and suddenly hear the personal voice of the poet:

I pulled those dreams out of the north wind

at the landfill site.

The north wind always brings cold, harsh weather to the UK and look at the irony of the *landfill site*: the artists' impressions had been full of environmental concerns, but these plans are not being recycled – they are going to be buried in the earth. And they are going to be buried (which surely suggests they are dead) with other such futures, which Armitage in the last line says are

all unlived in and now fully extinct.

Our dreams of a better future remain unfulfilled and the reality of the present reminds us that these dreams have not come true. The perfect *balsa-wood town* remains a dream, just a model. Once again, as he did in the first stanza, Armitage plays around with tenses here: he uses the past tense – *pulled those dreams out* – but they are stamped with today's date which suggests he should use the present tense. This suggests perhaps that the dreams and visions of a better future are credible in the past, when we are younger, but fade as we get older and understand the realities of life.

Why? This carefully constructed poem reveals

- a disillusionment with the dreams of the future imagined by architects and town planners.

- interestingly juxtaposes the language of architecture with the language of toys and childish games.

- demonstrates that reality does not always live up to our expectations.

The Moment – Margaret Atwood

Context

Born in 1939, Atwood is a Canadian poet and novelist. The history and geography of Canada are important influences in her writing. This poem was first published in 1976 and shows Atwood's growing interest in environmental issues. Since then she has become a strong supporter of the Canadian Green Party.

fissure – a narrow opening in rock, used here by Atwood as a verb meaning to crack apart.

Who? The poet narrates to the reader – *you* in line 3 - in the present tense. In the final stanza a personified nature talks to humanity in the past tense.

When? At the moment when you feel you have achieved something tangible, you can't breathe.

Where? It could be anywhere as line 4 suggests –*house, island, country*. This is a poem with global significance.

What? The poem shows the insignificance of human achievement compared with the power of nature.

Commentary

The opening stanza describes the sense of human achievement after a long period – *many years of hard work and a long voyage*. It focuses on the moment when you look around at your achievement and say *I own this*. Atwood deliberately uses language that can apply from the small-scale human achievement – getting your own room or house to much larger geo-political spaces like an island or a country. Whatever we think we own, she is going to suggest, is not really ours at all. She is even calling into question the idea of countries too – they are just lines on a map. Perhaps her use of the word *country* (which is where she stops) is intended to show that we do not think enough about the whole world.

The second stanza (still part of the poem's opening sentence) presents the world of nature personified and animated, and re-claiming the space you thought you had achieved and possessed through all those years of hard work. The realization of our true insignificance takes our breath away. Nature becomes itself once more in this stanza: the trees no longer protect us, the birds reclaim their language and the cliffs are eroded. This is not presented as a harsh or violent action – there is a preponderance of soft sounds in the stanza: the letters *m*, *f* and *l* create a consonance here which makes the process Atwood describes seem natural and gentle. Yet there is something almost sinister in the last line where you can't breathe. What is this moment? Is it an epiphany where we realize the truth – that all our achievements mean nothing? Not being able to breathe might even suggest death, when we also might look back and realize our material achievements – *room, house* – mean nothing

And then in the final stanza Atwood gives a voice to a personified nature. Human beings are accused of just being visitors: we own nothing. There is clearly a reference to the European colonization of the world in the phrase – *planting the flag* – and proclaiming that this or that land belonged to a particular country. Nature even suggests that human beings did not discover natural phenomena – they were always there, before they were 'discovered' and identified by Europeans. The use of the past tense by the personified voice of nature imagines a time when human beings will no longer exist: the earth will still be here.

Why?

The moment is the moment we realize all our accomplishments amount to nothing. This brief poem raises very economically and powerfully some important issues:

- We do not own the world; we must look after it.
- Human achievements are small compared with the force and enduring power of nature.
- Time: we are temporary – the world lives on.
- The natural world is more important than human beings.

Cold Knap Lake – Gillian Clarke

Context

Gillian Clarke who was born in 1937 in Cardiff is one of the leading poets of our time and is very much associated with Wales, where she has lived for most of her life. She and her husband live on a smallholding and keep sheep. You can find a lot of very useful material for students on her website, including comments on most of her poems. Her writing is deeply rooted in everyday experience – sometimes personal experience – but also touches on wider, deeper themes. Her poetry is widely studied in schools and she gives regular poetry readings and lectures about poetry. Cold Knap Lake is a man-made lake in Glamorgan.

for dead – as if dead. The people there assumed the girl was dead.

frock – dress.

dread – fear.

Who? The poet speaks as herself and recalls an incident from her childhood. The poem is written in the past tense, but then changes to the present in line 16 as Clarke ends her narrative to reflect on the significance of the event.

When? During the Second World War.

Where? At an artificial lake in Glamorgan.

What? The events of the poem are straightforward: a little girl is drowned in the lake and her body is pulled out; the poet's mother rescues the girl by giving her artificial resuscitation and the poet's father takes the girl back to her home. The voice of the poet watches these events and reflects on them. The rescued girl comes from a very poor family who beat her when she gets home as a punishment for nearly drowning. Then in the final two stanzas Clarke wonders whether she was there and witnessed the incident. In the final stanza Clarke says that she can't decide – she cannot remember whether she was there or not.

Commentary

Clarke herself has said of this poem

It is about the limitless way the mind takes in events and stories, laying down all that the mind encounters, enriching memory and imagination. It shows the importance of stories, nursery rhymes, poetry, pictures, alongside real events, in making us richly human. It is the picture of the human mind as made by the child in each of us. The lake, and the 'closing water' is memory.

Think about some of your childhood memories: do you have any which are imagined memories – ones which are based perhaps on stories or anecdotes that your parents have told about you but which you do not actually remember? There are certainly things from my childhood which I remember, but not because I really remember them – I have a visual image of them, because of the stories that have been passed down in my family or perhaps because of old photographs. So it is all a little muddled. Clarke herself has commented on this issue:

When you recapture a memory from early childhood, you're sometimes not sure if you were really there, if someone told you about it, or if you read it in a story. I'd read fairy stories and legends about people drowning in mysterious lakes.

Gillian Clarke was born in 1937 and the poem is set during the Second World War (her mother wears a *wartime frock* in line 7). In the opening lines we are shocked by the seriousness of death:

We watched a crowd

pull a drowned child from the lake.

'We' presumably meaning Clarke and her parents. The description of the girl is particularly effective and note how Clarke delays the most shocking word - *dead*- until the very end of the stanza:

Blue-lipped and dressed in water's long green silk

she lay for dead.

The length of the third line delays the shock of the last line, the water is personified and the image is quite beautiful, yet terrifying at the same time. *Long green silk* might be said to recall the death by drowning of Ophelia in Shakespeare's *Hamlet*.

Clarke's mother then gives the girl the kiss of life. But again Clarke withholds the most important part of the sentence until the end of line four. Clarke's mother is portrayed as a heroine. She kneels on the earth and

gave a stranger's child her breath.

This sounds like a miracle and *gave* suggests an act of extraordinary generosity – especially to *a stranger's child*. Note that Clarke's mother's *red head* has connotations here of life and contrasts with the girl who is *blue-lipped* and dressed in green, but will be *rosy* when she is given the kiss of life. In the last two lines of the stanza Clarke uses alliteration and a very short sentence to give the stanza impact:

The crowd stood silent

drawn by the dread of it.

It is only when we get to stanza three that we realize the girl lives. Again the alliteration foregrounds the language – *breathed, bleating* – and the child seems like a new born baby taking its first breath or a newly born lamb with its bleating. The final two lines are a complete juxtaposition because after the joy of saving a human life Clarke's father took her home where he

watched her thrashed for almost drowning.

We are not told why the girl was thrashed – perhaps her parents were angry about the trouble she had caused or perhaps it was a way of getting rid of their anxiety. In fact, there are lots of things we are not told: the rescued girl is anonymous; the people watching are just a crowd; the only individuals identified are Clarke and her parents. But, as we shall see, this is a poem about the nature of memory and it is appropriate that Clarke cannot remember or chooses not to give us these details.

That is the incident. The final two stanzas are Clarke's reflections on the incident. The first line of the fourth stanza sums up her dilemma: *Was I there?* And then a longer question follows. It is as if having recounted the incident Clarke is not really sure if she genuinely remembers it – or remembers it correctly. The *troubled surface* is obviously the lake, but also Clarke's memory – something about the incident is deeply troubling it seems. Under the surface of the lake and her memory there is something else *shadowy under the dipped fingers of willows*

where satiny mud blooms in cloudiness

after the treading, heavy webs of swans

as their wings beat and whistle on the air?

These striking lines are full of memorable sound effects and seem to combine great beauty – *satiny mud* (which might remind us of the *green silk* in the first stanza) - with confusion (*cloudiness*) and a sense of threat embodied in the swans: the assonance in *tre͟ading, he͟avy we͟bs* sounds especially ominous. The willows are personified and also feature assonance – *dipped fingers of willows*, while the lines are marked by repeated use of *s*, *l* and *w*. *Beat* and *whistle* are onomatopoeic. Overall the effect is mysterious, enchanting, frightening and confusing. Clarke has said of the swans:

Swans can be fierce, and pretty scary to a child who thinks they are beautiful beings out of legend. The little girl nearly drowned. Did the swans try to take her to their kingdom under the water? That's the kind of story that haunted me when I was a child.

And Clarke's word *haunted* seems to me exactly right. The poem's final two stanzas take on a dream-like quality in which Clarke's memory seems to fuse the water, the willows, the mud and the swans into a mysteriously important event – which, like the muddy water of the lake, refuses to become clear.

The final stanza is short, to-the-point and its more confident tone is enhanced by the poem's first full rhyme:

All lost things lie under the closing water

in that lake with the poor man's daughter.

This couplet is full of the letter *l* which gives it a fluid quality – like the water and like Clarke's memory. What does Clarke mean by *all lost things*? All the things we half-remember? All the things in our past? All the things we have forgotten? All the people in the world who have ever drowned and whose bodies lie beneath the surface of the water? All the things – memories, people and objects – that we once possessed but no longer have?

The poem touches on myth and fairy tale too. In the Bible God gives Adam (the first man) life by breathing into his nostrils. Swans often appear in fairy stories, but in reality their strength and violence is legendary. Children from poor backgrounds often feature in fairy stories too. The human attitude to water – over thousands of years – is important: water is always potentially dangerous, but we need it to grow crops, to wash things in and for certain technological processes. From ancient times human beings have been throwing things – often precious and valuable things - into water: even the fountains in my local shopping centre are full of coins that people have thrown in for good luck – and this is the 21st century! So it would seem that water – as a dangerous yet tempting element - has a central place in the human psyche.

Why?

This astonishingly beautiful and thought-provoking poem

- uses the lake to symbolize the shifting nature of memory.

- uses sounds and imagery to create a poignant feeling of beauty combined with danger.

- reveals the threat and attraction of water in human psychology.

- turns a miraculous but true story into an event with elements of dream and fairy tale.

- is hauntingly beautiful and mysterious like a dream.

Price We pay for the Sun – Grace Nichols

Context

Grace Nichols was born on the Caribbean island of Guyana in 1950. Since 1977 she has lived in Britain with her partner, John Agard. They are both poets and you can find other poems by both poets in other sections of this Anthology. Although she lives in the UK, she is very aware of her past and the traditions of Guyana, and many of her poems explore the clash or conflict between British or European values and those of her West Indian and African ancestors or, as this one does, they celebrate the life she left behind in Guyana. Nichols herself has said:

I am a writer across two worlds; I just can't forget my Caribbean culture and past, so there's this constant interaction between the two worlds: Britain and the Caribbean.

These two worlds are contrasted and juxtaposed in this poem.

unravelling – to take something apart.

croon – to sing or hum in an undertone.

Who? The poet, her mother, father and grandmother. The poem is addressed to tourists who have an idealized vision of the Caribbean.

When? The present.

Where? The Caribbean.

What? The poet contrasts the tourist image of the Caribbean with the reality.

Commentary

This poem vividly shows the difference between our image of a place and the reality. For many Europeans the West Indies are a beautiful holiday destination for a beach holiday: the weather is hot and the beaches are unspoilt and idyllic. Nichols is at pains throughout to show the reality that lies beneath this tourist image of the islands and her desire to tell the truth, to reveal the reality, even informs the language she chooses to write the poem in.

The poem begins with three stanzas of unequal length. In the first stanza which appears to be addressed to the tourist of line 3, Nichols asserts that the islands of the Caribbean are not just picture postcards: they are real:

more real

than flesh and blood.

She then sets up a pattern of three rhymes – *stone, foam, bone* – all features of the real, natural world with the final one associated with living things.

The second stanza is more personal in that it describes the reality of life in the Caribbean for the poet's mother, father and grandmother. Her mother's breasts are like *sleeping volcanoes*, but these volcanoes are not part of the tourist's itinerary because they hide *sulph-furious cancer*. The word play here continues the volcano simile (volcanoes produce sulphur) but include *furious* to suggest both the anger Nichols feels at the suffering of her mother because of breast cancer and the destructive effects of the cancer itself. The wind is

constantly whipping

my father's tears

to salty hurricanes.

These lines are cleverly compressed: destructive hurricanes are a feature of life in the Caribbean, but here are used metaphorically to suggest the father's tears. Why is he crying? Perhaps because of the mother's cancer or perhaps because life is hard and difficult and they face a constant battle against poverty, despite the image tourists have of the area. Meanwhile (and these different events are presented in one long continuous sentence) Nichols' grandmother is crooning (against a backdrop of sand, water and palm – which reminds us of the image of the Caribbean) and the final stanza repeats her words:

Poverty is the price

we pay for the sun girl

run come.

This contains the words that make up the title of the poem. Who are they addressed to? Nichols, her granddaughter? The tourist addressed in the opening stanza? The reader? All three, I think. The statement is made memorable by the alliteration on *p*. But what is really interesting is the final line – which is a complete paradox, almost an oxymoron. *Run* suggests that if you are from the Caribbean then you must get away in order to escape poverty and hurricanes and volcanoes; *come* might suggest the idea that tourists need to come in order to help relieve the poverty. On a more personal level, it may mean that the grandmother is urging Nichols to leave, to run, but, because she knows she will miss her, to come back to see her.

Nichols' use of free verse is important: it is a rejection of the ordered poetry (with a set number of syllables in the line and a rhyme scheme) which has been historically associated with the western European tradition. In addition, the language of this poem mixes standard English with Caribbean dialect and accent appropriately because she is writing about two different things - the image and the reality. Therefore, two different types of language reflect this opposition of ideas. Nichols also makes effective use of ellipsis to make her poem short and hard-hitting.

Why?

This short but powerful poem

- expresses anger at tourists who do not understand the reality of life in the Caribbean.

- evokes sadness for the suffering, disease and poverty of ordinary people.

- demonstrates the importance of family.

- evokes nostalgia for Nichols' Guyanese heritage.

- mixes standard and non-standard English with powerful metaphors.

Neighbours – Gillian Clarke

Context

Gillian Clarke who was born in 1937 in Cardiff is one of the leading poets of our time and is very much associated with Wales, where she has lived for most of her life. She and her husband live on a smallholding and keep sheep. You can find a lot of very useful material for students on her website, including comments on most of her poems. Her writing is deeply rooted in everyday experience – sometimes personal experience – but also touches on wider, deeper themes. Her poetry is widely studied in schools and she gives regular poetry readings and lectures about poetry.

This poem refers to the spring of 1986. On April 26th 1986 there was an accident at a Russian nuclear power plant called Chernobyl which is now in the Ukraine. Radiation from the plant leaked out and there were widespread fears all across Europe about the radiation being carried on the winds to affect nature and spread radiation sickness. The winds carried the fallout, the radioactive dust, to the north and then the west. Some was later found on sheep in Britain. Many ordinary Russians and Ukrainians died from the immediate effects of the accident – especially members of the emergency services who were sent in to rectify the accident and to bring the leak under control. In the Ukraine people are still dying from cancers caused by the radiation leak all those years ago.

There is another important part of the context to this poem. In 1986 Russia was still the Soviet Union, a country run in an authoritarian manner by the Russian Communist Party. The Cold War was not yet over and most of eastern Europe was part of the Soviet bloc. Contact with foreigners was discouraged, news was carefully controlled by the government and accidents like this one had a tendency to be covered up and never even heard about in western Europe. This was impossible in the case of Chernobyl – partly because in the days after the accident radiation began to be discovered on sheep in Finland and Norway, in the milk of cows in Poland – but also because things were changing inside the Soviet Union – their new president Mikhail Gorbachev (he came to power in 1985) was convinced that the communist system had to be reformed and had introduced a policy known by its Russian term – glasnost – which means openness and honesty. Clarke refers explicitly to this in the final line of the poem.

isobars – a line on a weather map, connecting places of equal barometric pressure. In the UK *shouldering isobars* on a weather map are usually a sign that rain and wind will be coming from the west. In the Chernobyl incident the radiation spread across northern and western Europe because the winds were coming from the east. The east wind in the UK always brings cold weather and is one explanation for Clarke's opening sentence – *That spring was late*. Spring was late because the wind was from the east and the temperatures were low, even before the accident at the nuclear power plant.

gall – bitterness.

caesium – a radioactive element which causes cancer.

toxin – poison.

Glasnost – a Russian word meaning 'openness' or 'honesty'.

Golau glas – a Welsh phrase meaning 'blue sky'.

Who? The poet starts in the past tense and then switches to the present for the final three stanzas. She uses the first person plural – *we*. There is a good case for saying that *we* refers to her and her family at the start of the poem, but by the end of the poem refers to the whole of humanity everywhere in the world.

When? In the spring of 1986 as the radiation from the Chernobyl nuclear plant spread across Europe and started to affect the environment.

Where? The opening four stanzas are set in different parts of Europe. By the end of the poem the words seek, as we shall see, to embrace the whole world.

What? The poet from her smallholding in Wales describes and reflects on the nuclear accident at Chernobyl in the Ukraine.

Commentary

This poem consists of seven stanzas; the first four are written in the past tense and each stanza is set in a different part of Europe. The final three stanzas are in the present tense. What the poem is actually about is not revealed until the fourth stanza, although we might sense that something is wrong before then.

The poem starts with a direct statement:

That spring was late.

We know that Clarke lives on a smallholding. People who work on the land are more aware of the seasons and Clarke and her family watch the sky and study the isobars in the hope that the weather will change and that spring will arrive. The *shouldering isobars* on the weather charts are signs that the weather might change. The birds don't reproduce because they are waiting for the weather to improve; lambs die and their corpses are eaten by the crows. The sentence that ends the first stanza combines the innocence of the lamb with the gruesome image of the crows:

Crows drank from the lamb's eye.

The second stanza concentrates on events in Finland where birds began dropping out of the sky. *Small birds fell* – is such an unusual collocation and the description of the song-thrushes:

Smudged signatures on light

is a phrase of overwhelming tenderness. *Signatures* suggest how recognizable these birds are because of their song; *smudged* suggest that something is wrong, that the birds cannot be seen clearly because of the radiation pollution. We might be reminded of a famous passage in the Bible where Jesus tells his disciples that God takes notice of every death of even the tiniest sparrow. This is the Gospel according to Matthew, Chapter 10, verses 26 – 32. God cares for every part of his creation and, Clarke implies, so should we.

The third stanza suggests that birds are dying in Norway which has fjords and we are given the first hint that something sinister has happened with Clarke's use of the word *gall*. There start to be public warnings about safety and in Poland milk which has been contaminated has to be thrown away.

Clarke and the reader finally reach the source of the problems in the fourth stanza. The environmental damage is due to

a mouthful of bitter air from the Ukraine

brought by the wind out of its box of sorrows.

These are important lines: if the wind had been blowing in a different direction (eastwards) then the people of western Europe might never have known about the accident at Chernobyl. All the damage to the environment would have been to the Ukraine and other parts of the old Soviet Union. The damage would still have been appalling in its scope, but it might have remained more obscure and also confined to the country which caused the accident. Note Clarke's use of alliteration here – *blowback, bitter, brought by, box* – the plosive *b*s give a strong sense of bitterness. *Box of sorrows* is an interesting phrase: in Greek mythology when Pandora's box was opened, it released death and suffering into the world, but one thing was left in the box – we will return to this at the end of the poem.

Clarke now changes to the present tense and to Wales:

a lamb sips caesium on a Welsh hill

and a child drinking rainwater

takes into her blood the poisoned arrow.

Once again, Clarke mixes images of innocence and extreme, deadly danger to create pathos.

We might detect irony in the opening of the sixth stanza:

Now we are all neighbourly.

Clarke mocks, but only slightly, the habit of towns to be twinned with other towns all over Europe (a practice which began after the Second World War in order to promote international understanding and in the hope of preventing another world war). Because radiation fall-out knows no national boundaries and goes wherever the wind blows it, Clarke is right – we are all twinned with Chernobyl because we all share the consequences of the accident. The stanza then focuses on Chernobyl itself – because it was in the vicinity of the nuclear reactor that the effects were felt most strongly. She mentions the *burnt firemen, the child on the Moscow train* – the immediate victims of the accident.

The penultimate stanza looks to the future. The opening sentence is brilliantly constructed:

In the democracy of the virus and the toxin

we wait.

Note how the verb and its subject (*we wait*) are withheld until the end of the sentence: the reader has to wait for them, just as Clarke is waiting to see what will happen. The *democracy of the virus* suggests solidarity with the whole of Europe, with everyone who has been affected by this environmental disaster. The word *democracy* is loaded with meaning too, because Gorbachev, the Soviet leader, and his reforms did finally lead to the end of the Cold War, the end of Communism and a form of democracy in eastern Europe. I think Clarke is less interested in these political concerns though and sees the *democracy of the virus* as humanity joined together to protect the environment and preserve the planet. In this sense political differences and national borders are relatively unimportant: the human race is connected by being human and by having the same home – the planet earth. Clarke and her family watch for spring migrations because they want to be sure that some of nature's rituals have survived the nuclear accident and that nature will return to normal.

The final stanza is an astonishing end to the poem. It is foregrounded by being only one line long, thus breaking the pattern of the poem. It also contains three languages:

Glasnost. Golau glas. A first break of blue.

Using words from three different languages is a way of showing our connections – simply because Clarke has put them there in that line. The meanings are important too. The process of *glasnost* was hastened by the events at Chernobyl. *Golau glas* (blue sky) is Welsh and the *glas* appears to echo *glasnost* – though its meaning is different. The blue sky that the Welsh and the English words refer to look forward with hope to a better time when nature has recovered from the radiation fallout, when there is more understanding between nations and when humanity takes more collective care of the planet.

And finally – Pandora's box – the one thing left in the box when it was opened was hope and this poem ends with an overwhelming feeling of hope, because of the way the last line combines three languages and looks to a better future.

Why?

This passionate poem about a real event

- expresses a faith in nature's ability to heal and to renew itself.

- expresses anger at our ability to damage nature.

- evokes enormous sympathy for the natural victims of man's mistakes.

- asserts that what connects us as human beings is more important than what divides us.

- ends on a note of hope for nature and for humanity.

Crossing the Loch – Kathleen Jamie

Context

Kathleen Jamie was born in Scotland in 1962 and has a growing reputation as one of Scotland's finest living poets. Scotland – its culture, landscape and traditions – is central to her work. This poem was published in 1999 in the collection *Jizzen*. 'Jizzen' is an old Scots term for childbed and many of the poems deal with birth of all kinds – the birth of Jamie's own children and the Scottish Parliament being established or 'born'.

loch – a lake in Scotland.

the race – a rapid current in water, either on a river or here in a lake.

nuclear hulls – sunken nuclear submarines which no-one knows about.

phosphorescence – something that shines in the dark.

blaeberries – a Scottish term for bilberry.

Who? The poet recalls an incident in her past using the past tense. The final stanza switches to the present tense. She addresses both the reader and the friends who were part of her youthful escapade.

When? Now – looking back at the past.

Where? On a tidal loch in Scotland.

What? After an evening in the pub, the poet and her friends row across the lake to the cottage they are staying in.

Commentary

The opening line invites us to *Remember* and the poet is addressing the friends who were with her on the night she describes in the rest of the poem. The poet remembers a night spent in the pub, after which she and her friends had taken a boat and rowed back across the loch to the cottage they were staying in. In this first stanza *the loch mouthed 'boat'* almost as if inviting them to row across it. They were probably slightly drunk too – it turns out in the next stanza that rowing across a tidal loch at night is not a very safe thing to do.

The second stanza starts with an abrupt caesura which signals a change in mood. They all go quiet and we hear through onomatopoeia the sound of the rowing – *splash, creak, spill* – enhanced by consonance on the letter *l* throughout this sentence. Then the poet was scared. The breeze and the hills are personified but in uninviting ways: the breeze is a *cold shawl*, the *hills hunched*. She wondered what lay beneath the surface of the water. Here the atmosphere becomes very sinister and frightening: Scotland has been home to Britain's fleet of nuclear submarines for decades and this has led to political protest near Faslane, the base where the submarines are kept, but also the possible damage to the environment should any accident or mishap occur. The poet uses the phrase *ticking nuclear hulls* and *ticking* suggests that these are dangerous bombs which may, at some future point, cause considerable damage to nature. This second stanza ends, then, on a note of chilling seriousness – which adds to the fear they feel.

The third stanza begins with the vagueness of memory: the poet cannot remember who rowed or who was silent. There is a vivid sense of being on the water at night – *salt-air, stars* – and then someone notices the phosphorescence in the loch. And the poem and the poet and the poet's memory are transformed from the fear of the previous stanza. The rest of the stanza is filled with a magical sense of the sheer beauty and magnificent transformative powers of nature. Note how many *s* or *sh* sounds there are after line 19 – this gives aural coherence to the lines and suggests the sound of water. Jamie uses two similes to describe herself and her friends: they are a *twittering nest/washed from the rushes* and an *astonished small boat of saints*. Both similes have religious associations: Moses was washed from the rushes and grew to be famous and influential; the boat of saints is a common motif in the history of Christianity: the earliest Christians spread the word of God by travelling around the Mediterranean in boats, often surviving terrible storms in the process; in more recent times, religious groups travelled to America in small boats in search of a place where they could practise their religion freely. I do not think this means that this is a poem about being a Christian – these are, after all, similes. But I do think the poet uses them to suggest that what they experienced on the loch with the phosphorescence was almost mystical, magical and a moment that changed them.

In the final stanza the poet switches to the present tense. She admits that what they did that night – drunkenly deciding to row across a potentially dangerous tidal loch – was foolhardy, but they survived and she and her friends now have families with people they have met since that frightening yet magical night. On reflection she now says it was a night when they were able to call their own:

the sky and salt-water, wounded hills

dark-starred by blueberries, the glimmering anklets

we wore in shallows.

And those *glimmering anklets* are a reminder of the phosphorescence that showed them the true beauty and magic of the natural world. The poem ends with an image from the past, as they jump out of the boat and they reach their destination by drawing

the boat safe, high at the cottage door.

And isn't it fitting that the poem should end as this exciting but slightly frightening youthful escapade comes to an end and they safely return to the cottage?

Why?

This poem recalls a foolish youthful event with affection and nostalgia and also

- shows the power of memory.

- celebrates the almost magical beauty of nature.

- warns of the dangers of the damage we can do the environment.

Hard Water – Jean Sprackland

Context

To fully understand this poem a little knowledge of what hard water is will help. Hard water is water that is rich in minerals because it has been in contact with the earth for a long time. On the other hand, soft water is water that has probably come from lakes or rivers and has not had time to pick up minerals. Most of England has hard water. Areas of the UK which have soft water are Scotland, Wales, the Lake District, Devon and Cornwall. With soft water soap becomes more foamy and drinks like tea and coffee will taste different. In hard water areas soap does not become especially foamy and the water itself may look a little cloudy when it is first poured from the tap (tiny traces of the minerals!), but this cloudy consistency will soon settle. Hard water tastes different too. Furthermore, some brewers deliberately added minerals to their water in order to improve the taste of the beer they produced: this adding of the mineral gypsum is called Burtonization – because brewers in Burton-on-Trent pioneered this adding of minerals.

You may be wondering what this has got to do with the poem, but you will soon see – Jean Sprackland comes from Burton-on-Trent and this is a poem that is not, in the end, about water, but takes the hard water of the famous breweries in Burton to explore the nature of our roots and identity.

Sprackland was born in 1962 and has published poems and short stories. This poem comes from the collection *Hard Water* published in 2003.

limestone – a sedimentary rock of calcium carbonate. Areas with limestone tend to have hard water.

gypsum – another soft mineral which helps to produce hard water.

alchemical – alchemy was an ancient form of Chemistry and its chief object was to try to turn ordinary metal into gold. Alchemists guarded their secrets jealously and I think Sprackland uses the word here to suggest that brewing has an element of mystery to it: master brewers keep some of their ingredients and processes secret.

mardy – a dialect word, meaning moody or irritable.

Who? The poet narrates this poem in the past tense.

When? Now.

Where? Burton-on-Trent.

What? The poet remembers being on holiday in Wales where the tap water is soft, but then says she prefers the hard water associated with her home town and explores the reason for this.

Commentary

The first stanza recalls the excitement of being on holiday in an area of soft water. It was

A mania of teadrinking and hairwashing.

Even the soap was *excitable.*

The second stanza starts with the word *but* – because despite the excitement of soft water, the poet loves coming back home. After an opening sentence of four lines the poem slows down in line 5. The poet says she likes the vowels, the language of her home town – *hey up me duck.* The next few lines describe the act of pouring a glass of hard water. The lines lovingly describe the qualities of hard water. Hard water causes problems and there is a hint of this in words such as *swimming-pool smell, anaesthetic, anxiety* – but Sprackland praises it for being *honest water*: it has *frankness.* It reminds her of various things *limestone, gypsum, sour steam* – but most of all, because this is the climax of the stanza:

The alchemical taste of brewing.   .

And this line is so important because it places the poem in Burton-on-Trent and nowhere else.

The final stanza continues her description of the water of home. After a night in the pub it rains and she turns up her face to the rain. The water contains a threat – the rainy nights are *pitiless*; she allows the rain to *scald my eyelids and lips*; the rain has *a payload of acid*; but she accepts it by opening her mouth and letting the rain-water in.

Line 20 is an important turning point. The poet with her mouth open is

speaking nothing

in spite of my book learning.

She says the rain of her home town has a *different cleverness* and she allows it to wash her tongue. She tells us it tastes of *work* and *early mornings*; and she then links the true taste of the rain with the language of her home town: *don't get mardy* and *too bloody deep for me.* For the poet this blunt rain and the language of her home town is

fierce lovely water that marked me for life

as belonging, regardless.

She has a sense of belonging, regardless of the fact that she has been away to university and received an education. The rain is *fierce* because it is hard water and throughout the poem it has certain admirable qualities as we can see from the words used to describe it – *straight, honest, frankness, the true taste.* It is lovely because of these qualities of honesty and down-to-earthness, but also simply because it is the water of home. She is also paying tribute to the ordinary people of Burton-on-Trent whose language she admires, like the water, as being honest and true. The phrase *too bloody deep for me* is especially important – it might be something that someone without Sprackland's education might well say of a challenging literary text.

So in the end, this is not really a poem about water; it is a poem about the importance of your roots and accepting them, of celebrating them and the way an education might separate you from your roots.

Why?

This poem takes a common phenomena (hard water) and

- celebrates the importance of our roots and our language.
- mocks the trappings of education (book learning).
- displays enormous affection for the poet's home town.
- pays tribute to the qualities of honesty and frankness.

The Literary Heritage

London – William Blake

Context

William Blake (1757 – 1827) is now seen as the foremost artist and poet of his time, but his work was largely unknown during his lifetime. He was a painter as well as a poet and you can see some of his paintings in art galleries like Tate Britain in London or the Fitzwilliam Museum in Cambridge. 'London' comes from a collection *Songs of Innocence and of Experience* which appeared together for the first time in 1794. *The Songs of Innocence* (which originally appeared on their own in 1789) are positive in tone and celebrate unspoilt nature, childhood and love. *The Songs of Experience* (from which 'London' comes) depicts a corrupt society in which the prevailing mood is one of despair and in which children are exploited and love is corrupted.

This poem is often read as a profound criticism of the society Blake lived in. Everything in London is owned (*chartered*) - even the River Thames which is a natural force which one might expect to be free. Blake was writing at a time when Britain was the wealthiest country in the world because of its global empire and because of the Industrial Revolution which produced goods which were exported all over the world. But not everyone shared in this enormous wealth; the gap between rich and poor was huge, with the poor suffering really terrible living and working conditions. This poem first 'appeared' (this term will be explained below) in 1794. The date of publication is crucial: Blake is partly seeing London in this way because of events in France. In 1789 the French Revolution began, changing French society forever and ushering in a new age of freedom, equality and brotherhood. Many English people saw what was happening in France and thought it was good to have a society based on greater equality; they looked critically at British society and saw appalling inequalities and injustices. For example, you may be aware that this was the period in British history that some people campaigned against slavery in the British Empire: what is less well-known is that forms of slavery existed in London. There are recorded cases of parents selling their sons to master chimneysweeps in London. The life of a chimney sweep was likely to be short: they were sent up the chimneys of large houses to clean them. Some suffocated; others were trapped in the confined space and died; sometimes their masters would light fires below them to encourage them to work faster – they sometimes were burnt alive. For those who survived, their health was affected: they suffered from terrible lung complaints as a result of breathing in coal dust and, because of poor hygiene, might also succumb to testicular cancer brought on by the accumulated layers of biting coal dust.

Blake had produced *Songs of Innocence* on its own in 1789, although we can tell from his surviving notebooks that he always intended to write *Songs of Experience*. I have used the term 'appeared' because they were not published in a conventional sense. Blake produced each copy of *Songs of Innocence and of Experience* at home by hand and copies were then given to friends and acquaintances. Part of this was Blake's own choice, but we can easily see that his views about Britain and its government would have been highly controversial, so open publication of them may have led to charges of sedition or treason. The British government at the time were terrified of a revolution here, like the one in France, and were doing everything they could to silence people like Blake who were critical of the society in which they lived.

Blake earned his living as an engraver. Before photographs and modern ways of reproducing images, engravings were the cheapest and easiest way of illustrating a book. Blake produced illustrations for other people's books throughout his life – that was how he earned a living. To create an engraving, the engraver has to carve, with a specialist knife, lines on a metal plate; when the plate is then covered in ink and pressed on paper the lines appear on the paper.

Blake used the same technique for reproducing his own poems. After coating the metal plate with ink and producing the outline, Blake coloured each page of each copy of *Songs of Innocence and of Experience* by hand with water colour paint. It is estimated that only 25 copies were produced in his lifetime. If you go to the British Museum you can see one copy: it is tiny and exquisitely detailed and, of course, very personal, because Blake coloured it by hand himself. In addition, to produce his poems in this way was time-consuming and arduous, since in order for the words to appear the right way round when the page was printed, they had to be written in mirror hand-writing on the plate – a painstaking process that must have taken hours and shows not only Blake's artistry, but also his devotion to hard work.

chartered – owned. The charter was a legal document proving possession.

mark – to notice.

marks – signs.

ban – a government edict banning people from doing something.

manacles – handcuffs or leg-irons.

hapless – unlucky.

harlot – prostitute.

marriage hearse – an oxymoron; Blake juxtaposes the idea of death (hearses carry the dead body to the graveyard) with life – marriage often produces children.

Who? The narrator recounts what he sees in the first stanza and in the next three stanzas what he hears as he wanders around London. The poem is written in the present tense which gives it an immediacy and greater impact.

When? 1794.

Where? London.

What? The narrator sees and hears a population suffering and full of pain and despair.

Commentary

The poem's narrator wanders through the streets of London looking at the suffering of his fellow citizens which is apparent on their faces. The first stanza concentrates on what he sees; the second stanza changes to the sounds he can hear and this continues until the end of the poem. Everywhere he goes he sees people who are repressed and downtrodden; in the third stanza he hears the cry of a chimney sweep and the sigh of a soldier; in the final stanza, at night, at midnight, he hears the curse of *the youthful harlot* (very young prostitute) whose *curse* rings out in the night and *blasts* the *marriage-hearse*. We might note that there is no interaction between Blake and the sights and sounds he sees; the only interaction that there is evidence of is the *new-born infant* in the final stanza – the product of a sexual act – but the baby cries and is born into a world of misery and degradation. Nowhere in the poem do we meet a complete human being: we see their marks and hear them, but there is no encounter with any complete human being, suggesting at once their isolation, but also their lack of completeness and community in this horrifying city.

In the first stanza Blake uses simple repetition of the word *chartered* and *marks* (although with a slightly different meaning). The oppression he sees is all-consuming – he sees it in every face he meets. Note the last line which uses parallelism of sound:

Marks of weakness, marks of woe.

The word *mark* is repeated and is then followed by two words which alliterate. This combination of the letter *m* and *w* is very soft and gentle and creates a sense of overwhelming sadness. Note how *mark* starts as a verb in a very innocuous sense and then becomes a repeated noun, suggesting that there is an indelible mark on all the citizens of London.

The second stanza picks up the word *every* and repeats it five times to suggest the situation he is describing is all–encompassing. Again the final line is significant. The manacles that imprison people are *mind-forged* – they are forged, made in the mind. Is Blake suggesting that the people of London are not even aware of their own oppression? Is it something in their mentality, their minds, which prevents them from protesting? Do they have too much faith in their own rulers? Do they not question the system? Note too how Blake delays the verb of the second stanza – *I hear* – until the very last two words of the stanza. Blake's use of repetition in the first two stanzas has another purpose: his language becomes as restricted and limited as the lives of the people he describes. The word *ban* often stirs some debate: you may read elsewhere that it is a reference to the marriage banns – the announcements of a couple's intention to marry. This ties in with the final stanza, but, according to the Oxford English Dictionary, marriage banns have never been spelt with a single *n*. Isn't it more likely that Blake means prohibitions, banning something? Such as public meetings to protest about the condition of the country?

The third stanza continues with the sounds of London: the cry of the chimney sweep and the sigh of the soldier. Why is the church *black'ning*? Some readers suggest that it is a result of pollution caused by industry, but it could be a comment on the moral corruption of the church – it is evil. Why? I think Blake would suggest it is hypocritical: it is appalled by the cry of the chimney sweep, but does nothing to stop slavery. The sibilance in lines 11 and 12 suggest the agony of the soldier. It is an astonishing image – sighs do not run in blood. But the soldier is badly wounded or dying – and he seems to be defending the palace or at least in the pay of the place where the royal family live. Blake uses synecdoche to great effect in this stanza with his use of the words *church* and *palace*: its use here is partly to protect Blake in the repressive society he lived in, but it also serves to distance the establishment and the royal family even further from their subjects.

The worst horrors are saved until the fourth stanza and Blake signals this by stating – *but most* – and what he hears most of all is the curse of the youthful harlot. You can sometimes read that this is a curse in the sense of a bad spell, but it might just as well be a shouted swear word (*curse* had that meaning too). Who she is cursing is unclear, but the curse *blasts the new-born infant's tear*. Perhaps this is an unwanted baby, another mouth to feed, its father one of her clients? The baby is crying and in the final cryptic, oxymoronic line, her curse

   blights with plagues the marriage hearse.

The phrase *marriage hearse* is an oxymoron because we normally associate marriage with new life and happiness, whereas we associate hearses with funerals and sadness, so to put the two ideas together is striking and original. Does Blake mean that some marriages are like death? Or that marriage is the death of love? Is marriage something that the youthful harlot will never know? Or is it the marriage of one of her clients? Why do married men visit prostitutes? Some readers even suggest that the curse of the harlot is some sort of sexually transmitted sexual disease which the harlot has given to her client who has then passed it on to his wife – this reading might be supported by the word *plagues*. But *plagues* can be a metaphor too – whatever interpretation you choose, it is wise not to be too dogmatic – the beauty and brilliance of Blake is that he is able to suggest all the above possibilities – and even more.

What is certain is that there is something very wrong with marriage in this final stanza and that the curse of the harlot is frightening and chilling: note Blake's use of harsh plosive consonants in *blasts, blights and plagues* – this is almost onomatopoeic in its presentation of a diseased, corrupt society and Blake's angry reaction to it. We have already mentioned the oxymoron with which the poem ends, but Blake in the third stanza had already juxtaposed things which are not normally associated with each other: the cry of the chimney sweep with the church, and the sigh of the soldier with the palace walls – both these images in a way are oxymoronic. Think back to our comments on 'The Sick Rose' in the introduction – this is a profound and moving criticism of Blake's society.

Finally, Blake's use of the ballad form is important. The ballad form is associated with the oral tradition and with anonymity – it is a more democratic form than the sonnet. However, traditional ballads have a strong narrative drive which this poem lacks. So we can say that Blake takes a form that is popular and egalitarian, and then turns its narrative conventions upside down by writing a poem that is descriptive.

The Final Unpublished Stanza

This is the stanza that was found in Blake's notebooks when he died and which some editions of his complete works publish. As you read it, think about why Blake did not publish this stanza during his lifetime:

Remove away that blackening church;

Remove away that marriage hearse;

Remove away that man of blood –

You'll quite remove the ancient curse!

This makes explicit what is implied in the poem: Blake is calling for a revolution which will *remove* the church and the monarchy: *man of blood* is a phrase famously used by Oliver Cromwell to describe Charles I, the English king who was executed after losing the English Civil War. One can only guess why Blake did not include this stanza, but we can speculate that in 1794 it was too dangerous and that Blake might have got in trouble with the authorities for publishing such a call. Artistically the stanza has its limitations: *remove away* is tautological and, because it makes completely clear Blake's attitude to the things described in the poem as we read it today, one can argue that takes away the cryptic, mysterious quality of Blake's poem as it first appeared. This cryptic nature of the poem encourages us to think and analyze what Blake is saying and thus we are encouraged by the poem to break out of our own *mind-forged manacles*, to expand our minds in order to realize the full impact, the complete implications of what Blake's view of London is. London needs to be changed urgently and by a revolution.

Why?

This very famous poem is remarkable.

- It is a political poem of protest against the authorities.

- This sense of protest makes it an angry and bitter poem.

- Blake speaks up for the marginalized in his society.

- It uses the ballad form in a revolutionary way.

- It is remarkable for its compression of language. Blake manages to pack so much meaning into so few words.

- Its use of simple repetition, sound effects and oxymoronic imagery make it memorable and striking.

Extract from *The Prelude* – William Wordsworth

Context

William Wordsworth was born in 1770 in Cockermouth on the edge of the English Lake District. He had a life-long fascination with nature and it is from the natural world that he took much of his inspiration. He died in 1850, having been made Poet Laureate in 1843. Wordsworth began to write *The Prelude* in 1798 and kept working on it and revising it until his death. It was not published until 1850, three months after his death. He published many poems during his own lifetime, but many readers feel that *The Prelude* is his finest work.

This extract is from *The Prelude*, a long autobiographical poem first finished in 1805. It is subtitled *The Growth of the Poet's Mind* – and Wordsworth tells the story of his life, but with the intention of showing his psychological development and also how he came to be a poet. Central to his development, he claims, was the influence of nature: Wordsworth grew up in the English Lake District – a national park and an area of outstanding natural beauty even today. It is not just that Wordsworth liked the beauty of nature – we perhaps all do that because we associate it with peace away from the hustle and bustle of urban or suburban life; he also believed that nature had a moral influence on him and had made him a better human being. He is at pains throughout *The Prelude* to try and prove this connection – that his experiences in the natural world made him a better person and a poet. You may elsewhere read references to Wordsworth's pantheism. Pantheists worship nature and feel that if there is a God then that God exists in every living thing, every part of the natural world: God is a spirit of the universe which exists in a rock or a daffodil as much as it does in a human being.

her – Nature.

elfin pinnace – a pinnace is a small boat; elfin means small and charming.

covert – secret.

bark – boat.

Who? The poet narrates in the past tense an incident from his childhood.

When? 1805. Wordsworth was a child in the late 18th century, but is recollecting this experience as an adult.

Where? On a lake in the English Lake District, generally thought to be Ullswater.

What? Wordsworth steals a boat and goes for a row on the lake. He explores the ramifications of this incident.

Commentary

This extract is written in blank verse. It narrates an incident. This extract comes from Book II of *The Prelude* which is entitled *Childhood and School-Time*. The opening sentence clearly shows the influence of Nature on the young Wordsworth:

One summer evening (led by her) I found

A little boat tied to a willow tree.

We know that *she* refers to nature from the preceding lines. The poet proceeds to unchain the boat and take it for an illicit row on the lake. In effect, Wordsworth is stealing the boat: he describes it as *an act of stealth* (he doesn't want to get caught) and uses an oxymoron - *troubled pleasure* – to show us that he has mixed feelings about what he is doing: he knows it is wrong. Lines 8–11 use a variety of sound effects and very positive vocabulary to present the initial experience of this escapade. He says the boat left behind her

still, on either side,

Small circles glittering idly in the moon,

Until they melted all into one track

Of sparkling light.

Listen to those lines: Wordsworth uses no figurative language, but there is a preponderance of *s*, *l* and *m* sounds which give a gentle, restful feeling which reinforces the meanings of the words. The lines are given more aural coherence by assonance: *side/idly/light* and by consonance - *track/sparkling*. Wordsworth has decided to row across the lake and has picked out a craggy ridge as his landmark towards which he is heading.

This positive tone and atmosphere continues up to line 20. The boat is an *elfin pinnace* – playful, mischievous (like an elf) – and the boat moves through the water *like a swan* – a beautiful, majestic bird.

And then the whole tone changes. By a trick of perspective, as Wordsworth rows across the lake, a huge peak comes into view. When you row, you face the direction you started from and the further Wordsworth rows from the shore of the lake, the mountains behind his starting point start to appear. Look at how the poet describes it and his response to it:

a huge peak, black and huge,

As if with voluntary power instinct,

Upreared its head. I struck and struck again,

And growing still in stature the grim shape

Towered up between me and the stars, and still,

For so it seemed, with purpose of its own

And measured motion like a living thing,

Strode after me.

Like nature, like the boat, the peak is personified and takes on a life of its own, but note also the way a sense of panic in the poet is created by simple repetition of *huge* and *struck*; these lines are full of sibilance too – which creates a sinister, hissing sound. Wordsworth's reaction is one of guilt and shame:

With trembling oars I turned,

And through the silent water stole my way.

He puts the boat back where he found it and then finds he is haunted by this experience for many days afterwards. He does not fully understand what has happened to him:

my brain

Worked with a dim and undetermined sense

Of unknown modes of being.

He is also depressed by the experience:

o'er my thoughts

There hung a darkness, call it solitude

Or blank desertion.

He cannot take his customary pleasure in nature – *No familiar shapes remained* – and his every waking thought and even his sleep is disturbed by

huge and mighty forms. That do not live

Like living men, moved slowly through the mind

By day, and were a trouble to my dreams.

How are we to interpret this poem? If some of the language towards the end of the extract seems a little vague, it is because Wordsworth himself – as a small boy – is struggling to make sense of what happened to him.

What is certain is that this experience is a formative one and leads to an epiphany: the poet is made to feel guilty for taking the boat and in that sense it is an important part of Wordsworth's intention – to show that we can learn morality from nature – not just from books or other people. And so nature is presented as beautiful and inspiring, but also frightening if you do something wrong or immoral. The huge and mighty forms that haunt the young boy's mind in the days that follow the incident seem to suggest that there is a divinity in nature, that the natural world (as Wordsworth sees it) is an expression of the existence of God and one which punishes us when we commit immoral acts – like stealing someone else's boat.

We can also see this extract as charting the passage from innocence to experience, from childhood to adulthood. In the first part of the extract Wordsworth is totally in control – of the boat, the situation and his emotions. What he is doing may be wrong but it is clearly enjoyable for a brief period: this can be seen as showing how attractive it is to sin – we are tempted to do wrong because some sins are very attractive and pleasurable. But the sudden appearance of the mountain changes everything and shows the young poet that he is not in control: there is a higher power that watches over us. In simpler terms we might say that the mountain symbolizes his guilty conscience.

Why?

This very famous extract:

• shows nature as a moral and spiritual guide.

- explores the psychology of a young boy.

- explores the attractiveness of wrong-doing, but also the effects of a guilty conscience.

- demonstrates a deep love of nature.

- focuses very closely on the individual and his relationship with nature.

The Wild Swans at Coole – W B Yeats

Context

William Butler Yeats (1865 – 1939) lived through a momentous period of Irish history as there were growing calls for independence from Britain, much violence and finally, in 1922, the establishment of the Irish Free State. Yeats was very interested in the pagan roots of Irish culture and ancient Irish myths, as well as the occult and mysticism. In 1898 he met the Irish playwright Lady Augusta Gregory and from then on spent his summers at her home at Coole Park, County Galway – which is the setting for this poem. Yeats once described Coole Park as the most beautiful place on earth. This poem was the title poem in the collection *The Wild Swans at Coole*, published in 1917.

Who? Yeats, his younger self and the swans on the lake. Yeats writes in the first person and the present tense, although he uses the past tense to look backwards and switches to the future tense in the final stanza.

When? October 1916. The poem was dated when it was first published. Yeats was 51 and still unmarried and childless.

Where? At the lake at Coole Park.

What? Yeats watches the swans and thinks about the first time he saw them and reflects on his life.

Commentary

The opening stanza is peaceful and describes the present. It is autumn and evening – there is a sense that things are coming to an end – the year and the day, but it is beautiful to look at. In the second stanza Yeats tells us that he first came to this lake 19 years ago and counted the swans, who rose up and flew away before he had finished. The third stanza starts to reveal the central idea of the poem: when Yeats first saw these swans he was younger and *trod with a lighter tread*; he was full of youthful optimism, but now his heart is *sore*. The swans, by way of contrast, are unchanged – *Their hearts have not grown old,* which implies that Yeats' heart has. He no longer has the energy for *passion* and *conquest* which still come naturally to the swans. The final stanza looks into the future and wonders where the swans will go next. There is certainty that they will delight men's eyes, but there will come a day when Yeats wakes up and the swans have gone.

The poem centres around two contrasts: Yeats as he is now compared with his younger self; and Yeats in contrast with the swans. The beauty and unchanging nature of the swans is emphasised throughout this poem. Compared to humans they have a beauty, power and grace which never changes. They almost become a symbol of the love that Yeats feels he has no energy for at his age and with a series of unsuccessful romances behind him. By contrast the swans are paired, *lover by lover*, but Yeats is alone and lonely. The swans are *brilliant creatures*: their wings are *clamorous*, like a bell-beat. They are *unwearied still*; *their hearts have not grown old*; they still have the energy for passion or conquest; they are beautiful and mysterious. They are also, as the title points out, *wild* – a word Yeats associated with passion and energy. Note the repetition of the word *still* throughout the poem: this suggests the unchanging nature of the swans and through the idea of stillness, the fact that we cannot tell what lies beneath the beautiful appearance of the lake and the scene: Yeats is deeply troubled and unhappy. The fact that the final stanza ends with a question shows Yeats' uncertainty about the future and his essential pessimism about love and growing old. Yeats has lost his youthful energy and passion. The second stanza expresses well the energy and passion of the swans:

> *All suddenly mount*
>
> *And scatter wheeling in great broken rings*
>
> *Upon their clamorous wings*

Here the verbs of motion - *mount, scatter, wheeling* – all suggest an energy which Yeats no longer has. If the swans are a symbol for love then the final sentence imagines a time when there will no love at all in Yeats' life. It is also interesting to note that Yeats was going through a period during which he was producing hardly any poetry, so that his creative block might also influence his mood in this poem.

Why?

This very famous poem has certain key themes:

- it identifies the unchanging energy and beauty of nature.

- it reflects on growing old.

- it is a poem that seems to be bidding farewell to love and relationships.

- it uses the swans as a symbol, a symbolic contrast to everything that Yeats is.

- it meditates on human memory and the passing of time.

Spellbound – **Emily Jane Brontë**

Context

Emily Brontë (1818 – 1848) was one of the three famous Brontë sisters who lived in the village of Haworth in Yorkshire. They are famous for their writing, but also because they all had tragically short lives, as did their brother Branwell. Emily's poems were first published in 1846 in a volume of poetry along with others by her sisters – Charlotte and Anne. They published under the assumed names of Ellis, Currer and Acton Bell – so readers would not know they were women and not judge their work harshly as a result of knowing their sex. All three sisters went on to publish novels which you may come across in your other reading in English. Emily published *Wuthering Heights* which is an astonishing book. It has been televised and made into several different film versions. Emily adored the wildness and rugged beauty of the Yorkshire moors and this can be seen in *Wuthering Heights* and this poem.

This poem was written in November 1837 when Emily was nineteen. This poem is usually thought of as belonging to Emily's 'Gondal' period; 'Gondal' was an imaginary world created by the Brontë children in which heroes and heroines battled against terrible and desperate situations. The Brontës (including their brother) wrote poems and short stories set in Gondal which are all linked and interwoven with each other. Fannie Ratchford in *Complete Poems of Emily Jane Brontë*, suggests that this poem refers to an earlier incident in the Gondal chronicles when one of the heroines exposes her child to die on the moors in winter. She cannot bear to watch the child die but she cannot tear herself away from the scene.

tyrant – an absolute ruler, an oppressor.

drear – dreary, gloomy, cheerless.

Who? An unidentified narrator – although the context above suggests it is a mother who has abandoned her baby.

When? At the start of the night. The poem is written in the present tense.

Where? Outdoors. The narrator is vulnerable to the storm which is coming. We might also say, given what we know, that the setting is the Yorkshire moors near Haworth.

What? The narrator, despite the awful weather conditions, cannot leave the moors.

Commentary

This poem is written in the first person and the present tense and this gives it an immediacy and vibrancy. The poem begins as night is falling; in the second stanza there is snow on the trees and the storm is coming; in the final stanza the narrator is surrounded by clouds and wastes. The narrator is held by *a tyrant spell*, but there is a progression in her attitude: in the first two stanzas she says she cannot go, but in the final line she expresses defiance – *I will not go* – the act of braving the storm has become a conscious act.

The fact that it is written in the ballad form is important too: it gives it the feel of something old and ancient as well as creating an insistent rhythm. This rhythm is re-enforced by heavy alliteration – *wild winds, bending... bare boughs* – simple repetition – *clouds* and *wastes* and *cannot* – and the consonance on the letter *l* especially in the first stanza, but throughout the poem. The speaker is encompassed by the storm – it is round her, above her and below her: there is no escape. The poem is given an added air of mystery by the *spell* – which like the trees – is personified.

If we accept the context of this poem suggested above – a mother who has abandoned her child on the moors – then this is a poem about the strength of maternal bonds and the fierceness and passion of a mother's love. Even this terrible storm cannot force her away from her baby. In this interpretation the storm may be seen as a pathetic fallacy for her own mental state at the abandonment of her baby.

However, it was published on its own, without any reference to the original setting of Gondal and the poem means something different, we might argue, on its own. In Victorian times women really were second class citizens. Once they married all their property automatically transferred to their husbands; they did not have the vote and would not get it until the 20th century. The Brontë sisters growing up in a genteel, middle class vicar's family would have been protected from the harsh realities of life and would have been expected to excel at needlework, drawing, playing musical instruments, water-colouring, painting. We know that Emily liked to wander around the moors near the family home, even in appalling weather conditions – and this was probably seen as slightly odd behaviour at the time.

So what? You are probably thinking. But if this is true, then 'Spellbound' becomes a poem of great courage and the wilful pursuit of risk and danger. It can be seen as an assertion of Brontë's determination to experience the full energy and force of the storm, to give herself up to elemental forces, to rebel against the protected, insulated life that was expected of middle-class Victorian ladies. Remember the last line which expresses her wilful determination – *I will not go*. This can be seen as a determined cry for independence and freedom – despite the risks that exist from being exposed to the storm.

Why?

This simple ballad powerfully communicates:

- a sense of the power of nature which inspires awe not fear.

- a woman's determined struggle for freedom from the stifling conditions of Victorian middle class existence.

- a sense of courage and resilience even when faced with the most hostile conditions.

- the narrator's sense of isolation.

- the narrator's desire for danger, risk and excitement.

Below the Green Corrie – Norman MacCaig

Context

Norman MacCaig (1910 – 1996) was a celebrated and well-known Scottish writer. He was a primary school teacher for a number of years before teaching creative writing in Scottish universities. He travelled widely, but the landscape and people of Scotland were an enduring influence on his poetry. He lived in Edinburgh, but had a holiday home in Assynt – a remote and beautiful area of the north west Highlands. This poem describes the landscape at a remote loch in the Highlands which MacCaig described as his favourite place in the world.

corrie – a semi-circular mountain recess.

infusion – the pouring of water over any substance in order to extract its essence.

swashbuckling – adventurous, exciting.

bandolier – a shoulder belt for storing ammunition.

Who? The poet narrates the poem in the first person. The landscape is personified, but he is alone, walking down the mountainside.

When? It is day time and MacCaig is looking back at the past and at the mountains of the Scottish Highlands. The poem is written in the past tense.

Where? At a remote spot in the Scottish Highlands.

What? MacCaig reflects on what the landscape of the Highlands has meant for him and how the area has influenced his life.

Commentary

One of the most important things to grasp about this poem initially is that it depends on a conceit or extended metaphor which begins in the second line and continues to the very end of the poem. It gives the poem a jaunty, light-hearted tone – but there is also a seriousness about the poem too.

The poem begins, perhaps, as a fairly conventional poem about nature with the mountains being personified:

The mountains gathered round me.

But the second line introduces the extended metaphor and might surprise us with an unusual simile - *like bandits.* Just look at all the words that MacCaig uses to re-enforce this extended comparison: *leader, swaggered, threats, thunders, stood and delivered, money and their lives, prowlers, swashbuckling, bandolier.* And the other unusual thing is that normally when nature is personified in poetry, it is usually seen as feminine – MacCaig turns those stereotypes on their head by making his nature male. The oxymoron in line 3 – *dark light* – suggests that the mountains are threatening but also benevolent.

The second stanza uses stereotypical phrases used by highwaymen in the past to extend the metaphor and to suggest that, despite their threatening nature, MacCaig took a lot from the mountains in terms of inspiration. These phrases – *stood and delivered, their money and their lives* – have a comic effect. Lots of poets write and pay tribute to nature: MacCaig's originality lies in the extended metaphor – the mountains as bandits, thieves, highway robbers and, in the third stanza, pirates – all figures outside the law.

The final stanza starts with the poet stating that his life has been enriched by an *infusion* of the mountains. He is walking down the mountainside in awful weather. He turns to say goodbye and returns to the metaphor – the mountains are *marvellous prowlers.* At that moment a *sunshaft* pierces the clouds and he sees that

their leader,

that swashbuckling mountain,

was wearing

a bandolier of light

This is such a striking and original phrase because it brings together two words which would not normally be associated with each other: *swashbuckling* and *mountain*. Note the consonance of the letter *l* as the poem comes to a conclusion, culminating in the word *light*. There has been a sense of threat throughout the poem, even though it is made light-hearted by the extended metaphor, but the tone of the last four lines suggests a moment of revelation and insight – an epiphany. How does MacCaig achieve this? Partly through the sounds and partly through the metaphor (in the last line - *bandolier*) juxtaposed with the word *light* – with all its very positive connotations.

Why?

This original and funny poem

- pays tribute to the inspiration MacCaig has found in the landscape of the Scottish highlands.

- reaches an epiphany in the final line.

- memorably portrays nature in an original and comic way while still showing its importance to the poet.

Storm in the Black Forest – D H Lawrence

Context

David Herbert Lawrence (1885 – 1930) is better known as novelist. He was born in the coal-mining town of Eastwood near Nottingham and came from a working class background. He travelled widely and also wrote over 800 poems, most of them in free verse. He also wrote some well-known short stories and three plays. Lawrence believed in spontaneity and naturalness, and many of his poems are about love and relationships or, as this one is, the power of nature. He felt that modern man was insulated by technology and civilization from his true self and from nature. This attitude can be seen in the final stanza of this poem.

We think this poem was written late in his life. In a notebook entry for July 20th 1929, Lawrence wrote: *Last night a long and lurid thunderstorm poured out endless white electricity.* He was staying at a hotel in Lichtenthal on the edge of the Black Forest in Germany.

cackle – to laugh.

uncouth – awkward, ungraceful.

subjugated – to be conquered or overpowered.

Who? The poet speaks as himself in the present tense.

When? It is almost night on July 19th 1929.

Where? On the edge of the Black Forest in Germany.

What? Lawrence describes the coming of a thunder storm.

Commentary

This poem is written in a very fluid free verse form with four stanzas of varying lengths. Lawrence liked to experiment and there is some truth in the observation that he was the first British-born poet in the twentieth century to embrace fully the lack of restrictions that free verse allows.

The first two stanzas describe the approach of the storm; the third single line stanza describes the rain which still has not started to fall; and the final stanza is Lawrence's comment on what he has seen.

The choice of free verse does seem especially suited to the subject matter here. The lines are very unequal in length; some are end-stopped; some use enjambment – it is all very unpredictable like the storm itself, like the natural world. The opening stanza describes the lightning in a series of beautiful and awe-filled phrases. Look at the combination of assonance and consonance in the opening line:

Now it is almost night, from the bronzey soft sky.

There is a tendency amongst some readers to think that free verse requires less skill and craft to write, but it can involve a very high level of patterning to do with sounds or repetition. Lawrence uses assonance again in lines two and three: the long *i* sounds of *white/fire/bright/white* and the shorter *i* sounds of *liquid/tipples/spills*. There is more assonance in *gold-bronze* and the unusual collocation *flutters bent*. The storm is alive.

The second stanza continues the metaphor of the lightning as *liquid fire* and introduces a new metaphor – the *white snake*. Here Lawrence continues to use assonance on short and long *i* sounds, and he combines it with verbs of great energy and movement – *pours, wriggles, spilled, tumbling, wriggling*. In the final line we hear the thunder:

And then the heavens cackle with uncouth sounds

and the alliteration on *c* and the longer vowel sounds in *cackle, uncouth* and *sounds* act as a contrast to the shorter sounds associated with the lightning – *electric liquid*. The heavens are personified here too and we cannot say that the lightning has been personified but it has been animated and brought alive.

Ironically the rain refuses to come. The final stanza represents a complete change of tone. Lawrence sounds amused - not at the storm and its lightning and thunder, but at the human assumption that we have somehow tamed electricity, that we can make nature do what we want. Lawrence seems delighted that nature cannot be mastered, cannot be chained by human beings. Lawrence uses the language of slavery to show the human desire to control nature, but laughs at our inability to do so.

Why?

Lawrence uses the extreme liberty of free verse to

- celebrate the power and majesty of nature.

- to mock human boasts that we can tame nature.

- to suggest that we should show a greater sense of awe and respect towards nature.

Wind – Ted Hughes

Context

Ted Hughes was born in 1930 and died in 1998. He was one of the most famous poets of his generation and was appointed Poet Laureate in 1984 – a position he held until his death. He was born in a small village near Halifax in West Yorkshire and the landscape of his birthplace influenced him throughout his life. Hughes was a prolific poet and also wrote several books for children. His private life increased his notoriety, as his first wife (the American poet Sylvia Plath) and his next partner both committed suicide. Much of his poetry is inspired by the power and beauty and mystery of nature. Hughes commented of this poem:

For quite a few years my parents lived in a house on top of a high ridge in West Yorkshire over the Calder Valley. Either side of this ridge the valleys just dived away out of sight, right down into a gorge and trees and streams...and then on the other side the hillsides rose up very steeply to the moors. This is a poem about a gale that went on for a few days and if you've ever been in a gale like that for a while, it gets into your head, begins to affect you.

brunt – the force of a blow.

guyrope – a rope on a tent which is attached to the ground to keep the tent in position.

grimace – an unpleasant distortion of the face.

the stones cry out – an allusion to the gospel of Luke in the Bible, chapter 19, verse 40. Jesus is told to prevent his disciples from speaking aloud and he replies that if they were to be silent *the stones would immediately cry out*.

Who? Hughes is the narrator of the poem, but he is not alone. *We grip/Our hearts* in lines 19-20.

When? The night and the day after a terrific storm. The poem starts in the past tense and moves to the present as the poem progresses.

Where? In a house on the top of a hill.

What? Hughes describes the power of the storm. This is largely a descriptive poem about man's relationship with nature.

Commentary

The first stanza uses a metaphor to compare the house to a ship which has been *out at sea all night*, because there has been so much rain and wind. Note the onomatopoeia in *crashing* and *booming*, and the metaphor which compares the winds to wild horses *stampeding*. Hughes also uses a lot of alliteration to create an impression of the sound of the storm: *woods, winds, window, wet; fields, floundering; black, blinding.*

Hughes skilfully uses enjambment from line 4 to 5 to mark the transition to dawn as our eyes mark the transition to a new stanza. In the daylight it seems that everything looks different and again Hughes makes use of alliteration – *wind wielded, blade, black*, as well as using consonance on the letter *l*. The wind in this stanza is personified and its *blade-light* (what a striking image – light as a sword!) flexes like *the lens of a mad eye*. We already get a sense of the enormous power of nature and the disorientating effects of a huge storm. Note the oxymoron of *luminous black* – this storm is so powerful it distorts our perceptions.

In the third stanza Hughes manages to get as far as the coal-house door, but note how he got there. He *scaled along the house-side*; we normally scale mountains so this gives us an impression of the enormous effort it must have taken. The hills are compared to tents. This metaphor suggests their shape, of course, but also their seeming fragility in these extreme weather conditions: like tents they might be blown away at any moment. Hughes also uses onomatopoeia – *brunt, drummed, strained* – and note the harsh repetition of the *nt* sound in *brunt, dented and tent.*

Stanza four continues the personification: it is as though the whole landscape is alive. The fields are *quivering* which suggests their fear; the skyline is *a grimace*. The tent metaphor is continued because the landscape threatens to *vanish with a flap*. Note too the onomatopoeia of *bang, flap* and *flung*. Even the birds cannot cope with the strength of the wind. Just read this carefully:

a black-

Back gull bent like an iron bar slowly.

Hughes uses alliteration, consonance (the repetition of *l*) and a simile (which also pays tribute to the wind's force) to make this line and a half memorable. The rhythm slows down too, because of the largely single syllable words – which is appropriate because this is happening slowly, as the last word reveals.

Once again enjambment leads us into stanza five. The house is in contrast to the landscape: it is not personified, but it is compared to a *fine green goblet* – which threatens to shatter because of the noise it is making. In line 19 there is a shift to the present tense which makes the poem more immediate. Hughes and his companion sit in front of the fire but cannot concentrate – not even on each other. Even the process of thinking has been destroyed by the storm.

Enjambment takes us onto the sixth and final stanza. The foundations (*roots*) of the house are moving and, from outside the house, the personified windows and stones *tremble* and *cry out*.

On the page this looks like a very regular poem: each stanza consists of four lines of roughly equal length – there appears to be order here in the chaos of the storm. But you will note when you read it aloud that the lines are very uneven. Furthermore, the experience of reading the poem lacks this order, because there is only one rhyme and Hughes makes use of enjambment between lines and between stanzas to suggest the chaotic energy of the storm. Some lines are end-stopped with commas, but only once is there a longer piece of punctuation – the colon that ends line 14. This gives the poem great pace which is like the speed and violence of the storm. (It is also interesting to contrast with 'Hawk Roosting', also by Hughes, which uses end-stopped lines to create a totally different effect and a much slower rhythm.)

Why?

This poem

- shows the sheer force and power of the storm.

- presents the storm is unstoppable and Hughes uses many poetic devices to display this to the readers.

- shows that human artistry (represented by the *fine green goblet*) is threatened by the power of nature.

- acts perhaps as a metaphor or symbol of the poet's stormy marriage to Sylvia Plath or for any stormy human relationship.

Place: Connecting the Poems

In this section I will be examining the specimen questions provided by AQA and going on to discuss other ways to connect the poems in this section. The difference between questions on Foundation Tier papers and Higher Tier papers is simple: the Foundation questions use bullet points to guide you in your response to the question.

These questions are for English Literature, Unit 2 entitled *Poetry across time*. You have one hour and 15 minutes to answer the paper. There are two questions on each section of the Anthology; you answer only one. There is also a question on an unseen poem. However, the question on the Anthology carries 36 marks and the advice on the paper is to spend 45 minutes on it. The unseen poem carries only 18 marks and you are advised to spend 30 minutes on it. I deal with the unseen poem at the end of this book. There is also general advice on answering questions in the examination at the end of the book. The questions that follow have been produced by AQA as specimen questions. My answers are simply suggestions.

Compare the places and how they are shown in 'A Vision' and one other poem from 'Place'.

Remember to compare:

- **the places in the poems.**
- **how the places are presented.**

Simon Armitage's 'A Vision' is about a town that never exists, because, although it is planned, the utopian future remains a dream. The language Armitage uses to present the vision is attractive and alluring, but the reality is different. William Blake's 'London' presents the city as a nightmarish vision of hell, and London in the poem is presented as a place of poverty, death and exploitation. Armitage's poem presents the town as a possible utopia in the planners' dreams; Blake presents London as a dystopian inferno.

In 'A Vision' the planners' vision of the future is very attractive. It was *a beautiful place* with *cities like dreams* where *people like us* drove around in electric cars after a trip to the *bottle bank* perhaps. But this vision of the future existed in the past and Armitage uses language associated with toys and childish games to hint that the vision is naive: there are *board-game suburbs* and the grass is made of *fuzzy felt*. This makes the belief that the future would be better seem childish.

By contrast, Blake describes a real place – London of the 1790s – as a place where everything is chartered and owned, even the River Thames. Every member of the population has *marks of weakness* and *marks of woe* – it is a place of oppression and sadness. As he walks around the great city, Blake hears everyone crying, trapped in their own *mind-forged manacles*. Where Armitage uses the imagery of toys and games, Blake uses repetition to show the all-pervasive gloom of the city. In the third stanza Blake writes more specifically about the victims of London – the chimney sweep whose cry *every blackening church appalls* and the soldier whose sigh *runs in blood down palace walls*. The church and the monarchy, Blake suggests, are responsible for the exploitation of Londoners. In the final stanza Blake's mood worsens: he hears the youthful harlot blast the *new-born infant's tear* and *blights with plagues the marriage hearse*. The plosive sounds of *blasts*, *blights* and *plagues* and the final oxymoron make Blake's anger at the state of affairs in London real and urgent. Even the state of marriage leads to death.

In the final stanza of 'A Vision' Armitage is clearly disillusioned and saddened. He finds the plans for the future in the landfill site and the north wind seems to blow such fanciful visions away

> *with other such futures*
>
> *all unlived in and now fully extinct.*

This can be taken as a sad and wistful comment on the unreality of human dreams. By contrast, Blake is angry and bitter and in his third stanza he names through synecdoche those who are to blame for the state of London – the church and the palace, organized religion and the monarchy. The fact that the French Revolution was at its height and that Blake sympathized with its ideals, makes his view of London so much more angry and political than Armitage's poem.

Compare the way feelings about nature are shown in 'Price We Pay for the Sun' and one other poem from 'Places'.

Remember to compare:

- **what the feelings about nature are in the poems.**

- **how the feelings are presented.**

Grace Nichols' 'Price We Pay for the Sun' and Emily Brontë's 'Spellbound' show different feelings about nature and for different reasons, but they both concentrate on the harsher, more destructive elements of nature.

Nichols' poem is addressed to a tourist to the Caribbean who has an image of a tropical paradise. Brontë's poem is written in the first person and describes an impending storm which the narrator is fascinated by and cannot tear herself away from.

Nichols' feelings about nature are that it can be hostile to human beings. The Caribbean may look nice but in reality they are not *picture postcards*. The struggle to make a living is a hard and gruelling one, and Nichols states quite clearly at the end of the poem that

Poverty is the price

we pay for the sun girl.

In the second stanza she writes about the sufferings of her family using metaphors drawn from nature. Her mother's breasts are *like sleeping volcanoes*, containing *sulph-furious cancer*; her father's tears (the result of a life of poverty and his wife's condition) are *salty hurricanes*; her grandmother's croon is *sifting sand* – insubstantial and not permanent.

'Spellbound' is a mysterious poem and we are told very little about the speaker. She is outside as a violent storm approaches and we are given a keen sense of the dangers she faces, but she *cannot, cannot go*. She seems transfixed by the power of the storm and by the end of the poem she has made a conscious decision to stay and endure the storm – *I will not, cannot go*. Like the volcanoes and hurricanes of Nichols' poem, the storm is frightening: the speaker is in a vulnerable position – *the night is darkening, the giant trees are bending*, above her are clouds, below her *wastes beyond wastes* – but she chooses to stay.

Both poets present feelings about nature which are far from idyllic and which they use to demonstrate human feelings and concerns. Nichols uses the natural phenomena of the Caribbean to mirror and draw attention to the sufferings of the native Guyanese who live in poverty and have to endure the reality of life there, unlike the tourists to whom the poem is addressed. Brontë, by contrast, writing in the first half of the 19th century, seems to use the storm as a metaphor for her desire to break free from the conventional behaviour expected of middle-class Victorian ladies. As such, she feels excited and enriched by the power of the storm.

Compare how the relationship between man and nature is shown in 'Below the Green Corrie' and one other poem from 'Place'.

'Below the Green Corrie' by Norman MacCaig and the extract from William Wordsworth's *The Prelude* show the relationship between man and nature in a completely different way and with a completely different effect. For example, Wordsworth personifies nature but in the traditional feminine way; by contrast MacCaig turns his back on tradition to personify nature as masculine and he uses imagery of outlaws, highway robbers and pirates. This give a slightly unscrupulous and comic atmosphere to the mountains he is describing. Wordsworth, starting off on the adventure of the stolen boat, led to it by nature, is about to embark on a moral discovery of some sort.

Another important difference between the two poems is that Wordsworth is writing as an adult looking back at a critical incident from his childhood and trying to explain its significance; MacCaig, on the other hand, is looking back with affection at the mountains that have inspired him throughout his adult life.

Once Wordsworth has stolen the boat, he begins to row across the lake and he describes his surroundings in positive and attractive terms: his oars leave

Small circles glittering idly in the moon,

Until they melted all into one track

Of sparkling light.

But the atmosphere soon changes and the appearance of the huge peak makes Wordsworth feel guilty and he feels alienated from nature. Some of the key words are emphasized through alliteration: *dim, undetermined, darkness, desertion* which replace Wordsworth's sense of *familiar shapes, pleasant images* and *colours*. Throughout the day he was haunted by *huge and mighty forms* and at night they were *a trouble to my dreams*. Nature has, by appearing so menacing to the young Wordsworth, taught him that it is wrong to steal.

If the extract from *The Prelude* moves from light to darkness, MacCaig's poem moves in the opposite direction. He is walking down the mountainside in rough weather. We might detect a note of dread in the opening line – *The mountains gathered round me* – but MacCaig's use of the extended metaphor makes them less threatening. They are dangerous – they are outlaws, pirates, criminals – but MacCaig has taken more from them than they have from him:

My life was enriched

with an infusion of theirs.

And, as he turns to *look goodbye*, there is a moment of beauty and revelation as their leader *was wearing/a bandolier of light*.

Both poets pay tribute to the human relationship with nature, and to the power and influence that nature has exerted over them, but the resulting poems differ in approach and tone. In Wordsworth's poem he is subservient to nature – the child to Mother Nature who must learn his lesson; MacCaig presents himself as on equal terms with his favourite mountains – *those marvellous prowlers*.

Readers like some poems and dislike others. Write about whether you like or dislike 'Cold Knap Lake' and compare your response to one other poem you either like or dislike. Remember to write about how the poems are written.

I like both Gillian Clarke's 'Cold Knap Lake' and Jean Sprackland's 'Hard Water', but they are very different poems, although water is an important motif in both poems.

Clarke's poem is magical and mysterious, and uses the water of the lake to symbolize the shifting, uncertainty of memory. The main event of the poem is presented as a miracle - a *blue-lipped* girl is brought back to life by Clarke's mother. The girl is described by Clarke as *dressed in water's long green silk* – an image which combines beauty with terror because water can kill through drowning.

My mother gave a stranger's child her breath

is a line that stands out for me because of its extraordinary generosity and because of its associations with the way God gave life to man in the Bible.

For me the poem really comes alive in the final two stanzas as Clarke reflects on this experience. On the one hand, this is something all readers can relate to – some of our earliest memories may be hazy and unreliable, influenced by what we have been told through family stories. However, Clarke uses the personified willows and the beautiful yet dangerous swans to create a modern fairy tale or myth, so that her closing couplet:

All lost things lie under the closing water

in that lake with the poor man's daughter

becomes a lament for all lost things and for all lost people everywhere.

Sprackland's poem begins in a similar way – with a memory of going on holiday to a soft water area. Where Clarke's poem deliberately invokes figures from fairy tale and myth – poor children and swans – Sprackland's vocabulary is drawn from rocks and brewing – *limestone, gypsum, alchemical.* Clarke uses the muddiness of the water to suggest the haziness of memory and the past; Sprackland uses the hardness of the water to celebrate the qualities of honesty and frankness that she associates with her home town. For her the water of Burton-on-Trent is

Flat. Straight. Like the vowels,

like the straight talk.

Sprackland also uses direct quotes from the people of her home town (in 'Cold Knap Lake' Clarke's is the only voice we hear): *hey up me duck, don't get mardy, too bloody deep for me.* Sprackland wants to assert her sense of belonging to her home town, despite her book-learning, and her poem is a tribute to the *fierce lovely water* that *marked me for life.*

Both poems present water in radically different ways. Clarke's poem mentions a specific place in the title, but her development of images from myth and fairy tale produce a poem that is emblematic of the human fascination with water. Sprackland's poem can only be about Burton-on-Trent, but I like the way she feels that she is still part of her roots. Clarke uses water as a mysterious, almost magical element, muddying the past and our perceptions of it; Sprackland uses it as a metaphor for honesty and frankness.

Other thoughts

Of course, you cannot predict what questions will come up in the examination, but you can do some thinking before the exam and select poems that work well together for various reasons. You will still need to do some quick thinking in the exam AND you must answer the question that has been asked: you cannot simply write about two poems that in your preparation you have decided go well together. What follows now are some brief notes which give some examples of poems that work well together, depending on the question. These are not exclusive – I am sure you can make connections which I have not spotted or thought of.

The extract from *The Prelude* would go very well with 'Crossing the Loch'. In both poems the narrators are out on the water; in both poems (for different reasons) they react with a mixture of emotions; both poems convey the awesome beauty of nature; and both poems reach an epiphany. In this connection too 'Cold Knap Lake' could also be used with either poem: all three deal with memory as well as our relationship with water.

'The Price We Pay for the Sun' and 'Neighbours' both explore the dangers of the world and see place in a pessimistic way: Nichols because of the natural climate of Guyana, Clarke because of man's unnatural development of nuclear power.

'A Vision' and 'London' might work very well together since both deal with urban landscapes and they both present a bleak vision of the way we live our lives. There are differences, of course: Armitage's poem is about how unreal dreams of life do not come true and do not match the reality; Blake's poem is directly about the reality of London in the late 18th century as he saw it.

'Hard Water' and 'The Price We Pay for the Sun' could be usefully linked because they both deal with the poet's roots in a way and the importance of those roots. You could draw out interesting broad similarities too between Nichols' use of her own accent and Sprackland's love of the phrases and vocabulary of Burton-on-Trent. Both poems are hymns of tribute to the place the poet calls 'home'. 'The Blackbird of Glanmore' might then go well with either of these poems since Heaney's poem is partly about the importance of home.

'Storm in the Black Forest', 'Wind' and 'Spellbound' all deal with the sheer power and ferocity of nature and can be linked in this way. In contrast to them all, 'Below the Green Corrie' pays tribute to nature and its influence on the poet, but does so in a very unusual way through a very original extended metaphor which has a humorous effect. For this reason too, and because it reaches a moment of epiphany at the end, 'Below the Green Corrie' might be good to compare with Wordsworth's extract, 'The Moment' or 'Cold Knap Lake' – all of which have a far more reverential attitude to nature than MacCaig. Equally MacCaig's presentation of nature as essentially benevolent and jocular contrasts well with the poems by Lawrence and Hughes.

'The Blackbird of Glanmore', The Wild Swans at Coole' and 'Spellbound' might work together well because, although place is important in each of these poems, the real subject matter could be said to be the poet and their feelings, and in the three poems the blackbird, the swans and the storm are all used to symbolize something important for the poet.

I think 'The Moment' and the extract from *The Prelude* would work well together. They are written in different ways, but both poems stress the smallness of humanity and the importance of nature. Writing about these poems would also allow you to display your understanding of the poets' very different contexts: Wordsworth's pantheism as opposed to Atwood's interest and involvement in the Green movement.

If you accept my reading of 'Spellbound' (Brontë rebelling against Victorian conventions) then you could write about it in connection with 'London', since both poets are rebelling against the status quo.

'The Blackbird of Glanmore' and 'Below the Green Corrie' might work well together. Both poems, while saying important things about place, are also genial and peaceful in tone, despite exploring vastly different ideas.

I would link 'A Vision' and 'Hard Water'. In Sprackland's poem the attractions of soft water are clear – just as the attractions of the town planners' blueprints present a better future. Neither the soft water nor the plans can last: Sprackland has to go home to her hard water area; the plans are merely dreams. The difference lies in the poets' reactions: Armitage seems upset and saddened by the reality of the present and the fact that the plans did not come true; Sprackland enjoys being back home in the reality of Burton-on-Trent.

Conflict

The poems in this section deal with conflict. Many of them are poems written about war. However, in the late 20th and early 21st centuries the nature of what we call 'war' has changed, so you will also find some very modern poems which use terrorism as their backdrop or which question the patriotism that war depends upon. Despite the fact that war and conflict cause death and injury, you will find a very wide range of emotional responses to the issue in this section.

Contemporary Poetry

Flag – John Agard

Context

John Agard was born in the former British colony of Guyana in 1949 and he has written many books for children and adults. He moved to Britain in 1977 and lives in Sussex with his partner Grace Nichols – who is also a poet. There are other poems by Agard and Nichols in the Anthology. Agard is well-known as a skilled and adept performer of his own poems and you may get the chance to see him perform his poems during your course. You should check out his performance of the poem 'Half- Caste' on YouTube, because his performance helps to bring the poem alive. In many of his poems he uses Caribbean accent and dialect to bring a Guyanese identity to his work, but he also uses Standard English in some poems – as he does in this one.

This poem appears in a collection entitled *Half Caste and Other Poems* published in 2005. Many of the poems are concerned with race and cultural identity as well as politics and relationships.

Flags are potent symbols of a nation. For example, in the USA schoolchildren every morning in school pledge an oath of allegiance to the flag; when something controversial happens in the world, protestors often burn the flag of the country they are protesting about; when flags are run up flagpoles, people have a tendency to salute them.

Who? The poet speaks as himself. He refers to the reader in line 14 as *my friend*.

When? No specific time – this poem has a timeless quality.

Where? No specific place – it has a universal relevance.

What? A series of questions are asked and answered.

Commentary

This poem's structure is a model of simplicity and economy. Each stanza is three lines long. The first line of each stanza is a question which begins with the same words, and is followed by a two line sentence which answers the question. The second line of each stanza remains the same. The first and third lines rhyme. As in many other poems in this Anthology, the pattern the poet creates is then broken in the final stanza – by breaking the pattern the poet draws attention to the final stanza: it is fore-grounded because it breaks the pattern. In the final stanza the opening question is worded slightly differently; it is followed by two separate sentences, not one, and the second and third lines rhyme. The title of the poem is referred to implicitly in each stanza, but the word *flag* is not used in the poem until the final stanza. In addition, in the final line of each stanza Agard always uses alliteration, consonance or assonance to make the line memorable and to foreground it: *nation/knees; guts/grow; gr<u>ow</u>/b<u>old</u>; <u>d</u>ares/cowar<u>d</u>; blood/bleed* – and the consonance on *l* in line 12.

Until the final stanza Agard refers to the flag dismissively and contemptuously as *just a piece of cloth*. But this piece of cloth can have remarkable powers over people:

- In the first stanza the piece of cloth *brings a nation to its knees* – an entire population falls down to worship the flag and perhaps go to war in its name.

- In the second stanza the cloth makes men brave.

- In the third stanza the power of the piece of cloth makes cowards *relent* and change – presumably to become courageous.

- In the fourth stanza Agard addresses the reader and reminds us of the consequences of war. The flag will *outlive the blood you bleed.*

The final stanza, as we have already noticed above, changes its structure and also provides a different perspective on the flag. The opening line seems to be spoken by an imaginary reader. In the second line Agard answers the reader and reveals that the piece of cloth is just a flag. Unlike all the other stanzas here the second line does not run on into the last line – it comes to an abrupt end, before Agard delivers the final line:

Then blind your conscience to the end.

Patriotism, Agard is suggesting, allows human beings to behave in ways that allow them to ignore their conscience and to do terrible things in the name of loyalty to their country, represented by the flag.

Why?

This simply-constructed, but very powerful poem

- mocks and satirizes patriotism.

- questions our loyalty to our country, any country.

- hints at the terrible, cruel and immoral things that can happen in wars.

- shows that our moral conscience might be in conflict with our patriotism.

Extract from *Out of the Blue* – Simon Armitage

Context

Simon Armitage was born in 1963 in the village of Marsden in West Yorkshire and has spent most of his life in that area. He is a very successful and highly-regarded poet, celebrated for his down-to-earth language and subject matter. Several of his poems are in the Anthology. His poetry often (but not always) deals with the ordinary incidents and events of modern life and appear to be based on personal experience.

What appears in the Anthology is an extract from a longer poem which tells the story of the terrorist attacks on the World Trade Centre Buildings in New York on September 11th 2001. It tells the story of the day from the point of view of an English businessman working in the North Tower on that day. Everything seems normal as his working day begins, but we see the impact of the attacks and the businessman's increasing realization that he will not be able to escape death. A very arresting, painful and poignant image from that day was of people trapped in the buildings throwing themselves out of the windows - preferring to fall to their deaths rather than wait to be burned alive or suffocated by smoke. Armitage has said of the poem that he wanted to avoid the political complications of the attacks and concentrate on writing a poem that was *commemorative and elegiac* and which would *give those inside a voice.* The poem was commissioned by Channel 5 and was used in a documentary televised on the fifth anniversary of the attacks. *Out of the Blue* was also used as the title for a collection of poems which includes this and two other long poems about conflict. On September 11th 2001 the terrorist organization Al-Qaeda launched various attacks on the USA. In New York two hi-jacked passenger planes were deliberately flown into the two parts of the World Trade Centre – or Twin Towers as they were known. The towers quickly collapsed and nearly 3,000 people died.

Who? An English business man who was in one of the Twin Towers on September 11th, 2001. This is the persona Armitage adopts: he writes in the present tense.

When? September 11th 2001.

Where? New York in the North Tower of the World Trade Centre.

What? The narrator describes his experience as he is caught between certain death in the tower through flames and fumes, and certain death by falling to his death,

Commentary

The poem begins with a mystery:

You have picked me out.

The identity of the person being addressed is not revealed until the last line of the poem. The next three lines offer us a distant perspective of what is happening:

Through a distant shot of a building burning

you have noticed now

that a white cotton shirt is twirling, turning.

The attacks on the Twin Towers were seen on TV by millions across the planet and newspapers the next day, in every country, were dominated by a picture of the moment one of the planes hit the first tower. Armitage's narrator is one of the people caught on the floors above the impact of the plane: they could not get out – the fire escapes were filled with fire and smoke – and they were too high to be rescued – the twin towers were huge sky-scrapers.

Throughout the poem Armitage uses short lines and short stanzas which give an impression of panic and fear, and also the man's breathlessness – he is nervous and full of fear and battling against the fumes of the burning building behind him. The use of the present tense gives the poem immediacy and a sense of urgency, and his repeated use of the present participle – the form of the verb ending in *-ing* – gives a sense of events happening as he speaks and continuing to happen. This is also enhanced by repetition – which suggest a mind panicking and unsure what to do. Armitage also uses the present participle to end many of his lines – this is known as a falling rhythm and is surely appropriate given what happens at the end of the poem. It is also said that a falling rhythm creates a sense of pathos and pity.

The second stanza reveals that the narrator is waving, but his isolation is such that he is unsure whether anyone is watching. The third stanza plaintively asks

So when will you come?

It is plaintive and poignant because we know that no-one came – the people caught on the floors above were doomed the moment the planes hit the towers. There are images of normality as the narrator imagines he could be mistaken for

a man shaking crumbs

or pegging out washing?

These images are important, I think, because they underline just how out of the ordinary the attacks were and they also emphasize the horror of what is happening by reminding us of normal, everyday activities like pegging out the washing.

The fourth stanza personifies the fire behind him: it is *bullying, driving*, but he has not quite given up hope:

the white of surrender is not yet flying.

And now his white shirt has become a possible white flag of surrender. The next stanza begins with a short sentence:

A bird goes by.

The bird is very important. It can be seen as an image of freedom, but it is ironic because birds can fly, but men cannot. It also reminds us that despite tragic human events of immense proportions, nature and the world just keep on going regardless, oblivious to human suffering. In this stanza we are made aware that others in his situation have jumped to their deaths. The horror of the fall is shown in the words

wind-milling, wheeling, spiralling, falling.

Gills in the next stanza suggest that the narrator is drowning in the fumes and the shocking, unexpectedness of the attacks is shown when he asks the person he is addressing

Are your eyes believing.

In the final stanza the narrator is nearing his death. He is *tiring, tiring*. He can hear the sirens of the emergency services below, but he is about to die – *failing, flagging*. And the last line reveals he has been addressing a loved one – wife, girlfriend, lover – in a way it does not matter. The end of the poem leaves it unclear whether he jumps or succumbs to the fire and smoke behind him – again the facts of his death are less important than the experience he has undergone and which has been shared with us by the poem.

Why?

This sensitive poem

- deals with an event of global significance from the perspective of one individual.

- gives an intimate account of a person on the brink of death.

- memorably shows the individual torn between two equally frightening ways to die.

- acts a memorial to all the deaths at the Twin Towers.

Mametz Wood – Owen Sheers

Context

Owen Sheers was born in 1974 and brought up in Wales. He was involved in a documentary film about two Welsh writers – Wyn Griffiths and David Jones who had both been in the 38th Welsh Division which took part in an attack on Mametz Wood in France. While he was at the battle site, a previously unknown grave containing twenty British soldiers was found and the memory of this forms the basis for this poem.

In 1916 during the First World War the British Army launched an offensive against German trenches in the Somme Valley in northern France. The battle began on the morning of July 1st at 7.30 in the morning and was to continue for four and a half months, costing over 200,000 British lives. The action at Mametz Wood started on the morning of July 7th and involved the Welsh soldiers attacking up a ridge at the top of which were the German trenches in a wood, heavily defended by machine guns. By July 12th Mametz Wood was under the control of the British Army – but at the cost of 4000 killed or wounded. This pattern – of huge loss of life to gain only a tiny piece of territory – was the pattern of a lot of the fighting in the First World War.

chit – unclear. A chit can be a small scrap of paper; but it can also mean a sprout – this would give the sense that the bones are alive and sprouting – certainly sprouts do reach the surface of the soil as the bones have done.

sentinel – guard.

mosaic – a design of small pieces of coloured glass or marble. Here the mosaic, if it were not broken, would make up the picture of the group of men as they were when alive.

dance-macabre – this was a very popular image in medieval poetry and art and consisted of a figure (usually a skeleton) representing death, leading dead people to hell.

Who? The poet.

When? On the day a new grave was uncovered.

Where? On the battlefield in northern France.

What? The poet is present at the discovery of a mass grave of dead soldiers and reflects on what he sees.

Commentary

This poem is organized into tercets but with lines of irregular length. There is one full rhyme in the final stanza which brings the poem to a close. The overall structure of the poem is interesting: line 1 refers to *them*, but their identity is not revealed until line 9 with the mention of machine guns. (Of course, the title would reveal this if you knew that Mametz Wood was the site of a famous battle.) The actual discovery of the grave is delayed until line 12 and the poem ends with the culmination of the poet's thoughts and reflections as he watches the grave and the soldiers' bodies being uncovered. There is an epiphany in the final stanza – for the poet and for the reader.

The poem's opening line has consonance on the letter *f* which is soft and gentle. This is matched by the image of the farmers who over the decades since the war have *tended the land back into itself*. 'To tend something' is to look after it, so the farmers are presented in a sympathetic light – looking after the land which has outlasted the soldiers and the war. The fragments of human skeletons that the ploughing of the fields turns up are described in the second stanza. The remains of human bones are fragile and fragmented – a finger, a shoulder blade – and they look like other things, so in death the skeletons have been broken up and are now not even recognizable as human remains or as individuals.

The third stanza introduces the battle that was fought for Mametz Wood and contains a reference to what is now seen as a terrible military blunder. Because the soldiers involved were mainly volunteers and had not seen action before, they were told to walk, not run, across no-man's land towards the enemy machine guns. This order was responsible for many, many deaths – the men were easy targets for the enemy machine gunners. Line 10 starts to personify nature which *stands sentinel* over the grave; *sentinel* is a word associated with the army and military life. Here, however, it suggests that the earth is kindly looking after the soldiers' bodies, just like the farmers who tend the land. The use of the word *wound* suggests not only that the deaths of the men were painful, but also that the earth was wounded and, by extension, that there is something deeply unnatural about war. Our bodies gradually force foreign bodies out and up to the surface of the skin: this image is used to show what the earth is doing – forcing the bodies of the soldiers to the surface so that they will be discovered. *Foreign bodies* is an interesting phrase – on the literal level, these bodies are foreign because they are Welsh soldiers buried in France; but the comparison with our own bodies forcing things to the surface of the skin suggests even more that these bodies are hurting the earth and that they do not belong there.

Stanza five moves to the description of the uncovered grave. The bodies are linked arm in arm perhaps suggesting the comradeship the men felt towards each other in life. The *broken mosaic of bone* suggests something beautiful (the mosaic) which is now broken. The poet is reminded of images of a dance-macabre – a reminder of human mortality.

Ironically, we are told in the sixth stanza, the leather of their boots has survived their physical decay. The images of what remains are grotesque: the heads are tilted back at an angle, their jaws are missing and in the final line the poet mentions their *absent tongues*.

The final stanza changes everything and produces a moment of insight and epiphany. The poet introduces an extended simile, imagining that the soldiers – their heads back, their mouths open – are singing again – but this time it is to remind us of their deaths and sacrifice. They are singing only now and it is as if the reality of the war has only now been made completely clear to the poet and to us as readers.

What is also interesting about this poem is what it leaves out. It does not mention what the men were fighting for or individual acts of heroism or even the awful suffering of the battle itself. It concentrates on what is left. The final image of the bodies appearing to sing now – at the moment their bodies are uncovered – suggest that it is the earth (which has been standing sentinel) pushing their bodies back to the surface so that we can be reminded of the waste of war. The way the earth is described is important too. The bodies have lain in the earth for decades. Sheers creates a comparison with the body pushing out something alien that does not belong there and by doing so he is suggesting that the earth has kept the bodies for this very moment – it has stood sentinel over them – so that the people who discovered them would remember the soldiers and they would be given a proper burial. The way the earth conspires in the revelation of the bodies suggest that war is unnatural and the earth knows this. And so we can say that the earth is presented by Sheers as a benevolent force which safeguards the bodies of the dead soldiers and allows them to be discovered so that they can be re-buried properly and so that they can act as a reminder of the past.

Why?

This poem, written nearly one hundred years after the deaths of the men discovered in this mass grave, shows us that:

- war is wasteful and unnatural.

- human life is fragile and brief.

- the earth and those who tend it have a permanence that the dead soldiers do not.

- we should always remember the deaths of soldiers in previous wars.

The Yellow Palm – Robert Minhinnick

Context

Robert Minhinnick was born in 1952 and writes poems, essays and novels. A lot of his poetry is based on his experiences of living in Wales, but he has travelled widely and visited Iraq in 1998. He has said of his writing

I think in images and I like to write in images. That is what writing is all about – the transforming image that provides even commonplace things with another dimension.

We will see the truth of this quotation when we look at this poem in more detail in the commentary. Minhinnick has also called this poem a ballad and we will examine this idea in the commentary.

Palestine Street is in Baghdad, the capital of Iraq, and it is an important road because it is wide and it runs through the eastern side of the city. The Tigris River flows through the centre of the city. This poem is a reflection on the last thirty-odd years of Iraqi history. Palestine Street was often used for official processions and celebrations of government achievements; since the Western occupation of Iraq it has often been the scene of attacks on American troops and the vehicles they travel in. However, you should remember that this poem was written after Minhinnick's visit to Iraq in 1998 and before the invasion of 2003. Minhinnick has said of this poem that it was Al-Rasheed Street that he was thinking of when he wrote the poem, but there is a certain resonance added to the poem by changing it to Palestine Street, because the name is more evocative.

Why? Well, the underlying reason for all the wars in the Middle East and even the existence of Islamic fundamentalism is that Palestine no longer exists. The land which was called Palestine was taken over by Jewish settlers who created the state of Israel in 1948. Some Palestinians remained in the new state, but most were forced into exile and they (largely supported by the Arabic and Islamic world) have been fighting ever since to get their land back. Jewish settlers created Israel as a Jewish state – a place where all Jews could feel safe – mainly in response to the Holocaust perpetrated by the Nazis in the Second World War. America and Britain have defended Israel's right to exist when some Islamic states were dedicated to its destruction –

which is why (even before the invasions of Iraq and Afghanistan) America and Britain were the targets of terrorist attacks. The invasions of Iraq and Afghanistan, it could be said, simply made a bad situation even worse.

A sense of some of the history of Iraq will be important for you and it is also relevant to the poem 'At the Border' by Choman Hardi.

Saddam Hussein was a Sunni Muslim and he persecuted the Shia Muslims in the south of Iraq, because he thought they were secretly in league with Iran – because in Iran most Muslims are Shia. These words – Sunni and Shia – describe different branches of Islam and they are only important to explain the bloodshed in the mosque in stanza two of the poem: Saddam Hussein discouraged strong religious belief – like that practised by Shia Muslims.

1979	Saddam Hussein becomes President of Iraq.
1980 – 88	Iraq and Iran fight a war over territorial disputes and ideological differences.
1990	Iraq invades Kuwait.
1991	the Iraqi Army is expelled from Kuwait by a British and American army.
2003	Iraq is invaded by a joint Anglo-American army and Saddam Hussein is overthrown.

poison gas – chemical weapons such as mustard gas and chlorine gas. Poison gas was used by Iraq in the long war against Iran and against its own Kurdish minority.

muezzin – in Islam the person who calls worshippers to the mosque for prayers.

dinars – money: the unit of currency in Iraq.

Imperial Guard – an army unit who originally were Saddam Hussein's personal bodyguards, but who then became élite troops in the Iraqi army.

Mother of all Wars – Saddam Hussein's term for the First Gulf War.

Tigris – river flowing through Baghdad.

Cruise missile – a guided rocket which can carry ordinary explosives, or chemical, biological or nuclear weapons. Both sides used Cruise missiles in the First Gulf War.

caravan – here, in the context of the Middle East, a company of people travelling together.

armistice – a treaty announcing peace.

Salaam – an Arabic greeting meaning 'peace'.

yellow palm – this tree is often mentioned in the Koran. It produces dates, but its leaves and bark are used to make timber, rope and fuel. Because of its usefulness it is sometimes taken as a sign of God's bounty and generosity to mankind.

Who? The poet narrates the poem in the past tense. He encounters various different Iraqi citizens on his walk.

When? Not specified, but we know that Minhinnick visited Iraq in 1998 and details in the poem suggest it is set before the 2003 invasion that toppled Saddam Hussein.

Where? The poet walks along Palestine Street in Baghdad.

What? Each stanza describes a different scene which reflects some aspect of life in Iraq.

Commentary

This poem is immediately memorable because it has a refrain which appears at the start of each verse, not at the end – the normal position for a refrain. Not only is each first line of each stanza exactly the same, but the second line of each stanza is grammatically the same (until the final stanza); each second line begins with *I* followed by something that the poet sees or hears or smells. We will see that the final stanza is different in many respects – not just in the way it changes the pattern that Minhinnick has set up. The use of repetition and a refrain are typical of ballads.

In each stanza lines 2, 4 and 6 rhyme which is what we expect in a ballad and helps to propel the poem forward – although unlike most ballads this poem does not tell one complete story about any of the characters. You might argue that it tells the story of modern-day Iraq. The rhyme helps to establish a regular rhythm too – which helps imitate the poet's walk down the street, as we tend to walk with a regular rhythm.

Each stanza paints a picture of one scene – which links with the poet's comment that he likes to write in images. Most of the stanzas juxtapose something good with something unpleasant. We should not, I think, imagine that the poet took one walk along Palestine Street during which he saw all these things; it is more that each stanza is based on a separate image which taken together chart the recent history of Iraq. Each stanza is also a complete sentence which re-enforces the notion that we are reading (or seeing) individual images or snapshots of Iraqi history.

In the first stanza the poet watches a funeral pass. The *women waving lilac stems* is a tender image, but it is undercut and destroyed in the final line of the stanza when we discover that the dead man is a victim of *poison gas*.

The second stanza switches from sight to hearing. The poet hears the call to prayer and the impressions are positive – *the golden mosque, the faithful* – but then the poet notices the *blood on the walls* and the *despair* in the priest's eyes.

The poet meets *two blind beggars* in the third stanza and gives them money – a kind, charitable gesture which is reinforced by the repetition of *hands* in line 15: this is the first human contact in the poem. Once again, however, this moment of generosity is spoilt when they salute him and he realizes they are veterans of the First Gulf War, who have been blinded in battle.

If the third stanza dealt with the sense of touch, the fourth uses smell. The poet smells the freshness of the Tigris River which *lifts the air*, but the sun is relentlessly hot – a *barbarian* – and does not surrender – *it knows no armistice* – a word deliberately chosen by the poet because of its normal associations with peace and the ending of warfare.

A Cruise missile is seen in the fifth stanza, seen by the poet and by a beggar child. From the ground it looks beautiful: it is *a slow and silver caravan* – and the repetition of *slow and silver* in the next line serve to emphasize its beauty. The beggar child in the street turns his face up to look at it and smiles at the missile. Note how this stanza has reversed the order of images, in the sense that here we begin with the disturbing image – the missile – and end with the child's smile.

The final stanza marks a change in so many ways. The opening line is the same, but the second is not – the usual opening of the second line being delayed until line 3. As we read on, we note that in this final stanza there are no images of violence or death. The yellow dates that the poet notices on the palms are *sweeter than salaams* and the beggar child reaches up to touch the dates – *the fruit fell in his arms* – a final line that expresses a hope and trust in the future and in nature's ability to provide for human beings.

Why?

This carefully structured and very visual poem

- shows the human pain and suffering that decades of war and internal strife can produce.

- juxtaposes peaceful images with images of death and images of tradition with images of modern life.

- gives a sharp sense of the poverty of Iraq.

- ends on a note of hope and optimism for the future.

The Right Word – Imtiaz Dharker

Context

Imtiaz Dharker was born in 1954 in Pakistan, but her parents emigrated to England and she grew up in Glasgow. As well as being a published poet, she is a successful film maker and book illustrator. This poem was published in 2006 in the collection *The terrorist at my table* and its general background is of political and religious tensions following the 2001 attacks on America, the Anglo-American invasion of Iraq in 2003 and the London tube bombings in July 2005.

guerrilla warrior – a guerrilla is an irregular soldier; here its conjunction with 'warrior' makes it sound especially heroic.

martyr – a person who is prepared to die for their cause.

Who? The poet; the shadowy presence outside the door; the reader – we are directly addressed in lines 24 and 28 and in line 13 the figure is said to be *outside your door*.

When? The poem is set in the 21st century at night.

Where? There is no specific location – it could be anywhere in the world – which is part of the poem's point.

What? The poet sees a figure outside in the shadows and wonders who he is. Finally she realizes it is just a child and invites him inside her house to eat.

Commentary

This is a remarkably brave and sensitive poem. 'Brave' because it deals directly with terrorism and the possibility of attacks by suicide bombers at a time when such things may fill us with fear or horror or even anger; 'sensitive' because the way the poem ends suggests a thoughtful, human and capacious response to its subject matter.

The poem is written in free verse, but is very carefully constructed with very precise use of repeated words and phrases, sometimes with subtle changes, as the poet and we deal with the problem of finding the right word. While exploring the complexities of international terrorism, the poem also builds up a sense of fear and dread, as we wonder about the identity of the figure outside the door.

Let us look at the first stanza:

Outside the door,

lurking in the shadows,

is a terrorist.

This sets up the pattern that Dharker goes on to vary as the poem progresses. The word *outside* occurs in every stanza except the last two, when the tone of the poem changes. *Lurking in the shadows* also contributes to the pattern of repetition: *shadows* or *shadow* occurs in the first six stanzas and is usually introduced by a participle (the form of the verb ending in –ing). The final line – *is a terrorist* – also occurs but the final word changes as Dharker searches for the right word. She is struggling for the right word because people have different attitudes: those who commit terrorist attacks against us are the ones we call terrorists, but to their supporters they may be freedom-fighters.

The word at the end of the stanza determines the verb in the stanza itself. The terrorist is *lurking*; the freedom fighter is *taking shelter*. The *shadows* that are in each stanza are important too: on the one hand, they create a sense of mystery and fear and they are real in the sense that someone is outside your front door in the dark; it may well be a bit shadowy, so you cannot clearly see who is there; on the other hand, they also reflect the uncertainty about what words to use to describe the person outside the door.

The first five stanzas alternate between positive words used to describe the stranger – *freedom-fighter, guerrilla warrior* – and words with more negative connotations – *terrorist, hostile militant, martyr*. The word you choose will depend on whose side you are on. There are other interesting variations on the first stanza. In stanza four he is waiting outside *your door* – so that the reader is implicated in this. The start of the fourth stanza compares words to *waving, wavering flags*. They are just labels that we use to define people and the words we use depend on our political affiliations.

Line 20 is a turning point in the poem. Dharker says

No words can help me now.

But in this poem we have already seen that words are not very helpful. They are just labels and no help in identifying the person in the shadows. In this stanza the figure is lost in shadows and turns out to be

a child who looks like mine.

Line 24 addresses the reader:

One word for you

and the final line reveals that the figure

is a boy who looks like your son too.

The final two stanzas change the whole tone and atmosphere of the poem. After all the speculation about who is outside the door, the poet opens the door and invites the child in to eat with the family. In the final stanza the child steps in and carefully removes his shoes, showing respect for the poet's house. Muslims take off their shoes when they enter a mosque, but I would not read too much into that - it is quite common in the UK for visitors to remove their shoes on entering someone's house in order not to get the carpets and floors dirty. It simply shows consideration for the house-owner.

You could argue that the right word in this poem is *'Come in.'* Dharker seems to be suggesting that if you see the human being behind the emotive words – terrorist, freedom fighter, martyr – you will discover the real human being beneath. We might say also that one part of the problem with terrorism (or whatever word we choose to describe that phenomenon) is that we fail to understand the humanity beneath the word and that we will only reach a solution if we are prepared to be conciliatory – if we are prepared to welcome them in to eat with us.

My answer to What? above is a little simple. This is not a real situation, but an imaginary one. There is not really a figure lurking outside a door – it is an imaginative way that Dharker uses to explore our attitudes to terrorists and freedom-fighters. Dharker has said in an interview that

Identity has nothing to do with nationality, or religion, or gender.

The ending of this poem is positive and optimistic because she expresses the belief that human beings can overcome their difficulties by a recognition of our shared humanity. What unites us as human beings is more important than the irrelevant differences that divide us.

Why?

This poem shows

- that the language and words we use are determined by our political attitudes.

- that we live in fear and dread of terrorist attacks.

- that language and the words that we use to label people are sometimes inadequate or do not tell the whole truth.

- that there is hope for peace and reconciliation through a recognition of our shared humanity.

At the Border, 1979 – Choman Hardi

Context

Choman Hardi is Kurdish and was born in 1974. Her family moved to Iran in 1975 and returned to Iraq in 1979. They had to flee Iraq in 1988 when Saddam Hussein started attacking the Kurds with chemical weapons. In 1993 she came to Britain as a refugee and is now a poet, translator and painter. She had collections of her poetry published in Kurdish before she started writing in English. This poem is autobiographical; the border is the border between Iran and Iraq. This poem was published in 2004 in the collection *Life for Us*.

The story of the Kurdish people is a sad one. The Kurds have their own language, culture and traditions which stretch back thousands of years but they live in five different countries: Turkey, Iraq, Iran, Syria and Armenia. So they exist as a people, an ethnic group, but they do not have their own country. Because they are a minority in the different countries in which they live, they have often been persecuted for being different and because they want to have more political independence in the countries in which they live. Because of this, many Kurds have gone into exile in order to escape persecution and oppression. Ideally, I suppose, they would want their own country, Kurdistan, which unites all the Kurdish people, but that is very unlikely to happen, because it would mean other countries giving up territory. In recent times they have have suffered most persecution in Iraq under the rule of Saddam Hussein.

You may feel you need to know a little about recent Iraqi history to fully understand the context of this poem. (This is also very good background material to 'The Yellow Palm' by Robert Minhinnick.) Saddam Hussein became the President of Iraq in 1979 and in 1980 started a war with neighbouring Iran. Iran had just had an Islamic Revolution and presumably Saddam Hussein thought he could benefit Iraq by waging war against an unstable neighbour. The war ended in 1988 and caused hundreds of thousands of deaths. During the war the loyalty of the Iraqi Kurds was called into question and they were attacked by Saddam's own troops.

In 1990 Iraq invaded Kuwait and the First Gulf War began in 1991: a mainly British and American army forced the Iraqis out of Kuwait; once again Saddam's regime used the Kurds as a scapegoat for the national failure and many Kurds escaped from Iraq into neighbouring Turkey. In 2003 a British and American army invaded Iraq and toppled Saddam from power. Iraq has been a troubled country ever since, but the Kurds in the north of Iraq do now have a measure of autonomy.

Who? The poet speaks as herself in the past tense. She is with her family and a large group of Kurds returning to Iraq. The border crossing is manned by border guards.

When? 1979 when the poet was five years old.

Where? On the border between Iraq and Iran.

What? The poet and her family wait at a border crossing to be allowed back into the country which they left.

Commentary

This poem uses simple language and simple sentences to evoke the perceptions of Hardi as she was at the age of five when this event took place. In general, the poem consists of a record of what she heard and saw; she faithfully recounts the words and actions of a variety of people. It is interesting to note that the poem uses direct speech a lot: we hear the direct speech of four different people, but the poet remains silent, simply observing and now telling us what she saw and heard. However, the poem uses her innocent perceptions to make a profound point at the end of the poem.

Although we know from Hardi's biography which border they are crossing, it is important that the poem itself does not name the border: it could be any border anywhere in the world, but as readers we do not realize that until the end of the poem, when the five year old child has a moment of sudden realization, an epiphany.

The poem opens dramatically with direct speech, a border guard telling them they have reached the last check-in point in this country. They (and at this point we do not know who *they* are) grab a drink and console themselves with the thought that

soon everything would taste different.

The short second stanza describes the chain which is returned to throughout the poem and which physically marks the border between the two countries. The poet notes that *the land under our feet continued* – despite the presence of the chain.

The next stanza introduces some childish humour. Hardi's sister straddles the chain so she has one foot in one country and the other foot in another. We are given her sister's direct speech which creates a vivid sense of the sharpness of this memory. She is told off by the border guards.

Stanza four concentrates on Hardi's mother. She is looking forward to returning to her own country and is convinced that when they are home everything will be better. At home even *the landscape is more beautiful*.

The next stanza makes us aware that Hardi and her family are part of a large group of people waiting to cross the border, anxious to return to their homeland, looking forward with great anticipation to being home. Somebody says they can *inhale home* and the mothers start to cry with joy. Silently the poet compares both sides of the border.

In the sixth stanza, without any explicit comment, we are told what the poet saw. She cannot tell the difference between one side of the border and the other. The soil has the same texture and colour, and it is raining on both sides of the chain.

The first four lines of the final stanza simply recount what happened before they were allowed to cross the border. Hardi reports that a man bent to kiss the earth of home. And then the moment of perception, towards which the whole poem has been building, arrives in the final line:

The same chain of mountains encompassed us all.

And here Hardi plays on the word *chain* – this is not the chain marking the border, but the chain or range of mountains. In the final line the poet suggests that borders are artificial and man-made, that the important things like the soil and the weather and the mountains are exactly the same on either side of the border. The border guards are Iranian, the people crossing are Iraqi, but the mountains surround all of them. The mountains are bigger than the petty lines on a map which mark the border.

Following on from this, we might say that even the notion of countries (which is why you need borders) are artificial and man-made. And if we pay too much attention to countries then we are likely to forget the common humanity that unites everyone on earth – no matter which 'country' they officially belong to. The word *chain* is very evocative: chains are also something used to imprison people. Perhaps the poet is suggesting that we are chained by our narrow attitudes to country and identity and fail to see the bigger picture – which is the immensity of nature and our common humanity.

The adults in this poem are presented very differently from the children. The border guards are doing their job, but tell the poet's sister off for a harmless bit of childish humour. The adults returning home are full of strong emotions – they cry, they are excited. The poet remains a dispassionate observer and this allows the insight of the final line to ring true – the five year old child cannot see what all the fuss is about and realizes that there is actually little difference between the two countries separated by the border.

Does this particular poem and the issues it addresses have a special force given that Hardi is a Kurd? I think it does. The Kurds have a language, a culture and strong traditions but no country. You may read references to Kurdistan, but that is the name of a region in Iraq – it is not an independent country. Besides it does not include the many Kurds who live in the countries called Turkey, Iran and Armenia. So it follows that it is especially appropriate for a Kurdish poet to stress the ridiculousness of man-made lines on a map that divide and separate us from each other.

Why?

This poem uses a child's language and perspective

- to show that national divisions are man-made and arbitrary.

- to argue that the borders between nations make us forget our common humanity and forget about the world, the landscape, the soil.

- to imply that we are imprisoned or chained in mental attitudes of patriotism.

Belfast Confetti – Ciaran Carson

Context

Carson was born in Belfast in 1948 and has lived there all his life. Violence and its effects are central to much of his writing – he has lived throughout the 'Troubles' - the name given to the last forty years of the history of Northern Ireland. During the Troubles terrorist groups representing both sides of the conflict attacked each other and the British Army, and planted bombs which deliberately targeted civilians too. This poem was written in 1990, but the term 'Belfast confetti' was already in use in speech and means the shrapnel (pieces of metal) placed around explosives that would fly out and injure people when the explosive was detonated.

There has been violence in Ireland ever since the English tried to conquer it and make it a colony in the 16th century. The most recent era of violence is known as the Troubles and flared up in the late 1960s. Tension between Catholic and Protestant communities erupted into violence and British troops were sent Northern Ireland to keep the peace, to keep the opposing sides apart. However, because of various factors, the violence escalated and terrorist groups on both sides of the sectarian divide became involved and increasingly powerful. There were many deaths and many bombings, and the violence continued into the late 1990s. Carson was brought up in the Falls Road area – one of the most dangerous areas of Belfast.

It is dangerous to generalize about Ireland, but essentially the Catholic community favoured unification with the Republic of Ireland, while the Protestant community wanted to remain as part of the United Kingdom. More immediately, in the 60s the Catholic community did not have equal rights because the Protestant majority dominated politics.

fount – this word means two things in this poem. It is a spring of water like a fountain, but it is also a fount of broken type: before computers, books and newspapers were printed using metal blocks to represent each letter and piece of punctuation which were laboriously put in position by hand. These metal blocks are not unlike the pieces of metal used as shrapnel.

Balaklava, Raglan, Inkerman, Odessa, Crimea – street names in the Falls Road area which ironically recall the Crimean War – another British imperial war, you might argue. You can read more about the Crimean War in the section devoted to *The Charge of the Light Brigade* by Alfred Tennyson.

Saracen – a British army armoured personnel carrier.

Kremlin-2 mesh – a type of mesh used over the windows of Saracens and designed to protect the windows from bombs and rockets.

Makrolon face-shields – Makrolon is a tough man-made substance which protects the face but is transparent.

fusillade – a continuous discharge of guns.

Who? The poet speaks as himself.

When? During the Troubles.

Where? In the Falls Road area of Belfast.

What? The poet is caught on the streets of Belfast when a bomb is detonated. He seems to get lost in the confusion and chaos after the explosion and describes the British Army's own confused reaction to the incident.

Commentary

This is a confused and confusing poem which you may struggle to make sense of – but it is deliberately written in this way to suggest that this sort of incident is frightening and confusing and it also demonstrates the inability of language to describe adequately what is going on. The title of the poem *Belfast Confetti* is an everyday, darkly-comic term for shrapnel. It becomes darkly comic because we normally associate confetti with weddings not bombings. The 'confetti'- the shrapnel - rains down on the streets of Belfast once the bomb has exploded.

In the first stanza the poet struggles to make sense of what is going on. He is caught up in a riot and then a bomb explodes, adding to the confusion. The very first word – *suddenly* – plunges us into the midst of the action. In the wake of the explosion the air is *raining exclamation marks*: this metaphor suggests the pieces of shrapnel flying through the air; the shouts and cries of people near the bomb's blast; and also the sheer sense of shock and fear that courses through the poet. Carson continues this metaphor of the shrapnel as pieces of punctuation to suggest that language and its tools – punctuation – cannot make sense of, or convey the reality of, the riot and the bomb. *This hyphenated line* becomes *a burst of rapid fire*. The poet tries to formulate a sentence in his head, but he cannot complete it – his sense of fear and panic and shock is so strong that he has lost the ability to communicate. To make matters worse, at the end of the stanza he cannot escape – everywhere is *blocked with stops and colons*.

In the second stanza the poet is lost in his home area. The tense switches to the present to give extra immediacy. He knows *this labyrinth so well*, but cannot escape. The list of street names adds to his sense of confusion. As I have already mentioned the names are highly ironic since they are named after places in the Crimea where the British Army fought; except Raglan Street which is named after Lord Raglan, the British army commander-in-chief during the Crimean War. Everywhere he finds a dead-end. The short sentences echo his confusion and also give us the sense that he is trying to move quickly in order to get off the streets to the safety of his home. Line 15 is full of references to British soldiers, but they are described in terms of their equipment – in a list like the street names. The soldiers are not presented as human and in line 16 they fire a series of questions at him – a *fusillade of question marks*. *Fusillade* is a brilliantly chosen metaphor which is appropriate since the soldiers are asking the questions, but also suggests how potentially dangerous these questions seem to the poet in his state of panic:

My name? Where am I coming from? Where am I going?

Clearly the soldiers are trying to catch the bombers and these are genuine questions which they might have asked someone running in the streets in the aftermath of a riot and a bombing, but they are more important than that. Carson's sense of total disorientation, his fear and total confusion, mean that he is unsure of who he is and where he's going, so great has been his sense of shock.

Why? This poem

- uses lists, questions and short, unfinished sentences to convey an atmosphere of fear and chaos.

- shows no interest in the political situation, but is wholly concerned with the reactions of one frightened and confused man.

- uses language to suggest the inability of language to adequately convey the reality of a riot and a subsequent bomb blast.

- enacts through its language and imagery the extreme sense of shock and disorientation that the poet feels.

Poppies – Jane Weir

Context

Weir grew up on the outskirts of Manchester and works as a poet, writer and textile designer. Her poetry has been highly praised. This poem was commissioned by Carol Ann Duffy along with nine other contemporary war poems in 2009, in response to the growing violence in Afghanistan and the inquiry into the invasion of Iraq. In an interview she commented:

I wrote this piece from a woman's perspective, which is quite rare, as most poets who write about war have been men. As the mother of two teenage boys, I tried to put across how I might feel if they were fighting in a war zone. I was subliminally thinking of Susan Owen [mother of Wilfred Owen – see the next poem] *and families of soldiers killed in any war when I wrote this poem.*

Armistice Sunday – the Sunday closest to November 11th, Remembrance Day, chosen because the First World War ended on November 11th, 1918.

tucks, darts, pleats – words associated the clothes and textiles.

Who? The poet speaks directly to a son who is taking leave of his mother, the narrator.

When? We are told it is three days before Armistice Sunday, but apart from that no specific time is mentioned and no specific war is mentioned which gives the poem a universal quality. It could be any war at any time and any mother bidding farewell to her son, unsure of what will happen to him. Having said that, Armistice Sunday has only been commemorated since the First World War, and the habit of wearing poppies to remember the sacrifice of dead soldiers is also a modern phenomenon, so this is a modern poem. We know it was published in 2009.

Where? The action begins at the narrator's home and ends in the local churchyard in front of the war memorial.

What? She pins a poppy on his lapel and says goodbye at the front door. Filled with memories of his childhood, she goes to her son's bedroom and then is led to the local churchyard and the poem ends with the mother gazing at the war memorial, thinking about her son.

Commentary

The opening sentence fixes the day: it is three days before Armistice Sunday. Before her son leaves, the narrator pins a poppy on the lapel of the person the poem is addressed to: it is her son, but this is only confirmed by later details. Even the gender of the speaker is not made explicit, but there are strong suggestions that it is his mother – which we will explore later. Armistice Sunday commemorates all those who have died in wars, but we might note that poppies have been placed on individual war graves to remind us that every serviceman who died was an individual. The final three lines of the first stanza use language which is rich in texture and sound qualities:

I pinned one onto your lapel, crimped petals,

spasms of paper red, disrupting a blockade

of yellow bias binding around your blazer.

Alliteration on *p* gives way to alliteration on *b*, and Weir also uses assonance to give further euphony to these lines: *pinned/crimped* and *spasms/paper/blazer* and *bias/binding*.

The second stanza gives us lots of recognizable domestic details: the mother (we assume that it is the mother because traditionally it is mothers who would fuss over a son's appearance in this way) the mother uses sellotape to remove the cat's hairs from her son's clothes and smoothes his collar down. The sellotape is *bandaged around* her hand – a hint perhaps that she is finding this leave-taking painful. The narrator says *I wanted* to rub noses with her son as they did when her son was younger, but she doesn't; she also had to resist the *impulse* to run her fingers through his hair. These details suggest that now her son is older she feels she cannot do these things that a parent might naturally do to their child when they are younger. So as our children grow up, it seems, we lose some of the intimacy we enjoyed when they were small children. Another detail which confirms that the son is older is probably the gelled blackthorns of his hair. He is old enough to make decisions about his appearance. The speaker clearly feels sad that her son is growing up: in lines 10 and 11 we are told she *steeled the softening of my face* and in line 18 she tells us *I was brave* – it is as if her face will soften with tears at her son's departure, but she manages to control her feelings in order not to embarrass her son – just as she has not rubbed noses with him or run her fingers through his hair.

The words she wants to say to him won't come; they are slowly *melting* in line 18. When she opens the front door the world is overflowing *like a treasure chest* and her son is *intoxicated*: leaving home may be sad for the parent, but it can be a time of excitement and opportunity for the child as these words suggest.

As soon as he has gone she goes to his bedroom and releases a song bird from its cage; I don't think we are meant to see this as literal, but it probably symbolizes the speaker's son being released into the intoxicating, *treasure chest* world – a good thing despite his mother's obvious sadness at saying goodbye.

Weir then introduces a dove which leads the mother to the churchyard. The mother is still distracted: her stomach is busy and her nervousness about her son is conveyed to us in imagery drawn from textiles and the manufacture of clothes – *tucks, darts, pleats*; she is obviously distracted too because, although it is November, she has no coat and wears no gloves. Weir is a textile designer and often uses such vocabulary in her poems. But the fact that she goes out improperly dressed is also a sign of her deep need to follow the dove and get to the war memorial.

Once in the churchyard the speaker traces the inscriptions on the war memorial while leaning against it *like a wishbone* – a simile that displays her fragility and which also raises the idea of wishes: presumably she would wish her son to be safe and happy. The dove flies above her and is described metaphorically as *an ornamental stitch* - and then the poem ends:

I listened, hoping to hear

your playground voice catching on the wind.

And that phrase - *playground voice* – suggests the speaker's nostalgia for her son's childhood and her regret that he has to grow up. *Playground* is a word we associate with primary schools and it is clear from earlier details in the poem that he is older and has left childish things behind.

This is a beautiful and powerful poem. The very writing of the poem can be seen to be a political act, because Weir is writing about a subject matter which is dominated by male poets, so to give a mother a voice is an important decision.

Some readers feel that the son is going off to war and that is why Weir is saying goodbye to him. I don't see the poem quite like that. Soldiers don't wear blazers; it is not a word used to describe what soldiers wear. I think Weir's son is going off to school – secondary school, perhaps even boarding school – and this poem is about a rite of passage for mother and for her son. A rite of passage is a ritual that marks a deep change in one's life: here it is all about sending your son off into the world, about not being able to rub noses with him because he is too old for that; it might contain the fear that later in the future he might join the army and his name might one day join the names on the war memorial.

And this fear of the future leads the mother to the war memorial, because on this day when she bids goodbye to her growing son, she feels real empathy for the mothers of the men listed on the war memorial. In their cases they said goodbye to their sons and never saw them again because they died in war. So the poppy on the lapel and the fact that this poem takes place three days before Armistice Sunday are crucial to the poem's impact. It is as if our commemoration of Armistice Sunday makes the speaker acutely aware of the much worse sacrifices that mothers make in times of war and alerts her to what might happen in the future if her son ever becomes a soldier. Becoming a soldier (or whatever your child's first job might be) would also be a rite of passage and death is the ultimate rite of passage.

And what are we to make of the dove? It is a symbol of peace, but in the final stanza the metaphor used to describe it is an ornamental stitch, a stitch which is ornamental, not practical, not serving a purpose. Does this suggest that our hopes for peace will always be ornamental and never real, never realized, never practical? Does it suggest that war will always be with us, because the dove will remain ornamental? This may seem a little fanciful to you, but the First World War which led to so many monuments in British towns and churchyards was once thought of as the 'war to end all wars', but Weir is writing in 2009 when British soldiers were dying regularly in Afghanistan. War has continued to blight human history.

Why?

This interesting modern poem

- allows a woman's voice to speak on the subject of war.

- uses symbols very effectively and evocatively.

- presents an inevitable rite of passage for any mother and her child.

- links this rite of passage with the commemoration of the war dead through poppies and on Armistice Day.

- uses the language of textiles to suggest the gender of the parent.

- movingly presents the way parent/child relationships change over time.

- is more powerful because the mother in the poem represses her emotions in front of her son.

- sees the growing up of children and their loss of innocence as inevitable, but sad.

The Literary Heritage

Futility – Wilfred Owen

Context

Wilfred Owen (1893 – 1918) is widely regarded as the leading British poet of the First World War. He died in action on November 4th 1918 – just seven days before the war finally came to an end. Owen was an officer and was awarded the Military Cross for leadership and bravery in October 1918. The shock of what he saw in the front-line moved him to produce a great many poems in a very short time – most of which were not published until after his death. He seems to have been particularly keen to ensure that the British public were told the horrific truth about the war. He developed his own use of half-rhyme which was to influence other poets for the whole of the 20th century.

'Futility' is one of only five poems that were published when Owen was alive. It was published in a magazine called *The Nation* in June 1918. The compassion that Owen reveals in this poem for the suffering of the ordinary soldier is typical of his work; some of his other poems though, are more brutal and horrific in their realism.

Owen was one of many British writers who felt moved to describe what they saw of the war in the trenches of France and Belgium – and it is a subject to which British writers have returned again and again. Why? Most people would agree that all wars are horrific and cause death and terrible injuries, so what was it about the First World War that so captures the imagination of generation after generation of writers? It seems that the First World War was unique because it caused huge numbers of deaths on all sides without any obvious effect on the course of the war; infantry troops were sent from their trenches to almost certain death and battles lasted for months with only a tiny movement of the front-line – so there was huge loss of life with no clear objective: it began to seem pointless to those involved in it and that pointlessness is echoed by this poem's title. Added to that, the conditions in the trenches – where the men lived and fought and often died – were appalling.

Futility – uselessness.

the clay – humanity. In the Bible God creates man from a lump of clay.

fatuous – foolish

Who? Owen speaks as himself.

When? In the present – *this morning, this snow*. But we know from the biographical context that this poem is set during the First World War – the poem itself contains no military detail at all.

Where? From the poem we know it is set in France; from our knowledge of Owen, we know that this is set in the trenches of the front-line.

What? A soldier has died. The speaker wants to move him into the sun, since that surely will bring him back to life. It doesn't, and the speaker reflects on the sadness and pity of the death as well as thinking about the bigger questions of human existence.

Commentary

The poem begins with an order - *Move him into the sun* - perhaps given by an officer. A soldier has died in the night – frozen to death in the snow it seems. In a sense, how he has died is irrelevant – it is the fact that he has died that Owen finds so shocking. He comes from the countryside and has always woken at dawn – *whispering of fields unsown* suggests that in Britain he worked on the land and had to sow seeds in fields, but this might also suggest the promise for the future growth that seeds contain. Because the sun had always woken him and had woken him gently, the speaker articulates an innocent trust that the *kind old sun* will wake him now. But, of course, it won't. The tone of this opening stanza is gentle with soft sounds; even the personified sun used to whisper to the young man.

The second stanza begins by pointing out that our solar system and our planet only exists because of the sun. Owen ends the stanza with three questions that simply cannot be answered without calling into doubt any religious faith and our very existence. Human beings are seen as the summit of evolution – *so dear achieved* – but the poet wonders why Creation occurred at all, if it will end in tragic deaths like this one: the sunbeams that helped create life on earth are *fatuous* and powerless. And this makes Owen question the whole point of human existence. Here in the second stanza the rhythm is broken up by the dashes and question marks which give a faltering, uncertain mood to the poem. Is Owen bitter or simply puzzled and confused about why we are here on this planet?

This is a very memorable poem in all sorts of ways. It uses half-rhyme to suggest that something very profound is wrong with what Owen describes, but it has no specific references to the First World War – apart from the word France. This perhaps gives the poem a timeless quality – it could apply to all deaths in all wars and the sense of futility that Owen feels could be applied to every death of a young person. It fits the definition of freshness of ideas because Owen uses one individual death to question the very nature of our existence on earth, the point of human existence and the nature of God – and he does so in only 12 lines – a remarkable feat of compression. This is a poem that is not just anti-war – it is also, one might say, anti-God because it questions why we are on earth if all that is going to happen is that we will die. It is a tender, poignant and gentle poem, full of a profound sadness at the thought of anyone dying before their time. Nature is important in the poem too: the dead soldier is at home in nature and at ease with the rhythms of nature, but that does not help him escape death.

Why?

This short gentle poem raises important issues:

- Life on earth seems pointless when we are faced with death, especially the deaths of young people.

- The sun (which might be symbolic of God and the creator of the planet) can create a whole world, but cannot bring one young man back to life.

- What is the purpose of human life on earth? The poet cannot accept that it is to kill each other in war.

- God – given the questions in the second stanza – seems not to exist or at least not to care about individual human deaths.

The Charge of the Light Brigade – Alfred Tennyson

Context

Alfred Tennyson was born in 1809 and died in 1892. His early work received a mixed reaction, but his *Poems* published in 1842 established him as the leading poet of his day. In 1850 he was made Poet Laureate and was given a peerage in 1884. This poem is not especially typical of his work. It was published in 1855 in a collection called *Maud* and was written in response to a British military disaster during the Battle of Balaklava in October 1854. It is said that Tennyson read the report of the disaster in *The Times* and was moved to write the poem.

The Crimean War was fought largely in the Crimean Peninsula – then part of the Russian Empire and now part of the Ukraine. Britain and its allies – France and the Ottoman Empire – were fighting Russia over who would control the Dardanelles – the narrow strip of sea in Turkey that connects the Aegean Sea to the Black Sea. It was important for British sea-routes and trade that Russia did not control the Dardanelles.

This is the report from *The Times* that Tennyson read:

At ten past eleven our Light Cavalry Brigade rushed to the front.....The whole brigade scarcely made one effective regiment, according to the numbers of continental armies; and yet it was more than we could spare. As they passed towards the front, the Russians opened on them from the guns in the redoubts on the right, with volleys of musketry and rifles.

They swept proudly past, glittering in the morning sun in all the pride and splendour of war. We could hardly believe the evidence of our senses! Surely that handful of men were not going to charge an army in position? Alas! it was too true – their desperate valour knew no bounds, and far indeed was it removed from its so called better part – discretion. They advanced in two lines, quickening their pace as they closed towards the enemy. A more fearful spectacle was never witnessed than by those who, without the power to aid, beheld their heroic countrymen rushing to the arms of death. At the distance of 1200 yards the whole line of the enemy belched forth, from thirty iron mouths, a flood of smoke and flame, through which hissed the deadly balls. Their flight was marked by instant gaps in our ranks, by dead men and horses, by steeds flying wounded or riderless across the plain. The first line was broken – it was joined by the second, they never halted or checked their speed an instant. With diminished ranks, thinned by those thirty guns, which the Russians had laid with the most deadly accuracy, with a halo of flashing steel above their heads, and with a cheer which was many a noble fellow's death cry, they flew into the smoke of the batteries; but ere they were lost from view, the plain was strewed with their bodies and with the carcasses of horses. They were exposed to an oblique fire from the batteries on the hills on both sides, as well as to a direct fire of musketry.

Through the clouds of smoke we could see their sabres flashing as they rode up to the guns and dashed between them, cutting down the gunners as they stood. The blaze of their steel, as an officer standing near me said, was 'like the turn of a shoal of mackerel'. We saw them riding through the guns, as I have said; to our delight we saw them returning, after breaking through a column of Russian infantry, and scattering them like chaff, when the flank fire of the battery on the hill swept them down, scattered and broken as they were. Wounded men and dismounted troopers flying towards us told the sad tale – demigods could not have done what they had failed to do.

At the very moment when they were about to retreat, an enormous mass of lancers was hurled upon their flank...With courage too great almost for credence, they were breaking their way through the columns which enveloped them, when there took place an act of atrocity without parallel in the modern warfare of civilized nations. The Russian gunners, when the storm of cavalry passed, returned to their guns. They saw their own cavalry mingled with the troopers who had just ridden over them, and to the eternal disgrace of the Russian name the miscreants poured a murderous volley of grape and canister on the mass of struggling men and horses, mingling friend and foe in one common ruin...At twenty five to twelve not a British soldier, except the dead and dying, was left in front of these bloody Muscovite guns.

And this is what *The Times* editorial said about the disaster:

Causeless and fruitless, it stands by itself as a grand heroic deed, surpassing even that spectacle of a shipwrecked regiment, setting down into the waves, each man still in his rank. The British soldier will do his duty, even to certain death, and is not paralyzed by feeling that he is the victim of some hideous blunder.

Why have I bothered to reprint this article? I think it is important for you to see the inspiration that Tennyson used. He had not been to the Crimea; he had never been on a battlefield; his only source was this article. *Some hideous blunder* is directly reflected in line 12 of the poem. Equally the reporter's assertion that the British soldier *will do his duty, even to certain death* is the main theme of the poem. The Light Brigade began the charge with 607 men; only 302 returned. I think *The Times* report is interesting – not simply because it is a first-hand account by a journalist who witnessed the event. The editorial admits there was *some hideous blunder*, but the overwhelming tone of the report and the editorial is admiration for the courage of the men who obeyed such a senseless order. We can see in Tennyson's poem a similar balance: he does admit it was a terrible mistake, but his emphasis is on the heroism of the men who simply obeyed their orders.

In reality, the incident was a complete failure and a pointless loss of life – it was a military disaster. However, it has become famous, partly through Tennyson's poem, but also because it moved other artists to produce work based on the incident. Perhaps it appealed to something that the public wanted to believe was part of being British – unflinching courage against the odds. Over the course of time, Tennyson's poem has lost some of its popularity perhaps because our attitudes to war have changed and we are more likely to question the justness of any war and the human cost of blindly following orders. In Tennyson's defence, one might say that as Poet Laureate it was his task to reflect the national mood at the time and it is certainly true that the men who charged on that day did display great courage

league – three miles.

Valley of Death – an allusion to Psalm 23 in the Bible and to a novel call *Pilgrim's Progress* by John Bunyan. In both texts faith in God encourages people to be brave in dangerous places.

Light Brigade – at school I was confused about this title. It means that the brigade were on horseback but were lightly armed – they carried only swords. And, yes – there was a Heavy Brigade who moved more slowly because they carried more weaponry.

sabres – the specific type of sword carried by the soldiers.

Cossack – an ethnic group from south-eastern Russia, famed for their fighting skills.

sunder'd – broken apart.

Back from the mouth of Hell – anthropologists have noted that in cultures all over the world there are stories about brave men who visit hell or the underworld or the world of the dead and return alive. For example, in Greek mythology Hercules visits the underworld, but returns unscathed, adding to his heroic qualities.

Who? Tennyson writes about the cavalrymen of the Light Brigade; the enemy are present in the poem, as is the person who gave the order to charge the Russian guns; the reader is addressed directly in the final stanza.

When? October 25th, 1854, although Tennyson wrote the poem a few days later having read the report in *The Times*.

Where? Outside the Russian town of Balaklava in the Crimean Peninsula.

What? Tennyson describes the charge of the cavalry and what happened to them.

Commentary

This very famous poem relies a great deal on repetition throughout its length. Tennyson also uses alliteration in many lines and, if you read it aloud, the rhythm of the poem seems to imitate the motion of the horses galloping forward. It is these features, I would suggest, which make the poem so memorable.

The opening stanza highlights the order the brigade was given in lines 5 and 6. The opening phrase is repeated three times; *Valley of Death* is repeated twice as is *the six hundred* – giving these phrases prominence and emphasising their relatively small numbers and the fact that they are going to die. The phrase *Valley of Death* would have been very evocative to a Christian audience because it comes from such a well-known psalm.

The second stanza is directly related to the report in *The Times*. Line 9 repeats line 5. Line 12 picks up the word used by the journalist, but makes the order anonymous – *Someone had blunder'd*. It is not part of Tennyson's aim to apportion blame for the order, but to praise the men who followed it. And it is important, in the poem, that the soldiers knew it was a blunder yet still went ahead and charged. Lines 13 to 15 use repetition, but also heap praise on their unquestioning obedience of the order, despite having a clear understanding that it would lead to death. The alliteration in line 15 – *do and die* – draws attention to their clear courage and willingness to die.

In stanza three Tennyson makes us aware of the enemy again, through simple repetition which here gives us a real sense of the situation into which they rode, facing cannon fire from three sides. Note the onomatopoeia of *thunder'd* and the alliteration in line 22. In lines 24 and 25 Tennyson uses synonyms for the Valley of Death – *the jaws of Death* and *the mouth of Hell*. Although he concentrates on their bravery, line 23 also mentions their skill. They rode *boldly* and *well*, despite the terrible situation they were in.

Stanza four describes what happened when the cavalry reached the Russian positions. Tennyson uses vivid verbs – *flash'd, charging, plunged* – to give us an impression of close quarter fighting. *Charging an army* reminds us of the impossible odds they faced, while *All the world wonder'd* might mean that the world looked on amazed at their courage or astonished at the stupidity of the order – it probably means both! They have some limited success when in close contact with the enemy: the Russians *reel'd* and were *shatter'd and sunder'd*. Finally, at the end of the stanza, they turn to ride back to the British positions – those that are left. Note Tennyson's repeated use of the phrase *the six hundred*, except that it is now preceded by *not*.

The brigade ride back to their own positions in stanza five. Again Tennyson repeats several lines and phrases from earlier in the poem. The first three lines are identical to the start of stanza three with only one word being altered. He uses more alliteration in line 44 and pays tribute to the soldiers with the word *hero* and by pointing out that they had fought so well.

The sixth stanza is short and directly addressed to the reader. It begins with a question which stresses their glory (and not the idiocy of the order); the second line is an exclamation of admiration and is followed by a line we have seen before which suggests their charge will become famous all over the world. The final three lines are imperatives, orders to the readers – we are told to honour the Light Brigade because they were so noble.

How attitudes have changed since 1854! Today if so many British soldiers died in an engagement that lasted only half an hour there would be a public outcry and calls for an enquiry – particularly if it emerged that they died because of an incompetent order or an order that was misinterpreted. But Tennyson is not interested in that side of this story. He wants to praise their unthinking bravery and willingness to die following orders. You may find it hard to agree with the attitudes in the poem, but there is no doubt that Tennyson uses all his poetic skills to create something memorable.

Why? This very well-known poem

- gives a vivid impression of the speed of the charge and the atmosphere of battle.

- glorifies the courage and heroism of the men who followed orders and made the charge.

- tells the reader to remember the dead and their noble deeds.

Bayonet Charge – Ted Hughes

Context

Ted Hughes was born in 1930 and died in 1998. He was one of the most famous poets of his generation and was appointed Poet Laureate in 1984 – a position he held until his death. He was born in a small village near Halifax in West Yorkshire and the landscape of his birthplace influenced him throughout his life. Hughes was a prolific poet and also wrote several books for children. His private life increased his notoriety, as his first wife (the American poet Sylvia Plath) and his next partner both committed suicide in a similar way. Much of his poetry is inspired by the power and beauty and mystery of nature. This poem, however, is perhaps influenced by the fact that Hughes' father was a First World War veteran.

Hughes' father fought in the First World War and, although the poem could be about any modern war, it is usually assumed that Hughes is writing about incidents or events that his father spoke about. The poem is written in the past tense.

Who? The poet acts as an observer and describes one unnamed man's experience of a charge towards the enemy armed with a rifle and a bayonet.

When? Unclear – it might be during the First World War. What the poem has to tell us about the experience of war is universal and applicable to all wars.

Where? A battlefield. Infantry soldiers are charging a hedge where the enemy are.

What? The poem describes the sensations of one soldier as he charges into battle.

Commentary

The poem is divided into three distinct stanzas. The first stanza describes the start of the charge towards the enemy positions. In the second the soldier seems to be frozen in time. In the final stanza the action resumes. Hughes writes in free verse and in long sentences with much use of enjambment – all this suggests the speed at which events occur in battle. There is no time to think when you are under fire and the words give us an impression of this.

With the first word - *suddenly* - we are plunged immediately into the centre of the action. As soon as the soldier awoke he was running. Hughes uses powerful harsh and vivid words to convey the experience. Everything conspires to slow him down: his sweat is heavy; he is not running but stumbling; the field is full of clods; his rifle becomes heavy:

He lugged a rifle numb as a smashed arm.

The simile subtly reminding us of the dangers he faces and the assonance on *u* in *lugged/numb* gives in sound an impression of its heaviness. And all the time as he runs towards the hedge – which *dazzled with rifle fire* – around him bullets are

smacking the belly out of the air.

Smacking is onomatopoeic and we might notice that much of the imagery in this first stanza comes from the human body – *belly, arm, eye* – this soldier is being shot at and it is his body which is being attacked. In the final two lines of the stanza Hughes tells us that the patriotism which once motivated him has gone, to be replaced by *molten iron* sweating *from the centre of his chest* – another thing to slow him down.

The start of the second stanza almost comes to a stop as the soldier suffers a sense of *bewilderment*. He starts to question exactly WHY he is running towards the enemy guns:

In what cold clockwork of the stars and the nations

Was he the hand pointing that second?

The mention of the *stars* suggest that this is partly his fate to be there at that particular moment, but the *nations* reveals that this very human and individual experience is actually happening because of international politics and the habit of countries to wage war against each other. *Cold clockwork* suggests something mechanical and *cold* suggests a lack of feeling for the individual. The soldier is frozen in an appalled epiphany:

his foot hung like

Statuary in mid-stride.

The third stanza introduces a hare which appears out of the *shot-slashed furrows*: *slot-slashed* combining consonance and onomatopoeia to become very memorable. The hare is a victim of the bullets: it is clearly in agony (*rolled like a flame*) and in a state of extreme trauma and shock:

its mouth wide

Open silent, its eyes standing out.

The hare is important in the poem: on the one hand, it is symbolic of the soldier's own pain and lack of understanding; on a deeper level, Hughes uses it to suggest that war is man-made and unnatural. This is not simply to show that innocent animals can be the victims of a war; much more importantly, Hughes is suggesting that it is unnatural for human beings to take part in war too.

The soldier carries on running towards the hedge and, as he runs, he drops what Hughes compares in a simile to *luxuries:*

King, honour, human dignity, etcetera.

He is no longer running for some of the conventional reasons that men fight. Having seen the hare and had his moment of epiphany, he is running to survive, to stay alive – no other reason. Note Hughes' dismissive use of the word *etcetera* – all the reasons given for waging war are irrelevant. Hughes ends the poem with a graphic reminder of the reality of the battlefield and the soldier's fear and his instinctive desire

To get out of that blue crackling air

His terror's touchy dynamite.

Note the onomatopoeic *crackling* and the way Hughes uses the consonance and alliteration on *t* to suggest the knife-edge of tension which the soldier feels.

This is a very powerful and physical poem dealing with the experience of the individual soldier in battle. And it IS an individual soldier – Hughes makes no mention of any other soldier being involved, so the individual's fear and isolation are given prominence.

Why?

This interesting poem about the experience of fighting

- unusually has the moment of epiphany in the middle of the poem, not the end.

- destroys the myths about why men fight – patriotism, King and country, etcetera.

- uses harsh violent imagery to convey the soldier's fear.

- uses nature, in the form of the hare, to condemn war as unnatural.

The Falling Leaves – **Margaret Postgate Cole**

Context

Born in 1893 into a firmly Anglican family, Margaret Postgate began to question her religious beliefs as a student at Cambridge. She became a socialist, a feminist and an atheist. Her brother, Raymond, was put in prison during the First World War because he was a conscientious objector – someone who refused to fight because it is against their principles of pacifism. He was eventually forced to sign up, but was declared medically unfit to be a soldier. Nonetheless, her brother's stand influenced Margaret and she became a pacifist and began to campaign against conscription or forced enlistment. It was through this work that she met her husband, G D H Cole.

The date of the poem is important. The early summer of 1915 saw the Second Battle of Ypres in Flanders, a region of Belgium. In the battle it became clear that the First World War battles would produce many casualties as men armed with rifles and bayonets were sent to take enemy positions guarded by rapid-fire machine guns and artillery. It was also during the Second Battle of Ypres where the German Army used poison gas in battle against British, Canadian and French soldiers for the very first time (the Germans had already used it against the Russian Army in the east). The battle lasted a month, but resulted in over 105,000 men from both armies being killed or wounded.

It was not only the men who suffered during the First World War. The women at home were the mothers, wives, sweethearts and sisters of the men dying in such huge numbers in France and Belgium, and many women poets responded to the war by writing poems.

thence – from that place.

gallant – brave, courageous.

multitude – a great many.

pestilence – a plague.

strewed – scattered loosely.

Flemish – of or belonging to Flanders.

Who? The poet writes in the first person and the present tense.

When? November 1915.

Where? The poet is riding on a horse in the English countryside.

What? She sees the leaves falling from the trees and this makes her think about the dead soldiers in Belgium.

Commentary

This is a peaceful and gentle poem, full of a tender sadness at the sheer number of deaths occurring in the First World War. The scene of the English countryside on a still afternoon is in contrast to what must be happening in Europe on the battlefields. The falling leaves are symbolic of all the young men dying in France and Belgium. It is written as one long verse paragraph which is one long sentence, but with lines of unequal length, suggesting that the thoughts of the poet are uneven or with the short lines suggesting the short lives of the soldiers which have literally been cut short. There is a rhyme scheme too, but it is unobtrusive because of the irregular line length and enjambment.

Autumn is often used as a time of reflection by poets on the inevitability of death and decay – the season shows that the year is dying and the use of snowflakes twice as a simile re-enforces the sense that winter is coming and perhaps that there will be more deaths as the war continues. But the poem is gentle in tone because of the frequent use of words beginning with *w* and *l* and *f* – all very soft consonants. These mean that the combined effect of the alliteration is to create euphony and a mood that is wistful and elegiac. The poet has no experience of warfare and there is no first-hand detail of warfare in the poem. The dead are praised – they are *gallant* and have *beauty* - and there is no distinction between British and German soldiers. The leaves are so numerous that they are like snowflakes *wiping out the noon* – that phrase *wiping out* being especially appropriate to the deaths in the war, but it also emphasises through hyperbole the staggering number of deaths that can wipe out the sun; this seems to be connected with the autumnal mood and the sense of everything ending as the year draws to its close and is an example of pathetic fallacy. The leaves, like the soldiers, are *withering* – but the poet makes clear they have not been killed by something natural like *age* or *pestilence* – this slaughter is man-made. The final line:

Like snowflakes falling on the Flemish clay

is astonishingly beautiful and poignant. The alliteration on *f*, the consonance on *l*, the fragility of the leaves and the snowflakes and the reference to *clay* (remember God created man out of clay according to Christian myth) all give a sense of sadness and pointless loss which ends the poem on a note of gentle compassion and pity.

Why?

- This poem is a lament for the many deaths caused in the First World War.

- It expresses great compassion and pity for the *gallant multitude*.

- Its tone is sad and elegiac.

- It uses pathetic fallacy.

- It reminds us of the inevitability of death through its use of natural imagery.

'Come On, Come Back' – Stevie Smith

Context

Florence Margaret Smith (known as Stevie) was born in 1902 and died in 1971. She published three novels and nine collections of poetry. Her poetry is very quirky, individual and distinctive. Her poems often address questions of loneliness, war, religion and loss of faith. She can draw heavily on ideas of myth and fairy tales – as she does in this poem. As a child she was often separated from her mother because of illness and long periods in hospital and she suffered from depression for most of her adult life. In an interview with the BBC she said that she thought of death as a release from 'the pressure of despair' that she felt about life.

Austerlitz – this is the site of a famous battle in 1805 at which Napoleon defeated a combined Russian and Austrian army. Why has Smith chosen this as a setting? Perhaps to suggest that although the technology of war changes, its essential facts do not.

Memel Conference – an imaginary conference which had graded the substance M.L.5. Memel is a real place, however. The town of Memel came under German control in the Napoleonic era. It is in Lithuania. After the First World War in 1923 the Memel Convention established it as the centre of an autonomous area called Memelland. In 1939 the Germans conquered the area and the town's 1300 Jews were exterminated. It was re-taken by Soviet forces in 1945.

M.L.5 – this is called *the first of all human exterminators*. It is obviously some future weapon used to kill people.

sentinel – guard.

Who? Vaudevue, a female soldier in a future war. An enemy sentinel appears later in the poem. The poet speaks in the present tense as an observer of what happens. The poem concentrates on one individual – the girl soldier Vaudevue.

When? In the future during a war. The poem is written in the present tense. This poem was written during the 1950s during the Cold War when a Third World War seemed a possibility, and when the

West and the Soviet Union were developing more and more sophisticated technology to kill people.

Where? At Austerlitz.

What? Vaudevue, a soldier, has been exposed to M.L.5 and her mind has been destroyed. She seeks comfort by swimming in a nearby lake. An enemy soldier spots her discarded clothes and sits down to wait for her to emerge from the lake.

Commentary

Because it is set in the future and mentions imaginary weapons as if they were real, this poem has a strange dream-like quality – very much like the other poem by Smith in this Anthology: 'The River God', discussed above on page 67.

In the first verse we find the girl soldier Vaudevue sitting on the battlefield alone. When the poem was written it was not the norm for women to be combatants, so we are clearly in the future (although two armies in the world of the 1950s allowed women to have fighting roles – the Israeli Defence Force and the Red Army of the Soviet Union – so it did happen). It is midnight and in the aftermath of battle everything is peaceful. Look at the coherence of line 5 – *midnight/moonlight* and *alone/stone.*

The second verse reveals that she has been exposed to M.L.5 – some awful new weapon which has left her just alive and has obliterated her memory. She remembers nothing

and cries, Ah me why am I here?

Barely able to walk – *staggering* – she approaches a lake, strips off her clothes and dives into the icy waters. Her action is instinctive:

As a child, an idiot, as one without memory

and the lake is *adorable*. The view is attractive – *a ribbon of white moonlight* lies on the water. What are human beings without our memory? Smith uses similes to convey the mental blankness that M.L.5 has caused in Vaudevue. The waters are *as black as her mind* and

Her mind is as secret from her

As the water on which she swims.

As secret as profound as ominous.

Without memory she has no identity, no power of thought and so she does what is instinctive.

In the fifth stanza Vaudevue drowns. She is aware of her mental blankness and weeps for it. She swims

Until a treacherous undercurrent

Seizing her in an icy-amorous embrace

takes her down below the surface of the water. The undercurrent is treacherous, but note that its embrace is *icy-amorous* – in her mental state, death appears to be a release and the water seems to love her. To kill her seems an act of mercy.

Line 34 introduces another character – an enemy sentinel who notices Vaudevue's abandoned clothes and sits down to wait for her return. Line 37 introduces the words of the title to the poem – 'Come On, Come Back' and we will return to these words as the poem ends with them too. As he waits, the enemy soldier whittles a pipe from reeds growing at the lake's edge and at dawn he plays the melody of the song 'Come On, Come Back.' This act for me gives the poem a timeless quality: men have been whittling pipes out of reeds for thousands of years.

The final stanza reveals the mystery of the title. Vaudevue is dead – in the current's *close embrace* and cannot hear the enemy sentinel playing the tune of 'Come On, Come Back' which, Smith now reveals, was

Favourite of all the troops of all the armies

Favourite of Vaudevue

For she has sung it too

Marching to Austerlitz,

'Come On, Come Back.'

I have quoted this at length because it seems to me to be crucial to our understanding of the poem. As a song title it is ambiguous: it might be the sort of song that civilians sing urging their loved ones – the soldiers - to come back safely from the war; within the poem itself we might even see it as death or the lake calling to Vaudevue to put her out of the misery of living with her mental suffering; and at one point it is the sentinel calling her out of the water by playing the notes of the song on his pipe. The final line is plaintive and poignant because Vaudevue, and all the other soldiers exposed to M.L.5, are dead - they cannot come back. And, because Smith has alluded to wars of the past, we might be tempted to say that it is a lament for all the war dead ever.

The fact that soldiers from both sides sing the same popular song suggests that they have a lot in common and suggests that war is pointless – a decision made by politicians. The unnaturalness of war is suggested by the juxtaposition of Vaudevue's suffering with calm, tranquil images of nature. The allusions to past wars and the fact that this poem is set in the future demonstrates perhaps the inevitability of war.

Why?

This dream-like haunting poem

- suggests that there will always be wars.

- shows the tranquillity of nature as a contrast to human destructiveness and a haven for Vaudevue.

- presents death as preferable to a life without memory and identity.

- shows that both opposing armies have a lot in common.

- despite being set in the future has a timeless quality because of its allusions to past battles and wars and the evocative song it imagines.

- becomes a plangent lament for all those who have died in war through the ages.

next to of course god america i – E E Cummings

Context

Edward Estlin Cummings was born in 1894 to liberal, highly educated parents; he died in 1962. He was a prolific writer, with over 2900 poems published as well as two autobiographical novels and four plays. He divided his life between America and Europe: he felt especially at home in Paris.

Cummings uses traditional forms of poetry, but also experimented with form, punctuation, capital letters, spelling and lay out to create poems with a very distinct visual appearance. Indeed, he was published throughout his life as e e cummings. His style is often playful and a lot of his poems deal with love, sex and war.

'Land of the pilgrims' – a phrase from the original American national anthem, called 'America'. The full phrase is 'land of the pilgrims' pride'.

Say can you see by the dawn's early – the opening line of the current American national anthem, 'The Star Spangled Banner'.

My country 'tis of thee – another phrase from 'America'.

Who? The inverted commas at the start of the poem tell us that this is not the poet who is speaking. The speaker appears to be an American politician.

When? The poem was published in 1926. Cummings took part in the First World War, but the point of the poem could be applied to any war in any period.

Where? No specific location.

What? The politician makes his speech. Only the last line is the voice of the poet.

Commentary

This is an unusual sonnet at first sight and you may struggle to get to grips with it, but it is actually fairly easy to understand once you realize what is going on.

Cummings is satirizing patriotism and politicians who manipulate words in order to justify going to war and sending young men to their deaths. The first thirteen lines of the poem do not make complete sense: this is part of the satire because Cummings is suggesting that the things politicians say do not make sense – their speeches are full of meaningless rhetoric which uses a few recognizable phrases which appeal to their audience.

The first four lines contain a quotation from *The Star Spangled Banner* (which is the American national anthem) and two quotations from *America* (which had been the American national anthem). The first line mentions *God* and *America*, linking patriotism with religion: American coins still bear the inscription 'In God We Trust'. *Land of the pilgrims'* (the next word is pride) reminds us of the original English settlers of America – the founding fathers as they are known in the USA. Cummings leaves off *pride* because an American reader would know the word that follows, because it comes from a well-known patriotic song, but also to suggest the speaker is talking nonsense – in the poem it is followed by *and so forth* – as if the speaker cannot be bothered to complete the quotation. He knows that just a phrase from such a song is enough to stir his audience.

The second quatrain makes very little sense. There are points where it is about to make sense, but then the speaker breaks down into nonsense again.

Thy sons acclaim thy glorious name

does make sense: he is talking about the name of America and how appeals to patriotism will work, but this is followed by a list of childish exclamations – *by gorry by jingo by gee by gosh by gum.*

Line 9 starts with a rhetorical question – *why talk of beauty* - and could be said to be the turn in the sonnet at the start of the sestet. For a few lines the poem makes sense: the speaker describes the happiness of the soldiers as they rushed towards death:

these heroic happy dead

Who rushed like lions to the roaring slaughter

The conventional phrase is 'like lambs to the slaughter'; *lions* suggests their bravery and courage. But it is hard to believe that any soldier is happy to die. The speaker also says that they did not stop to think – which from a politician's point of view is perfect: soldiers who obey orders without thinking about the consequences or the justice of the war they are fighting in. In the final line the speaker throws in another empty phrase – *the voice of liberty* – empty because it is being used as an excuse for the deaths of the young men and because it is in a poem which does not make sense.

The final line of the sonnet is separated from the rest and the poet comments on the politician's speech. Is his rapid drinking of a glass of water a nervous reaction because he knows he has spoken nonsense? Is it in relief because he has got away with spouting such nonsense?

Here the lack of punctuation and the lack of anything that makes complete grammatical sense in the octave suggest a complete lack of thought and argument. In a way Cummings is showing the power that certain words and phrases (like the quotations from patriotic songs) can have over people. The speed of the poem – obviously helped by the lack of punctuation – suggests that the politician is glib and insincere.

Why? This unconventional poem:

- satirizes the way politicians manipulate language to appeal to patriotism.
- satirizes patriotism itself.
- criticizes politicians who lead us into wars by appealing to national glory and by claiming that somehow death is heroic.

Hawk Roosting – Ted Hughes

Context

Ted Hughes was born in 1930 and died in 1998. He was one of the most famous poets of his generation and was appointed Poet Laureate in 1984 – a position he held until his death. He was born in a small village near Halifax in West Yorkshire and the landscape of his birthplace influenced him throughout his life. Hughes was a prolific poet and also wrote several books for children. His private life increased his notoriety, as his first wife (the American poet Sylvia Plath) and his next partner both committed suicide in the same way. Much of his poetry is inspired by the power and beauty and mystery of nature.

sophistry – false logic.

the allotment of death – the act of deciding who will die.

Who? The poet adopts the voice of a hawk who is in a tree, looking down at the world.

When? Not specified. In a sense the poem is deliberately timeless.

Where? There is a generalized natural setting.

What? The hawk looks down at the world and reflects on himself and his relationship with what he sees.

Commentary

Many of Hughes' other poems, especially from early in his career, deal with the violent and wild aspects of nature and this poem is typical in that sense. It is unusual, however, because it adopts the persona of the hawk who speaks in the first person.

The first stanza finds the hawk sitting in a tree with its eyes closed. Unlike humanity he does not suffer from inaction and there is

no falsifying dream

Between my hooked head and hooked feet.

In other words, he does not dream of doing things – he does them. Even in sleep he rehearses *perfect kills*.

In the second stanza the hawk suggests that everything in the world has been created for his convenience. He begins with an exclamation:

The convenience of the high trees!

Hawks appear to glide on the air while they watch the ground, looking for some tiny animal to eat. The air, the sun, even the earth's face seem to be designed for the hawk to be a hawk and to make it easier for him to prey on weaker animals.

The third stanza sees the hawk as the zenith of Creation. Hughes uses repetition – *Creation* –and alliteration: *foot, feather, foot*. The hawk has evolved slowly into a perfect killing machine and now, he asserts

I hold Creation in my foot.

He has the power of life and death over other animals below him in the food chain.

Line 13 is interesting. We all know that the world is constantly spinning. Here the hawk says that he revolves it all slowly – his arrogance is such that he says he turns the planet, so that he can see his prey. His power is such that he owns everything:

I kill where I please because it is all mine.

The next two lines are very interesting because they juxtapose words that we associate with human behaviour – *sophistry* and *manners* – and contrast them with the hawk's more direct methods:

My manners are tearing off heads.

This implies a contrast between nature and humanity which we will return to when we discuss the poem's impact and meaning.

The fifth stanza also uses a word connected with humans and our use of reason – *arguments*. Lines 18 and 19 show that the hawk acts without thought and Hughes uses enjambment cleverly:

the one path of my flight is direct

Through the bones of the living.

Just like the hawk's flight which is direct, the words of this sentence burst through the end of line 18 to continue through into line 19 – the enjambment here supports the sense.

The final stanza is an appropriate culmination to the poem. Each of its four lines is a complete sentence, so the rhythm of the poem is slow and confident. The stanza introduces no new ideas but repeats concepts the hawk has already expressed: nothing in Creation has changed because he has permitted no change and he is *going to keep things like this*.

How is the hawk presented by Hughes? It is selfish and self-centred and arrogant; it is cruel and savage; it is designed by evolution to kill. The words *I, me, my* and *mine* occur in every stanza which proves his self-centredness.

Stylistically this poem is in complete contrast to 'Wind' (in the 'Place' section of the Anthology). Its rhythm is slow and measured – largely because here Hughes writes in short sentences with heavy caesuras and every little enjambment. The effect of this is to slow the poem down and that helps give a sense of the hawk's control and his easy confidence. The hawk's strong, short statements convey his arrogance and power. Hughes' word choice is interesting, however, and can also be contrasted to 'Wind'. Here he uses several long, Latinate words which serve to suggest that the hawk is clever, wise and knowing. We associate Latinate vocabulary with learning and intellectual superiority.

There is little general agreement about the full meaning of this poem. Most readers agree that it is a poem which shows the destructive, instinctive power of nature and that it is narrated by an arrogant hawk, but after that, agreement breaks down. In moral terms the hawk is loathsome; as a machine built for killing the hawk is perfect. There are some political readings of the poem which see the hawk as representing a fanatical, power-crazed dictator who can do what he likes because of his power. In a more philosophical sense, Hughes seems to be satirizing the human need to think before acting; our habit of prevarication and procrastination. The hawk has no such misgivings and acts on instinct; as he says:

There is no sophistry in my body.

So perhaps Hughes is arguing that we need to be truer to our instincts and not let our thoughts get in the way of action.

Why?

In this well-known poem Hughes may be suggesting a variety of things:

- animals have the ability to act instinctively and without mercy.

- human beings are held back by sophistry and manners.

- nature's predators should be treated with respect – they are perfectly designed killing machines.

- political tyrants are primitive animals at heart and have paranoid, delusional tendencies.

- the human world of morality and conscience are completely removed from the world of nature.

Conflict: Connecting the Poems

In this section I will be examining the specimen questions provided by AQA and going on to discuss other ways to connect the poems in this section. The difference between questions on Foundation Tier papers and Higher Tier papers is simple: the Foundation questions use bullet points to guide you in your response to the question.

These questions are for English Literature, Unit 2 entitled *Poetry across time*. You have one hour and 15 minutes to answer the paper. There are two questions on each section of the Anthology; you answer only one. There is also a question on an unseen poem. However, the question on the Anthology carries 36 marks and the advice on the paper is to spend 45 minutes on it. The unseen poem carries only 18 marks and you are advised to spend 30 minutes on it. I deal with the unseen poem at the end of this book. There is also general advice on answering questions in the examination at the end of the book. These questions have been produced by AQA as specimen questions. My answers are simply suggestions.

Compare how war is shown in 'The Charge of the Light Brigade' and one other poem from 'Conflict'.

Remember to compare:

- **the war in the poems.**
- **how the war is presented in the poems.**

Alfred Tennyson' 'The Charge of the Light Brigade' and Ted Hughes' 'Bayonet Charge' are linked by the same word in their titles – *charge* – but they show the experience of war in completely different ways.

Tennyson's poem was written in 1854 and deals with a military disaster involving the Light Brigade – a group of cavalry who were given an ill-thought-out order, but who obeyed it regardless. Hughes' poem deals with an individual infantry soldier on foot; it is not even clear which army the soldier is fighting for. It is interesting to note that neither poet had first-hand experience of combat.

Tennyson admits that the order was a foolish one – *Some one had blunder'd* – but his main concern is to celebrate the heroic bravery of the men who made the charge against such difficult odds and in the knowledge that they were doomed. He asserts the unquestioning obedience of the soldiers:

> *Theirs not to reason why,*
>
> *Theirs but to do and die.*

Above all, by his repetition of the phrase *the six hundred* Tennyson is stressing that the action was a group effort and is paying tribute to all the cavalrymen – the survivors and the dead. Tennyson idealizes everything they did: he emphasizes the appalling odds they faced; he tells us they rode *boldly* and *well*; when they finally reach the Russian lines they cause havoc amongst the defending Russians and Cossacks.

By contrast, Hughes' individual soldier is completely alone. There is no acknowledgment in the poem that he is part of a larger group who are charging. In addition, Tennyson's poem is about a world-famous military action; Hughes's soldier is anonymous and the action he takes part in is unremarkable. We get a very vivid impression of the physical effects of the charge: the soldier's sweat is heavy; he is stumbling across the field; he almost stops in bewilderment and, then starts to question why he is there. Hughes tells us that he dropped *King*, *honour*, *human dignity* as reasons for being there; he continues the charge in order to get out of that *blue crackling air*. This is a direct contrast with Tennyson – he does not mention these things specifically, but we can imagine that the Light Brigade follow their orders unthinkingly because of their belief in Queen/King and in honour.

Both poems use rhythm in different ways. Tennyson's rhythm imitates the noise of charging horses, while Hughes' use of three long sentences reflects the agonizing slowness of the charge.

Modern readers may feel that Tennyson's glorification of heroism is slightly old-fashioned, but it could be argued that he was merely reflecting the public mood at the time; his tone is not very different from *The Times'* report which was his only source. Hughes, by contrast, is writing in the second half of the 20th century after two world wars which resulted in millions of deaths and which changed forever the public perception of war.

Compare how attitudes to conflict are shown in 'Flag' and one other poem from 'Conflict'.

Remember to compare:

- **the attitudes in the poems.**
- **how the attitudes are presented.**

John Agard's 'Flag' and E E Cummings 'next of course to god america i' show similar attitudes to conflict, but present this attitude in very different ways. Both Agard and Cummings attack the patriotic feelings that are used to justify wars or to encourage people to join the armed forces, but their poems could hardly be more different in tone and form.

Cummings chooses to write a sonnet, a type of poem which is highly patterned, but there are parts of the poem which barely make complete sense. The speaker in Cummings' poem is an American politician and he uses brief phrases from patriotic American songs to stir his audience and appeal to their patriotism: *land of the pilgrims'*, *say can you see by the dawn's early, my country 'tis of thee* – the point, though, is that quotations remain unfinished: they are so well-known to Americans that they don't need to be finished, but also, Cummings is suggesting, politicians use these phrases casually and without coherence because they know that the call to patriotism can be very strong. The fact that much of Cummings' poem does not make logical sense, especially the line *by jingo by gee by gosh by gum*, shows that Cummings feels that patriotism is nonsensical – like the politician's speech. He goes on to claim that the dead are heroic and happy to die - a ridiculous notion given the numbers of the dead in the First World War.

Agard's poem is much more controlled, but he is speaking as himself, unlike Cummings who is imitating and satirizing a politician. Agard repeats the dismissive statement – *It's just a piece of cloth* – in the second line of the first four stanzas, and the final line of each stanza tells us what this piece of cloth can do: it can bring *a nation to its knees*, make *men grow bold*, force *the coward to relent*, and it *will outlive the blood you bleed*. We can guess that the piece of cloth is a flag because of the poem's title, but this is confirmed by line 14. As soon as you have a flag, Agard asserts, you can *blind your conscience to the end,*

which suggests all the horrific acts of violence that are done in war under the cloak of patriotism, symbolized by the flag.

Both poems share the same attitude to conflict: it is wrong and it is encouraged by patriotism – either through the rhetoric of lying politicians or by appeals to the flag as a national symbol. Cummings' poem pokes fun at the politician and is deeply sarcastic about the politician's use of patriotic clichés; Agard's much more strictly-controlled poem seems to be full of controlled anger and outrage. Both poems have an almost universal timeless quality and could be applied to any conflict: patriotism and flags, both poets are suggesting, are simply excuses for the appalling nature of war.

Compare how the results of war are shown in 'Futility' and one other poem from 'Conflict'.

'Futility' by Wilfred Owen and 'The Yellow Palm' by Robert Minhinnick show the results of war in radically different ways and have a very different effect on the reader. In 'Futility' Owen describes the death of just one soldier and his reaction to it. In 'The Yellow Palm' Minhinnick shows the wider social effects of war on just one country – Iraq under Saddam Hussein. They both end with very different views of war.

The title of Owen's poem suggests the pointlessness of that individual soldier's death and, perhaps, of the whole war. The soldier has died in the night and in the first stanza the officer orders the men to move him into the sun in the naive hope that the kind old sun will wake him and bring him back to life. When he was alive, we learn, the soldier had a special affinity with the sun; it would wake him

At home, whispering of fields unsown.

The futility of the soldier's death forces Owen to question why we are here on earth at all if it is only to die in the way this soldier has done. The sun began life in our solar system by waking *the clays of a cold star*, but, Owen asks in the second stanza, why did the *fatuous sunbeams* bother *to break earth's sleep* by creating life, if young soldiers die before their time.

Minhinnick's 'The Yellow Palm' has a completely different structure from 'Futility'. Owen shows the results of war through one anonymous soldier; Minhinnick, as he wanders down Palestine Street, shows the results of war on a whole society, and a very specific society

- Iraq under the dictator Saddam Hussein. In each of the stanzas of 'The Yellow Palm' we witness the results of war, but these are juxtaposed with images of normality and ordinary Iraqi life. In the first stanza we see a victim of Hussein's poison gas attacks on his own people; in the second blood on the wall of a mosque – the result of sectarian violence; the blind beggars the speaker gives money to in the third stanza turn out to be veterans of the First Gulf War. Even the sun is a barbarian that knows no armistice, unlike the *kind old sun* in 'Futility'.

However, Minhinnick's poem ends on a note of optimism. The image of the yellow dates which fall into the child's arms suggests a belief in the power of nature to renew and bring better times for the country. Owen's poem ends with questions about human life on earth and the way that the results of war make him question his belief in God. He has no answers. It is interesting that Minhinnick uses full rhyme throughout 'The Yellow Palm', but Owen uses half-rhyme – a sign that something is terribly wrong.

Compare how attitudes to conflict are shown in 'The Charge of the Light Brigade' and one other poem from 'Conflict'.

Attitudes to conflict in 'The Charge of the Light Brigade' by Alfred Tennyson and in 'Belfast Confetti' are shown to be very different. Of course, Tennyson's poem dates from the mid-19th century and is about a conventional war, while Carson's is set in Belfast at the height of the recent Troubles. Tennyson is writing as Poet Laureate of Great Britain, while Carson is describing his experience of being caught up in a riot in his home area when a bomb goes off. In addition, Tennyson had no first-hand experience of battle and based what he wrote on the report of the incident which he read in *The Times*. Carson has lived all his life in Belfast.

Both poets seek to convey the reality of conflict, but do so in very different ways and with very different effects. 'The Charge of the Light Brigade' is written from the point of view of the British Army; 'Belfast Confetti' is written from the point of view of someone facing the British Army on the streets of a British city.

Tennyson's attitude to conflict is that it is a way for men to show courage, obedience to orders and to gain honour through death. Tennyson emphasizes their bravery by stressing the terrible odds against them: they were *charging an army* and were *storm'd at with shot and shell*; their obedience is shown in lines 13 to 15; and in his final verse Tennyson exhorts his readers (the British public) to

Honour the charge they made!

Honour the Light Brigade!

Tennyson's attitude to conflict can be summed up by the first line of the last stanza – *When can their glory fade?* Conflict is a way of obtaining glory – even through death. The regular rhythm of 'The Charge of the Light Brigade' clearly suggests the rhythm of horses charging, but its very regularity also suggests a sense of order and Tennyson's overwhelmingly positive attitude to the charge itself.

There is no honour or glory in 'Belfast Confetti'. Instead Carson is keen to demonstrate through imagery and structure, the fear and panic he felt during the riot and subsequent explosion. The poem has a deliberately chaotic structure starting *Suddenly* and moving quickly form image to image which are expressed as metaphors of punctuation – it is as if language itself has lost the ability to communicate the truth of what is going on. There is a pervading sense of menace: Carson is lost in a *labyrinth* of streets, despite the fact that he knows this area so well. He feels trapped and the images of the British soldiers he encounters make them seem inhuman: he can't see their faces because of the Makrolon face shields. Stopped by the soldiers, he is bombarded with a fusillade of questions. He is scared, afraid and panicky.

There two very different poems represent two different attitudes to conflict. Tennyson is writing in the 19th century as the Poet Laureate and is keen to stress the nobility and courage of the soldiers. Carson is writing as a civilian caught up in a street riot: his use of long lines, sudden pauses, long lists and, finally, questions reflects his sheer panic at being trapped and lost.

Other thoughts

Of course, you cannot predict what questions will come up in the examination, but you can do some thinking before the exam and select poems that work well together for various reasons. You will still need to do some quick thinking in the exam AND you must answer the question that has been asked: you cannot simply write about two poems that in your preparation you have decided go well together. What follows now are some brief notes which give some examples of poems that work well together, depending on the question. These are not exclusive – I am sure you can make connections which I have not spotted or thought of.

'Flag' and 'next of course to america i' would make a good pairing because they are written very differently, but both are satirical about patriotism. And either of them would make an excellent contrast with 'Hawk Roosting' where we appear to get the point of view of someone in authority. At the same time they would also work quite well alongside 'The Charge of the Light Brigade' because of Tennyson's view of unthinking heroism – something Cummings' speaker would approve of, but which Cummings himself satirizes.

'Poppies' and 'The Falling Leaves' would work well as a pair because they are both tender, gentle poems about loss; they are both written by women; and they both use symbolism.

'Out of the Blue' and 'The Right Word' go well together because they both deal, in very different ways and from different perspectives with the problem of terrorism.

'Belfast Confetti' and 'Bayonet Charge' would work well together because both are about the experience of being in conflict, in a life-threatening situation. Either of these might also go very well with 'The Charge of the Light Brigade' because it too describes battle – although without emphasizing the fear that the Light Brigade felt. 'Out of the Blue' also is a first-hand account of what it is like to be in a situation where you will die.

'Mametz Wood' might work well with 'Futility'. They are very different, but share a First World War connection, and for this reason either of them might work well with either 'Poppies' or 'The Falling Leaves.'

'The Yellow Palm', 'At the Border, 1979' and 'The Right Word' all share a positive ending which would make them good to pair, depending on the question asked. The first two deal with issues with Iraq as well, and because 'The Right Word' deals with terrorism you may feel that this is another link. 'Out of the Blue' could also be paired in this way with any of these three because it shows the effects of terrorism.

Equally, from a different point of view, any of those three – 'The Yellow Palm', 'At the Border, 1979' and 'The Right Word' – because they end with insight and hope, could be used to contrast with any poem about the suffering of those in war, because they tend to end in despair and pity.

Although they are very different poems, one almost timeless, the other set in an imagined future, I think 'Futility' and 'Come On, Come Back' would go well together because they both have a quality of tender pity and poignant regret, and both present the natural world as benign.

'Poppies' and 'The Right Word' might go well together: they are both written by women and, although one is about saying goodbye to a son and the other is about welcoming a child into your home to eat, they share a domestic atmosphere and are, in different ways, full of generosity and love.

'At the Border, 1979' would go well with either 'Flag' or 'next of course to god america i' because all three undermine the concept of patriotism, but Hardi's poem is very different from the other two in the way it presents a personal account of an incident from childhood, but comes to the same conclusion – *The same chain of mountains encompassed us all.*

'Hawk Roosting' and 'next of course to god america i' would work well together. Cummings' poem shows the public face of the politician; Hughes' poem, it could be argued, shows the private thoughts of someone in power. In addition they are very differently written with Cummings' poem threatening all the time to break down into nonsense and Hughes's poem, by contrast, written in a very carefully controlled way – reflecting the sense of control and power that the speaker feels.

Relationships

The poems in this section deal with the relationships between people and those they are close to. Many of the poems explore love, but many different types of love: happy, fulfilled love; unfulfilled love; love breaking down into hatred and recrimination; the love between men and women, between parents and children, between brothers and between friends.

Contemporary Poetry

The Manhunt – Simon Armitage

Context

Simon Armitage was born in 1963 in the village of Marsden in West Yorkshire and has spent most of his life in that area. He is a very successful and highly-regarded poet, celebrated for his down-to-earth language and subject matter. Several of his poems are in the Anthology. His poetry often (but not always) deals with the ordinary incidents and events of modern life and appear to be based on personal experience.

This poem was originally written for a television documentary (Channel 4 – *Forgotten Heroes: The Not Dead*) about soldiers who live with the long-term effects of being involved in warfare and suffering from post-traumatic stress syndrome. In the documentary the poem is read by Laura Beddoes, whose husband Eddie had served as a peace-keeper with the British Army in Bosnia. For this reason the poem is sometimes called 'Manhunt: Laura's Story'. Eddie was discharged because of injury and depression and the poem explores the impact this had on his marriage. Armitage listened to many accounts by soldiers of their experiences in order to get the inspiration for this poem. He has said:

Never having been to the front line, turning the words, phrases and experiences of these soldiers into verse has been the closest I've ever come to writing 'real' war poetry, and as close as I ever want to get.

Bosnia was once part of Yugoslavia. When the Communist system all over eastern Europe fell, in Yugoslavia ethnic and religious tensions which had been controlled and suppressed under communism came to the surface. By the mid 1990s the different ethnic groups began fighting each other and committing acts of genocide. The United Kingdom and other NATO countries responded by sending troops to the region to act as peace-keepers and to keep the warring factions apart. In particular, they were attempting to protect Bosnia from attacks by its more powerful neighbour – Serbia.

Who? Armitage adopts the voice of Laura who narrates the poem in the past tense.

When? After Eddie has returned injured, physically and mentally, from war.

Where? No specific location.

What? Laura explains how she very slowly discovered the man that Eddie had become.

Commentary

This poem is written in free verse with frequent use of rhyme and half rhyme. On the page it is divided into separate two line couplets but the lines are of unequal length. This immediately suggests that it looks like a normal poem, but it isn't. In the poem we will find that Eddie's mental wounds are much worse than his physical ones – so he may look normal but underneath the surface he is suffering a terrible trauma because of what he has seen at war. Note the deliberate ambiguity of the title: if you are looking for an escaped soldier or airman you launch a manhunt. Laura is on a manhunt, but for the man she used to know before he went to war.

The repetition of *then* and *and* is very important in the poem: it suggests that each step in renewing her love for Eddie, in trying to find him again, in trying to understand what he had suffered, is a step in a very slow process. They quickly re-establish a physical relationship with

passionate nights and intimate days.

And she then starts to explore his physical wounds by touching his wounds and scars. In these lines the human body's fragility is emphasized in the metaphors – *porcelain collar-bone, parachute silk* –

and his body is seen in terms of machines which do not quite work - *broken hinge, fractured rudder*. In some ways these images are reassuring because broken hinges can be fixed.

But line 16 mentions Eddie's *grazed heart* and the rest of the poem becomes more difficult in the sense that his mental wounds are invisible and more permanent. Does his *grazed heart* suggest he has lost the ability to love? The fragments left by the bullet are a *metal foetus* – a metaphor that suggests something is growing inside him. Laura then widened the search (remember she is still on a manhunt for the man she used to know) – and finds

a sweating, unexploded mine

buried deep in his mind, around which

every nerve in his body had tightened and closed.

And this confirms that what really makes Eddie so distant is his mental trauma at the sights and sounds of war, the suffering he witnessed that he now cannot forget. And

Then, and only then, did I come close.

And so the poem ends with the manhunt unsuccessful: Laura does not find him – she only comes close. And comes close to what? The man that Eddie now is? An understanding of what he has been through? What he has seen and heard in Bosnia?

Armitage gives Laura a voice of incredible sensitivity and feeling in this poem. She remains loyal to her lover, despite the difficulty she has in renewing her relationship with him. Eddie remains throughout the poem passive, silent and unknown – which actually makes his mental torments more terrible because they remain hidden and unknown, perhaps unknowable.

This contemporary poem raises with powerful sensitivity

- the long-term effects of warfare on soldiers and their loved ones.

- how the human mind can cope with images and memories of suffering.

- the traumatizing mental scars that ex-soldiers carry with them and which affect their relationships.

Hour - Carol Ann Duffy

Context

Carol Ann Duffy is one of the UK's most successful and best-known living poets. Her poems have a very wide appeal. On May 1st 2009 she became the nation's Poet Laureate – the first woman ever to hold the position. There are several poems by Duffy in this Anthology and her poems are often set for study by the examination boards – because they are thought of very highly and because many of them are very accessible. Her poems often use very modern and everyday language, but in fresh, funny and witty ways. She uses traditional forms like the sonnet and the dramatic monologue but succeeds in breathing new life into these old forms by the modernity of her writing and subject matter. The accessibility of many of her poems may obscure the fact that she is highly skilled at a very intricate and ingenious manipulation of language.

This poem comes from a collection of poems called *Rapture* – which are all love poems and which show all the different aspects of what it is to be in love – including the break up and things going wrong in a relationship.

Midas – a famous figure in Greek myth who was granted the wish that everything he touched should turn to gold. In this poem it is used as a metaphor for the sunlight which transforms the poet's lover's legs.

cuckoo spit – a white, sappy substance that appears on some plants during early summer. It has nothing to do with spit or cuckoos.

Love spins gold from straw – in the story 'Rumpelstiltskin', the heroine is given the impossible task of spinning straw into gold.

Who? The poet addresses her lover directly in the present tense with occasional use of the future tense.

When? As the title suggests this is the record of one hour that the lovers spend together.

Where? In the countryside.

What? The poet describes an hour spent with her lover and celebrates the love they are enjoying together in a magical period of the relationship.

Commentary

This beautiful modern sonnet describes one hour in a relationship where everything is going perfectly. The sonnet explores love in relation to time, uses imagery to do with wealth and riches to suggest the extreme pleasure the lovers feel, and also shows the transforming power of love. It also mocks the stereotypical ephemera that we habitually associate with love – because in this relationship, the lovers simply need each other.

The opening statement:

Love's time's beggar

is bold and confident. *Love* IS *time's beggar* because when love is at its best you simply do not have enough time to spend with your lover: every moment is precious and you don't want to waste a single second, so you need to beg Time for more. Because of this even a single hour is as *bright as a dropped coin* and *makes love rich.* Duffy and her lover find an hour together and spend it not on flowers or wine (conventional gifts, perhaps, that we might give our loved ones), but simply together with

the whole of the summer sky and a grass ditch.

There is a rich texture to this opening quatrain: Love and Time are personified; there is the simile of the *dropped coin* (dropped as you might drop it into a beggar's collecting cup); and Duffy plays with the two senses of spending: spending money (on flowers and wine) and spending time together.

In the second quatrain time seems to stand still because the lovers are so absorbed in each other:

For thousands of seconds we kiss.

Note how the main verb there – *kiss* - is delayed until the end of the unit of sense. Duffy's lover is transformed: her hair is like *treasure* and the sunshine (*the Midas light*) turns her limbs to gold. And because of the richness of the imagery – *treasure, golden limbs* – and because *Love's time's beggar*, Time slows and *we are millionaires.*

They have enough time to enjoy each other and they seem to have the power, the poem states, to delay the onset of night, so that this rich and magical moment will last forever:

so nothing dark will end our shining hour.

That word *so* marks the turn of the sonnet and Duffy goes on to reject other things that the lovers do not need. Lines ten and eleven are interesting:

no jewel hold a candle to the cuckoo spit

hung from the blade of grass at your ear.

Lovers often exchange jewels as tokens of love and because it is on the lover's ear it suggests an ear-ring. But these lovers have no need of jewels. *Hold a candle to* is a colloquial expression meaning that no jewel can be better than the cuckoo spit that hangs from the blade of grass at your ear. But by introducing the word *candle* Duffy is reminding us of the conventional props of romance (candle-lit dinners) and also reminding us that the lovers are already lit by the *Midas light* of the sun: in comparison a candle seems useless and unnecessary. The quatrain continues, asserting that no chandelier or spotlight is needed because the lover looks perfect – *here. Now* – in the sunlight.

The final couplet repays close attention:

Time hates love, wants love poor,

but love spins gold, gold, gold from straw.

There is a suggestion that time will destroy love: perhaps that over time, feelings change, people change and love may die. That is one reason why the poem celebrates the perfect hour that the lovers spend together. The final line, however, shows the power of love: love can take ordinary things – straw – and turn them into gold; it can turn cuckoo spit into an ear-ring; it can transform the lover into the most beautiful person on the planet. The image of spinning straw comes from the fairytale 'Rumpelstiltskin' and this is appropriate because this poem describes a perfect hour spent alone with one's lover where there is nothing to spoil the lovers' total absorption in one another – it really is like a fairytale. The epizeuxis of gold conveys delight and joy.

One of the things I find most appealing about this poem is the way it rejects the trappings of love – flowers, wine, jewels, chandeliers, candles, spotlights – and places the lovers in a very ordinary setting – *summer sky, ditch, cuckoo spit, blade of grass*. This shows the power of love at its peak – all the lovers need is time and each other.

However, do the references to fairy tale and myth suggest something darker – that this hour might be perfect, but it cannot last? Fairy tales and myths are only fairy tales, after all. 'Rumpelstiltskin' as a story has dark elements. The poem takes place on a summer's day, but summer will turn to autumn. In this reading, the epizeuxis on gold becomes a desperate (desperate because it is repeated) attempt to assert that this love WILL last forever.

Why? This beautiful modern sonnet

- captures the joy and intense pleasure of love at its best.
- uses an extended metaphor to show the richness of the experience of love.
- shows how time slows down when we are in love and every second is precious.
- rejects the clichés of romance to imply that this love is genuine.
- celebrates the intensity and transforming power of love.
- uses allusions to myth and fairy tale to suggest the magical feeling that true love can give.
- perhaps hints that this moment of sheer delight and joy will not last.

In Paris with You – James Fenton

Context

James Fenton was born in 1949 and has won wide recognition for his poetry. He has worked as a war journalist, political commentator and reviewer. He has said that the English poet W H Auden has been his biggest influence and this poem is very reminiscent of Auden. Like Auden, Fenton tends to use traditional forms, like the sonnet or the ballad, to explore contemporary life. In addition, Auden often presents what we call 'love' in a light-hearted tone with the emphasis, not on the emotional side of love, but the sheer physical pleasure.

Another part of this poem's context is the image that British people have of Paris. I think it is true to say that we associate it with romance and love: travel firms offer 'Romantic Breaks' in Paris and the city has a certain meaning for people in the UK that Frankfurt and Brussels do not have. So Fenton uses our assumption that Paris is a city of love and romance; it is also a city full of tourist sites or places of interest that are world famous and an integral part of the tourist experience. *Maroonded* – Fenton's deliberately incorrect version of *marooned* adds to the light hearted tone. Technically this is a neologism – a made up word. He makes it up in order to get a rhyme with *wounded*.

bamboozled – puzzled or mystified.

on the rebound – looking for a new relationship very quickly after the break up of another one.

The Louvre – the most-visited art gallery and museum in the world.

Notre Dame – the cathedral of Paris, a huge and iconic building.

Champs Elysées – the most famous avenue in Paris; filled with exclusive shops and also used for important processions.

all points south – in bodily terms, the lower part of the human body, below the waist.

Who? The poet narrates the poem and it is addressed to his new lover in the second person – *you*.

When? The exact time is not specified, but he is on the rebound, so it is after the end of a relationship.

Where? Paris – in a seedy hotel room.

What? The narrator of the poem pleads with his lover to ignore the tourist attractions on offer in Paris in order to stay in the hotel room and explore each other.

Commentary

This richly-comic poem covers a wide range of tones and uses a jaunty rhythm and internal rhymes to establish a humorous tone. It uses rhyme on more than one syllable as well – *Elysées/sleazy* – which often has a comic effect in English.

The opening sentence is an abrupt command:

Don't talk to me of love.

The reason why Fenton does not want to talk about love becomes clear as the first two stanzas proceed: he has just finished an intense relationship which has left him *tearful*, *bamboozled* and *resentful*. He is on the rebound and in Paris with, we assume, a new girlfriend/lover. The break-up of a relationship can be a painful thing : but this poem is funny. The internal rhyme of *earful* and *tearful*; the play on words – *talking wounded* (in wars the phrase is normally *walking wounded*); the neologism of *maroonded*; the unusual, slightly archaic *bamboozled* – all these help make the poem less than serious. The final line of the opening two stanzas suggest Fenton's priorities:

I am in Paris with you.

He wants to immerse himself in his new relationship.

The third verse changes its structure, but the chatty, conversational tone remains: because his priority is his new lover he sounds irritated and grouchy at the thought of having to visit all the tourist sites in Paris. The Louvre is possibly the greatest art gallery and museum in the world, so not to go to it if you are in Paris strikes me as funny. The line

If we say sod off to sodding Notre Dame

is also colloquial and cynical at the same time with the repetition of *sod/sodding* demonstrating Fenton's grouchiness. What does he want to do instead? He wants to stay in the hotel room:

Doing this and that

To what and to whom

Learning who you are,

Learning what I am.

He means he wants to stay in the hotel room and have sex, learning about his new lover through physical action. *Doing this and that* clearly suggests the whole range of sexual activities that are open to them.

The fourth stanza changes the pattern that Fenton established at the start.

Don't talk to me of love. Let's talk of Paris.

But the Paris he wants to explore is not the world-famous tourist site, but

The little bit of Paris in our view.

In other words, the bedroom that the lovers are in.

The final stanza reaches a climax with the excited repetition of Paris and the phrase *I'm in Paris with....* It is clear that Paris as a tourist destination is not what Fenton is excited about. He is excited by the prospect of his new relationship and the relationship seems to have the freshness and enthusiasm that comes at the start of a new love affair. He is obsessed and fascinated with *the slightest thing you do* and cannot stop looking at *your eyes, your mouth*. His intentions are clear – he is most interested in *all points south*; he is looking forward to sex with his new lover.

This is a poem about lust and desire. Having just ended a relationship, Fenton seems desperate to have sex with his new lover. *Don't talk to me of love* refers to the relationship that has just ended and by which he has been hurt, but is also a statement about the new relationship: he does not want to complicate things by talking of 'love', he seems to want intense, casual sex and is prepared to ignore the tourist attractions of Paris in order to get it. In short, he doesn't want to talk about love – he wants to do it!

Why? This funny, chatty poem

- celebrates the excitement of a new relationship.

- puts the emphasis on sex and physical desire.

- rejects the conventional activities of the tourist in an off-hand and humorous fashion.

- suggests that 'love' can be painful, but that sex can be all-consuming.

- skilfully uses a range of poetic devices and colloquial language to suggest a light-hearted tone.

Quickdraw – Carol Ann Duffy

Context

Carol Ann Duffy is one of the UK's most successful and best-known living poets. Her poems have a very wide appeal. On May 1st 2009 she became the nation's Poet Laureate – the first woman ever to hold the position. There are several poems by Duffy in this Anthology and her poems are often set for study by the examination boards – because they are thought of very highly and because many of them are very accessible. Her poems often use very modern and everyday language, but in fresh, funny and witty ways. She uses traditional forms like the sonnet and the dramatic monologue but succeeds in breathing new life into these old forms by the modernity of her writing and subject matter. The accessibility of many of her poems may obscure the fact that she is highly skilled at a very intricate and ingenious manipulation of language.

This poem, like 'Hour', also comes from *Rapture*. It makes lots of allusions to Western films. This was (until the 1970s) a very popular type of film, but fewer and fewer are being made now. Set in the American West during the 19th century, they often portrayed cowboys and Indians or outlaws being brought to justice by dedicated, heroic sheriffs and marshals – the upholders of law and justice. They often culminated in a gun-fight – usually with the odds stacked heavily against the good guys.

high noon – *High Noon* (1952) is a very famous Western movie. Gary Cooper (the marshal in a frontier town in the American West) waits for the arrival of a notorious criminal gang who have just been released from jail and are headed back to town to wreak revenge on the people who sent them to jail. The film culminates in a gun-fight.

calamity – a calamity is a disaster or difficult situation. It may also be an allusion to Calamity Jane, a famous American frontierswoman from the 19th century who fought against the native Americans and outlaws.

the old Last Chance Saloon – a frequently-used name for bars in America in the 19th century. They were named in this way because some parts of America banned alcohol, so the bar might be the last chance you had of having a drink before you entered the next state. Alternatively, they might be the last chance of having a drink because what lay in front of you was wilderness. The term has passed into the English language as a figurative expression which is used to mean your absolutely final chance of resolving a problem.

Sheriff – like a marshal, a law-enforcement officer in America.

Who? The poet and her lover are communicating by phone and talking, but also texting each other.

When? No specific time, but the poem is a modern one. The relationship is having problems.

Where? The poet is at home, her lover absent.

What? This poem describes an argument conducted by phone and text and which presents the break up or disintegration of a relationship.

Commentary

This is ultimately a comic poem about the break-up of a relationship. There are painful elements too, as there are when any couple break up, but it is essentially light-hearted. The poem is about two lovers who are arguing and communicating both by a landline phone and by text, so their communication is a mixture of speech and text messages.

What gives the poem a light-hearted edge is Duffy's use of an extended metaphor or conceit based on Western movies and gun-fights in them. Even the title is a reference to Westerns because to be quick on the draw (to get your gun out of your holster quicker than your opponent) ensured your survival, provided your aim was good. The opening sentence introduces this metaphor: the speaker is wearing the mobile and the landline

like guns, slung from the pockets of my hips.

The phones are metaphorically transformed into guns because we can say and text hurtful things in the course of an argument like this. Then her lover phones and says something hurtful: it is a *pellet* in the speaker's ear and makes her *groan*. The lover phones again. But Duffy does not answer and the lover leaves a message after the tone. Duffy twirls the phone: this is an image taken from gun-fighting where the gunfighter might twirl his hand gun on his finger, using the trigger and its guard as a fulcrum. The speaker makes some hurtful, wounding remark: she squeezes

> *the trigger of my tongue*

But it's *wide of the mark*, suggesting it doesn't have the intended hurtful effect. The lover, by contrast, chooses her spot and blasts the speaker through the heart.

The third stanza plays on references to Western films while at the same time – with the reference to *High Noon* – suggests that this is the final showdown of the breaking relationship. Duffy continues the extended metaphor by showing the mobile to *the Sheriff*, but, sneakily, she has another one concealed in her boot.

In the final stanza, the lover texts both phones at once, causing the poet to *reel*. Duffy, like a dying gunfighter, is down on her knees and the text messages are called *the silver bullets of your kiss*. This is an astonishing image: we expect kisses to be a sign of love and affection, but these kisses are *silver bullets* – special bullets which in myth and folklore are the only type of bullet said to be effective against werewolves, witches and other types of monster. Has the lover texted a series of kisses – xxxxx – and is the speaker of the poem a witch in this lovers' argument? If they are kisses, then they are unexpected in the heat of an argument and take the speaker off-guard – which is, perhaps, why she sinks to her knees. And then the poem ends:

> *Take this...*
>
> *And this... and this... and this... and this....*

These words work on two levels: the repetition imitates gunshots being fired at your opponent in a gunfight, but also imitates the thumb pressing on your mobile as you punch in the letters you are sending or perhaps repeatedly pressing 'send'. And what is the speaker sending? Kisses? It is unclear – but the repetition and the context of Western gunfights suggest violence, while the lack of clarity suggests that we do not know whether the relationship will recover.

This poem presents love as a battle or gunfight with the messages presented as bullets that wound the two lovers. The relationship descends into a slanging match and the poem is disjointed with rhyme occurring sporadically and internally and with lots of short statements reflecting the short text messages that they exchange; the frequent caesuras enhance this disjointedness and give the reader sudden halts and pauses. However, the extended metaphor is cleverly and consistently used and I think introduces a comic element into the poem: the text messages do hurt, but they won't really kill you!

Why?

This clever and well-written modern poem

- presents the bitter and devastating disintegration of a relationship.

- uses an extended metaphor to add an ironic distance and to add humour.

- cleverly uses caesuras and to mirror the modern technology of text messages.

- shows how human beings need relationships and love to give their lives meaning.

Ghazal – Mimi Khalvati

Context

Mimi Khalvati was born in 1944 in Tehran, the capital of Iran (known for centuries before as Persia). She was educated in Britain and moved here permanently in 1969. Some of her work explores the tensions between Persian and British culture, and, although she writes in English, she often uses traditional Persian forms of poetry.

The ghazal (pronounced *garzzle*) is an Arabic form that was first used by poets in the 6th century. It has very strict rules that govern the way it is written. A ghazal must have:

- Five or more two line stanzas.

- The even numbered lines must rhyme with each other.

- There can be no enjambment between the stanzas; each couplet must be a complete sentence (or several sentences) in itself.

- In the first couplet the two lines should rhyme with each other.

- In the final couplet the two lines should rhyme with each other and they should contain some sort of word play involving the name of the poet.

The term *ghazal* is not specific to any one language and ghazals have been written for centuries in Arabic, Pashtun, Kurdish, Turkish, Kashmiri, Urdu and Persian, and in European languages during the last two hundred years – they were a popular form in German 19th century literature. Traditionally the ghazal deals with love – usually unrequited love which will never be attained. In the Islamic world this unattainable love might be for a higher being or for a woman: the dream of a perfect union is the same. Some ghazals may be sexually quite explicit or they may be very spiritual. This type of poem is always written from the point of view of the unsatisfied lover; metaphors, sometimes violent or very forceful, are common. We shall see that Khalvati follows very closely the form and subject matter of a strictly traditional ghazal.

venomous – poisonous.

Shamsuddin – a close friend of Rumi who wrote down many of Rumi's poems.

Rumi – a famous 13th century Persian poet and mystic. Rumi wrote about Shamsuddin in a ghazal:

Why should I seek? I am the same as

He. His essence speaks through me.

I have been looking for myself.

Who? Khalvati is the narrator of the poem which is addressed to her lover. It is written in the present tense.

When? A time is not specified. It is not even clear whether this poem describes a relationship which already exists or one that the poet would like to exist. I don't think this matters at all: what matters is the astonishing imagery that the poet uses to describe and imagine their love, their union.

Where? There is no specific location.

What? Through a series of vivid and extravagant metaphors Khalvati expresses her desire to have a relationship with her unnamed, unidentified lover.

Commentary

This poem oozes a sense of the pleasure of sex and sexual desire. The speaker repeatedly expresses the urge to be united – physically and emotionally - with her unnamed lover and the poem is rich in imagery which suggests the pleasure and the fulfilment that will come from their union. This poem demonstrates the sheer intensity of desire and love, and also expresses the desire to be united both physically and spiritually. Many of the couplets begin with the word *If* – so it seems that Khalvati is imagining or fantasizing about what she wants to happen in this relationship. The metaphors she uses are sometimes things which go naturally together – two things that are closely associated with each other; sometimes they are two halves of one thing; and sometimes they are opposites.

The poem consists of ten stanzas, each of two lines. The first couplet rhymes, as does the last and in between the even-numbered lines rhyme. The final couplet contains a pun on the poet's name because the lines end in *me* and *me* which together sound like Mimi. So Khalvati conforms to the conventional form of the ghazal and that in itself is a tribute to a centuries-old tradition of Persian love poetry. The way the even lines rhyme on more than one syllable is called mosaic rhyme and it gives the poem a mesmerizing, hypnotic quality. This is enhanced because Khalvati often uses alliteration, repetition and internal rhyme in the even lines as well.

In the first couplet the poet is the grass and her lover the breeze; she invites him to blow through her. Then she is a rose and he is a bird; he is invited to woo her. These images are very romantic and intimate.

The second couplet refers to poetry. Her lover is the *rhyme* and she is the *refrain* – and in this poem she really is, because the word *me* is used at the end of every couplet and could be described as a refrain. She instructs him – *don't hang on my lips*. To hang on someone's lips means to give close, admiring attention to someone. Khalvati does not want this; she wants action and invites her lover to

come and I'll come too when you cue me.

The alliteration here gives the words coherence and we night note the sexual sense of this line: she wants to achieve mutual, simultaneous orgasm.

The third couplet introduces harder imagery. The lover has an iron fist in the velvet glove and the poet invites him to tattoo her – another very intimate act. She also states

when the arrow flies, the heart is pierced.

The image of Cupid firing arrows is familiar to western culture and, while this is not a reference to Cupid, it still shows the effect that love can have – you heart can be pierced with the intensity of the emotion.

Khalvati describes herself in the fourth couplet as a *venomous snake*, but invites her lover to charm her into submission

weave a spell and subdue me.

Crowns of laurel leaves have been awarded as signs of prowess and accomplishment for centuries in various human cultures. Khalvati imagines herself as the laurel leaf in her lover's crown – his 'reward' for loving her, so to speak. In the second line of this couplet she becomes the laurel tree herself, imagining his arms around her bark.

The sixth couplet begins with an exclamation:

Oh would I were that bark!

And then her lover would become the dew in her shade *to bedew me!* The meaning of *bedew* and its associations with moisture convey a clear sexual intent.

Her desire for her lover is so great that in the seventh couplet she says she is willing to take on any shape to *marry your own* and to encourage him to *pursue* her. She will be the *shadow* to his *hawk*, the *flame* to his *moth*. These are interesting images: when a hawk flies the shadow that it casts obviously moves with it and this suggests Khalvati and her lover will move and act in complete synchronicity. Moths cannot resist flames and this image seems to express the hope that her lover will find her irresistible. Most people find flames attractive visually and they give off heat, which might suggest the burning passion for her lover that Khalvati feels.

In the next couplet she and her lover are opposites – east and west – but east and west cannot exist without each other. Line 15 is perfectly balanced:

If I rise in the east as you die in the west.

In this couplet both lovers are the sun, but at different times of the day. The second line of the stanza plays on the centuries-old meaning of *die* – to reach sexual orgasm and, by doing so, Khalvati says, her lover will *every night renew me.*

In the next couplet Khalvati foresees the end of the relationship, but this is very amicable: the lovers will remain good friends and she invokes the famous relationship between Shamsuddin and Rumi placing the poem even more firmly in its Persian context. She imagines that her lover will continue to be her *muse... and guide.*

The ending of the poem reiterates the need Khalvati has expressed for her lover. She wants her lover to be *heaven and earth to me*; in return she will *be twice the me I am* (twice me is me-me or Mimi), thus punning on her name which we know is a characteristic of the ghazal. Her final statement – *only half the world you are to me* – is a compliment to her lover; he is the world to her, but she can only be half that.

Why? This unusual poem

- celebrates and follows a traditional form – the ghazal – and the traditions behind it.

- uses rich imagery to suggest the attractions of love, both sexual and spiritual.

- expresses a longing for complete union with her lover.

- looks forward to the friendship and affinity that will follow love.

- mixes gentle imagery with violent images to suggest the wonderful variety of sexuality.

Brothers – Andrew Forster

Context

Andrew Forster was born in 1964 and brought up in South Yorkshire – a fact which is reflected in this poem with the references to local football teams. A lot of his poetry is autobiographical and based on his memories of growing up. Forster made this comment about the writing of *Brothers*:

The more I wrote the more the memories just kept on coming. I'm sure that all of us who have brothers and sisters have occasionally behaved in ways we've later regretted. As a poet I'm interested in exploring tiny moments that seem to have huge significance. The incident in 'Brothers' seemed to be one of those moments.

tank-top – a sleeveless pullover, popular in the 70s, noted for their garish colours and bizarre patterns.

Who? The poet, his younger brother, the poet's older brother Paul and 'Mum' (line 7). The poem is addressed to the poet's unnamed younger brother.

When? 1973, when Forster was nine. The poem looks back into the past with regret.

Where? The poet's hometown in South Yorkshire.

What? The poet and Paul manage to shake off their younger brother in order to go into town on their own without the inconvenience of their younger brother.

Commentary

In this poem Forster explores his relationship with his younger brother by looking back at their childhood and one day in particular. From this very ordinary incident expressed in ordinary language, he constructs a moving and reflective poem about his relationship with his brother.

The first stanza explains the situation. The poet and Paul are *saddled* with the younger brother – they begrudge having to look after him for the afternoon simply because he is younger. They walk slowly (*amble*) across the field to the bus stop; this opening stanza is one long sentence, perhaps reflecting the slow amble across the field. Paul and the poet are talking about football. The words used to describe the six-year-old brother show that at the time he thinks his brother is childish; the younger brother *skipped*, his tank-top is *ridiculous* and he is *spouting six-year-old views* on football – that word *spouting* suggesting that his views are worthless. The younger brother seems full of life – he is obviously delighted to be in the company of his older brothers.

The second stanza introduces some urgency: there is a caesura after *froze* and line 6 is a complete sentence. The brother (unnamed) realizes he has no money for the bus, so the poet sends him home to get money from their mother. The brother *windmilled* home – again showing his age but also his pleasure at the prospect of an afternoon with his older brothers. This is the turning point of the poem: the poet and Paul look at each other and smile and take the decision to go to town on their own:

His smile, like mine, said I was nine and he was ten

and we must stroll the town, doing what grown-ups do.

The repetition of *and* reminds us that the poet and Paul are still only children, whatever they like to think, and the first line of the final stanza confirms this: as they run for the bus they chased *Olympic Gold* – their heads are full of childish fantasies. This detail is important: by fantasizing about winning Olympic Gold it shows that the poet is as childish as his younger brother, so, from an adult perspective, he is even more wrong to resent his younger brother's company.

At this moment the poet looks back to their house and sees his younger brother returning with money in his hand, but the poet does not wait and runs on to catch the bus, leaving his younger brother at home:

I ran on, unable to close the distance I'd set in motion.

This final line has a literal meaning: they are a long way apart because the poet is nearly at the bus stop and his younger brother is at the gate of the house. But the line can be seen metaphorically too: that the act of betrayal when they were just children has created an emotional distance between them now they are adults.

Why?

This poem concentrates on a very ordinary incident in very ordinary language to reveal a moment of epiphany which

- shows how rifts in families can stem from very trivial incidents.

- shows that children act without thought and only later realize the consequences.

- implies the importance of family through the poet's tone of regret in the final line.

Praise Song for My Mother – Grace Nichols

Context

Grace Nichols was born on the Caribbean island of Guyana in 1950. Since 1977she has lived in Britain with her partner, John Agard. They are both poets and you can find other poems by both poets in other sections of this Anthology. Although she lives in the UK, she is very aware of her past and the traditions of Guyana, and many of her poems explore the clash or conflict between British or European values and those of her West Indian and African ancestors or, as this one does, they celebrate the life she left behind in Guyana. Nichols herself has said:

I am a writer across two worlds; I just can't forget my Caribbean culture and past, so there's this constant interaction between the two worlds: Britain and the Caribbean.

Praise songs are a type of poem from Africa and celebrate the life of the person they are about. Nichols celebrates the strengths and qualities of her mother in this poem. Elsewhere she has written of her mother that she was a

warm, intelligent, loving woman who was full of stories, anecdotes and songs from her own childhood. People loved being around her and I can't remember a single day when our home wasn't visited by some friend, neighbour or relative who had dropped in 'just feh minute' but ended up staying hours.

plantain – an edible fruit, similar to a wild banana.

flame tree – a tree found in the Caribbean with bright red flowers and a wide, over-arching spread.

replenishing – to fill again, to fill completely.

Who? The poet and her mother to whom this poem is addressed.

Where? In Guyana, the reference to the flame-tree and fried plantains makes this clear.

When? Looking back into the past with nostalgia, until the last line looks to the future.

What? The first four verses are a tribute to Nichols' mother's qualities and what she meant for her daughter; the final line gives her mother's advice.

Commentary

This poem is written in free verse, but it is an interesting example of how a poet can create their own pattern in free verse but using repetition or the same sequence of words, and then break that pattern to create an effect. You should note the lack of punctuation and capital letters too – as well as choosing free verse (and so rejecting all the traditional ways of structuring a poem) Nichols also rejects the conventions of normal punctuation – this is a common feature of some modern poems, but particularly of post-colonial poems. The lack of punctuation allows the poem to speed up, so that the words come out as a burst of language which matches here the enthusiasm which Nichols feels for her mother. The first three stanzas have the same grammatical structure and rely on repetition. The first line is *You were* which is also repeated in line 10; the second line introduces a metaphor and ends with the words *to me*; the final line consists of three adjectives joined by *and* with the last word in each line ending in *-ing–* so although this is a free verse poem, Nichols imposes her own pattern on it.

Note the metaphors Nichols chooses – *water, moon's eye, sunrise* – all natural phenomena which suggest that the mother's love and care for her were natural, powerful and inevitable. The fourth stanza breaks the pattern as lines 11, 12 and 13 contain metaphors to express the mother's influence on Nichols. In this stanza the poet introduces metaphors based on food and which are also (in some cases) associated with life in Guyana. The breaking of her own pattern suggests her sheer excitement at recalling all these things that her mother gave her - and this fourth stanza concentrates on the most essential thing a parent can give a child – food. The speed is also suggested in the line:

the crab's leg/the fried plantain smell,

where Nichols uses a forward slash instead of more conventional punctuation which suggests enthusiasm. The metaphor of the *flame tree's spread* suggests an overwhelming sense of protection and care for her daughter. These details – the flame tree, the fried plantain – fix the poem as being about Guyana and suggest that the mother has not just given her daughter food, but also a culture, a way of life. The repetition of *replenishing* again suggests intensity of emotion while echoing the structure of the end of the first three stanzas, and also suggests that the mother's care of her daughter is life-long.

Finally in the last line Nichols gives her mother a voice and she says:

Go to your wide futures,

which is her final gift to her daughter – the act of letting her go. It is a final line which is full of hope and optimism, and foresees Nichols' move to the United Kingdom and her future success as a poet. We might also see it perhaps as a belief that one day black people will be treated more equally than has been the case in the past.

Why?

- This is a poem of celebration of the love and protection that a mother gives.

- It is also nostalgic about the poet's childhood in Guyana.

- It ends on a note of boundless optimism about the future.

- It celebrates human harmony with nature.

- It equates a mother's care with the kindness and benevolence of nature.

Harmonium – Simon Armitage

Context

Simon Armitage was born in 1963 in the village of Marsden in West Yorkshire and has spent most of his life in that area. He is a very successful and highly-regarded poet, celebrated for his down-to-earth language and subject matter. Several of his poems are in the Anthology. His poetry often (but not always) deals with the ordinary incidents and events of modern life and appear to be based on personal experience. Several of his poems explore his relationship with his father – as does this one.

As a young boy Armitage was a choirboy and his family were often involved in performances at their local church. Armitage has said of his father:

My dad has always been confident and quick-witted. He says it there and then, right off, while I have to go away and think about it and then put it down on paper.

Remember this quotation as we look at the final stanza.

Harmonium – a type of organ.

Farrand Chaplette – the firm that made the harmonium.

Marsden Church – the church in Armitage's home village.

for a song – very cheaply.

beatify – to make blessed or happy.

treadles – a pedal or foot-lever; here for working the harmonium.

dottled – spots left by tobacco.

nave – the central aisle of a church.

freight – cargo.

sorry – weak, pathetic.

Who? Armitage and his father.

When? The day they go to move the harmonium from the church. The first three stanzas are in the past tense and then the poet switches to the present tense in the final stanza.

Where? In Marsden Church.

What? The poet describes the harmonium and then he and his father moving it out of the church.

Commentary

The first stanza explains the situation: the harmonium is unwanted and Armitage can get it cheaply. The opening sentence is filled with assonance on the *a* sound which makes a memorable opening – along with the unfamiliar name of the harmonium itself. But note the colloquial language in the second sentence – *bundled off, for a song* – fixing this as a poem based on an everyday incident.

The second stanza describes the harmonium. The emphasis is on its decay and decrepitude: the case is aged, the keys yellowed, one of its notes is broken and there are holes in both the treadles. Note how the stanza begins with a lot of alliteration on *s* and the transforming image of *sunlight through stained glass* which Armitage claims, using hyperbole, can *beatify saints and raise the dead*. By the end of the stanza we have returned to the down-to-earth details of the *grey woollen socks* and *leather-soled shoes* of the organist's feet. Once again these details mark this out as a poem rooted in the ordinary and the everyday.

The third stanza presents a different point of view and explains one of the reasons why Armitage feels that he wanted the harmonium. The mixed alliteration on *h* and *s* in the opening sentence and at the end of the stanza the first metaphor – *gilded finches* – add a vivid sense of why this instrument matters: Armitage and his father had both been choristers in this church.

The final stanza introduces the poet's father and switches to the present tense. His father is helping Armitage carry the harmonium away. There is a note of affection in the opening description of his father whose smoker's fingers remind us of the yellowed keys of the harmonium itself.

And we carry it flat laid on its back

and the position of the harmonium and the fact that they are carrying it through the church, prompts Armitage's father to say jokily that the next box that Armitage will carry along the nave of the church will be his father's coffin. We might note how close father and son are: Armitage can almost predict what his father will say:

and he being him can't help but say

There seems to be a grudging bit of affectionate admiration for his father's quick wit. In comparison Armitage makes some inadequate response:

and I, being me, then mouth in reply

some shallow or sorry phrase or word

too starved of breath to make itself heard.

A lot is going on in these lines. We know from what Armitage has said that he regards his father as confident and quick-witted, while he himself is not (he seems slightly embarrassed that he can only mouth in reply *some sorry phrase*). In addition, he may be a little breathless from the effort of carrying the harmonium. Is it not possible too that the thought of his father dying is so emotionally shocking that Armitage is momentarily lost for words? What his father clearly meant as a joke, has made the poet think about his father's death in the future.

The harmonium can be seen as a symbol of the father and of Armitage's relationship with him. Like the harmonium, the father is old and past his best; he too will be carried along the nave in his coffin at some point in the future; they are joined together in the poem by the act of carrying the harmonium out of the church. But the very word 'harmonium' brings to mind questions of harmony in a relationship and, despite, their awkward exchange of words at the very end, this poem presents father and son helping each other in harmony.

The poem is written in free verse, but is given unity by alliteration and assonance both of which create a harmony of sound. As we have observed, most of Armitage's words are colloquial, but there is clever word play in the use of idiomatic expressions such as *going for a song* and *struck a chord*. There is assonance in *stained, saints, raise,* in *opened their throats* and throughout the final stanza – *away, carry, flat, laid, back, say, nave*; alliteration in *hummed harmonics* and in *some shallow...sorry* and in *still struck, stood, stalls, son, streamed*; and internal rhyme in line 24. The poem's final rhyming couplet brings the poem to a neat and satisfying conclusion.

Why?

This is a poem which

• celebrates the close relationship between a son and his father.

- shows that family traditions (like singing in a choir) can create important bonds.

- touches on the forthcoming death of a person close to you.

- uses resolutely down-to-earth and everyday language to probe deeper feelings.

- uses free verse but uses the sounds of words cleverly to give the poem unity.

The Literary Heritage

Sonnet 116 – William Shakespeare

Context

Shakespeare is the most famous writer England has ever produced and his plays are known throughout the world. 'Sonnet 116' by William Shakespeare is part of a sonnet sequence of 154 sonnets – also known as a sonnet cycle. Readers have commented that in the sonnets as a whole, Shakespeare covers every aspect of arguably the most important and strongest human emotion – love - as well as our most powerful instinct – sexual desire and the whole range of what happens in what we now call human relationships. Unlike Shakespeare's plays (most of which were unpublished during his lifetime), the sonnets were published in 1609. What does this tell us? We are not entirely sure: it is generally felt that it shows that poetry was held in higher regard than writing plays, so perhaps Shakespeare published the sonnets to achieve fame and wealth; there is also the fact that in Shakespeare's era there were no copyright laws – so once a play was published, there was nothing to stop any theatre putting a play on without giving the writer any performance fees.

Of the 154 sonnets some are very famous and appear in many anthologies. These very famous ones are well-known by the general public too: in the past, BBC Radio 4 has sometimes run public surveys to discover the nation's favourite poem or the nation's favourite love poem and Shakespeare's sonnets are frequently voted into the top ten. If you like 'Sonnet 116', then you might like to read some of his others. They are readily available on-line and are known by their number and the first line:

Sonnet 18 – Shall I compare thee to a summer's day?

Sonnet 29 – When in disgrace with Fortune and men's eyes

Sonnet 55 – Not marble or the gilded monuments

Sonnet 57 – Being your slave what should I do?

Sonnet 71 – No longer mourn for me when I am dead

Sonnet 91 – Some glory in their birth, some in their skill

Sonnet 129 – The expense of spirit in a waste of shame

Sonnet 130 – My mistress' eyes are nothing like the sun

Because so little is known about Shakespeare's private life, there has been endless speculation about who the sonnets are addressed to – but none of this speculation helps us get any closer to the individual sonnets and their meaning and impact. Personally I find it of no interest whatsoever, because for me the words are what make the sonnets memorable and worth reading now – over four hundred years since they were first published.

'Sonnet 116' is often used in modern marriage services (nowadays some churches allow couples considerable freedom in choosing some of the words they use during the service) and I have even seen cards for sale which reproduce the words of the sonnet – these cards are intended to be sent to people who are getting married. The whole sonnet presents a love that is steadfast and loyal and unchanging in the face of other changes. We will look closely at the language and tone of the sonnet, but also consider a deeper and darker interpretation.

impediments – obstacles.

or...remove – or ends when one person leaves or stops the relationship.

ever-fixèd – permanent, not moving.

bark – ship.

time's fool – the fool of time, subject to time and ageing.

bending sickle – a scythe and its curved shape; the Grim Reaper carries a sickle; sickles and scythes are long-handled tools used for chopping down tall crops or weeds; here it is used metaphorically – Time chops us down because we succumb to age and finally death.

compass – range.

bears it out – endures it.

doom – Doomsday, the end of the world in Christian mythology, the day of Final Judgement when Christ will come to earth again and decide who goes to Heaven and who to Hell. Shakespeare uses this to suggest that love will last forever – until the end of time or the end of the world.

Who? The voice of the poet – but the commentary that follows suggests the implied presence of other people.

When? The sonnets were published in 1609, but most scholars believe that Shakespeare began to write them in the 1590s. Within the poem no particular time is specified.

Where? No particular place is specified, so the location does not seem important.

What? Shakespeare states that true love will never change and then explores this assertion through a series of images in order to prove or demonstrate that love will never change.

Commentary

The opening sentence of the sonnet is justly famous: the recurrence of the letter *m* which both alliterates and is within certain words, and the way the first line runs on into the second:

Let me not to the marriage of true minds

Admit impediments

creates a gentle, calm, mellifluous tone which is appropriate to the sense: consonance on the letter *l* allows creates euphony, which is all enhanced by the enjambment. The next sentence too:

Love is not love

Which alters when it alteration finds.

is often quoted on its own and offered as a universal truth: true love never changes no matter what happens. This second sentence is memorable not just because of the sentiment but because of the words: the repetition of the word *love* as well as *alter/alteration* and the soft sounds of the letter *l* and *w* and *f*. So far the sonnet is quite clearly concerned with marriage and *alters* is a pun on what we find at the eastern end of a church - the altar. *Impediment* too is a word, a very important word, in the Church of England marriage service. In the marriage service the priest says to the congregation, before the couple exchange their vows of marriage:

Does anyone know of any just cause or impediment why these two should not be joined together in holy matrimony?

Impediment here means an obstacle. At this point in the service, centuries ago, this was the moment when someone in the congregation could mention an obstacle – such one of the couple being already married or promised to someone else or below the legal age to marry or whatever. The final line of the quatrain continues this pattern of repetition – *remover/remove*.

The second quatrain introduces new images in an effort to define what love is. Line 5 begins with a dramatic exclamation – *O no* – and then introduces a metaphor based on ships and navigation. Love is *ever-fixèd*: it never changes and can endure the fury of tempests without being shaken; love is like a star that guides sailors who would otherwise be lost (*wandering*) and they measure the height of the star (love) even before they understand whether the star will help them navigate. Shakespeare uses assonance – *star* assonates with the rhyme words *bark* and *mark* – and *whose worth's unknown* – repeats the same sound with *o* – which also goes back to the exclamation at the start of the quatrain. This creates a sort of aural harmony even though he is writing about potentially dangerous things – tempests, and ships that are lost.

The third quatrain changes the line of thought again. It starts with a bold statement – *Love's not Time's fool*; Shakespeare means that true love will not alter even though time changes our physical appearance as we age. Time destroys *rosy lips and cheeks*. Note the consonance on *c* in *si*c*kle's* *c*ompass *c*ome. Line 11 deliberately echoes the opening quatrain with its use of *alters*. The whole quatrain is held together not just by sense and subject matter and rhyme, but also alliteration – *bending, brief, but bears*. The final line says that love will last until Doomsday, the end of time.

The sonnet ends with an assertive couplet. Shakespeare states that if he is wrong – that if love is impermanent or transitory, then it follows that he, the poet, never wrote a word and no human being ever really loved.

This poem is usually read as a definition of love or true love: an emotion that survives time and tempests, that will never change, no matter what happens. This is why it is so popular in connection with marriages – it serves, people think, as a vow of love that will last forever. Perhaps its power has a lot to do with its sounds: we have noted the clever use of repetition; the euphony created by the soft consonants in the opening quatrain; and, perhaps, its appeal has something to do with Shakespeare's straightforward imagery of stars and ships, rosy cheeks, death personified with his bending sickle.

However, a closer reading will show that there is another possibility, another way to interpret this very famous poem.

Remember that in the first sentence Shakespeare had said he was not going to admit impediments – he is going to say nothing at this point of the marriage service. This suggests that Shakespeare is writing about the marriage of someone else and asserting that he still loves that person and his love will never change, despite the fact that they are marrying someone else and not him. It is ironic, isn't it, that the sonnet is so often used in marriage services: this is a poem about the end of a relationship – a relationship that is ending because one of the people involved in the relationship is getting married. Consequently, the speaker's feelings are of sadness and a sense of betrayal, but they are controlled by the strict form of the sonnet which helps to restrain the terrible sadness the speaker feels.

In the light of this reading of the poem, the poem's imagery still fits with what I wrote earlier in the summary, but some of the images take on a darker, sadder tone and atmosphere. The simile involving the *wandering bark* works as a simile, but it might also suggest Shakespeare's emotional state now that his former lover has rejected him to marry someone else – he is like a ship drifting. Love that bears it out until the edge of doom, means a love that will never die and will keep going until Doomsday, but that word *doom* perhaps suggest the terrible sadness that Shakespeare feels at the end of the relationship: in a sense it is almost like the end of the world for him. *Bears it out* suggests a determination to keep going despite the heartbreak he feels – and he does, in a sense, keep going, because the sonnet reaches its conclusion.

Why?

This world-famous poem

- offers a definition of love which many readers have found comforting and inspiring.

- asserts that true love lasts forever and will endure absence and time and even death.

- uses simple repetition and wonderfully crafted combinations of sound to create euphony.

BUT it might also be read as

- a poem full of heartbreak and sadness at the loss of a loved one who marries someone else.

Sonnet 43 – **Elizabeth Barrett Browning**

Context

Elizabeth Barrett Browning was born into a wealthy family in 1806. At the age of 14 she suffered from a lung complaint and the following year damaged her spine in a riding accident; she was to be plagued with poor health for the rest of her life. Elizabeth had started to publish poetry anonymously and was starting to become famous. In 1838 her brother Edward drowned off the coast of Devon and for the next five years Elizabeth became a recluse, hardly leaving her bedroom in her father's house. However, she continued to write poetry and began a long correspondence with the poet Robert Browning, who began writing to her after reading her poems. Between 1844 and 1846 they wrote 574 letters to each other and finally ran away to Italy to get married. They had to flee to Italy because Elizabeth's father was violently opposed to the marriage. She and her father never spoke again and he disinherited her. Her health improved in Italy and she gave birth to a son in 1849. She died in her husband's arms in 1861.

'Sonnet 43' is from the sonnet cycle *Sonnets from the Portuguese* which she wrote during their correspondence and before their marriage. (*Sonnets from the Portuguese* is simply the title she chose – they are not translations and do not exist in Portuguese!). This sonnet cycle explores the development and growth of her love for Browning and, although she wrote many other poems, it is these sonnets for which she is mainly remembered today. What is interesting and rarely mentioned in guides like this, is that the earlier poems in the sonnet cycle were not as confident as 'Sonnet 43'. In the earlier sonnets she is afraid of the consequences of her love for Browning and unsure about her own feelings: 'Sonnet 43' is towards the end of the cycle and represents the achievement of a confident, mature love.

thee – you.

Grace – the Grace of God.

my lost Saints – perhaps a reference to members of the poet's family who have died or to her former strong religious belief which has been replaced by love for Browning.

Who? The poet addresses her future husband.

When? From the period before they were married.

Where? The location is not specified.

What? The poet explores the many ways in which she loves her husband-to-be.

Commentary

Although this poem is a Petrarchan sonnet in form, it is unlike many sonnets because there is no turn in line 9 – there is no conflict or problem to be resolved because Barrett Browning's tone is assertive, confident and strong: she is expressing her love for Browning without doubt or hesitation.

The opening sentence – given more prominence by the poet's dramatic use of the caesura – asks a question which the following thirteen lines attempt to answer. In all there are eight different aspects of love identified. As the poem goes on each different type of love is introduced by the words *I love thee* – which is a very simple device of repetition, but may explain why so many readers find this a memorable poem. In the first quatrain the poet moves on to speak of the spiritual aspect of her love; the second quatrain deals with the love that enriches ordinary, everyday life. Her love is given *freely* she says in line 7 and *purely* – line 8: her love is given unselfishly and modestly, in the way someone might turn away from praise.

In the sestet the poet analyses her love in three more ways: she loves him with Passion – an emotion she once expended on grief and with the fidelity of a child. She loves him with the same passion she once reserved for religion. She then states that her love is completely overwhelming – it is like breathing and continues through good and bad times – *smiles, tears, of all my life*. The poem ends by stating that if it is God's will, then her love will continue after death and exist in the after-life – another answer to her opening question.

Apart from the lack of a turn or problem to be resolved, which sets it apart from many sonnets, Barrett Browning uses hardly any imagery, no metaphors or similes. She takes an abstract concept 'love' and defines it largely through other abstract concepts – Grace, Right. The words *I love thee* are repeated nine times in the course of the sonnet and this simple use of repetition has made the poem so well-known and popular. This repetition also shows the strength and confidence of her feelings.

So how does she love her husband?

- She loves him with her soul when it is searching for the meaning of life (*the ends of Being*) and the mystery of God (*Ideal Grace*).

- She loves him in an ordinary down-to-earth way – *the level of everyday's most quiet need*.

- She loves him *freely* – in the same way that humans seek morality (*Right*).

- She loves him purely and modestly (*as men turn from Praise*).

- She loves him with the passion she once expended on *my old griefs*.

- She loves him with the faith of childhood.

- She loves him with the love she seemed to lose with her lost Saints (the siblings who had died when she was younger).

- She loves him with the breath of all her life.

- She will love him better after death.

This famous poem is very simple in its use of language – and perhaps that is its appeal. There are no metaphors to confuse or to analyze; the imagery is limited and where it occurs it is very simple – *sun, candlelight, smiles, tears*; it is clearly written in the Christian tradition and some readers may find her certainty and faith comforting.

To His Coy Mistress – **Andrew Marvell**

Context

Andrew Marvell was born in a village near Hull in 1621. His father was a Church of England vicar. Marvell went to Cambridge where he wrote some of his first poems in Latin and Greek and it is believed he then travelled widely in Europe. The 1640s were turbulent and violent years in the history of England. A destructive Civil War between Parliament and the King was fought out with the King's forces finally being defeated in 1645 at the Battle of Naseby. Charles I was eventually put on trial, found guilty of treason and executed by parliament on January 29th 1649: England became a republic.

Marvell was closely associated with the Parliamentary side: in the late 1640s he was employed as tutor to Mary Fairfax, the daughter of Sir Thomas Fairfax, Commander in Chief of the parliamentary army and then in the 1650s he worked in Cromwell's government. In 1659 he became MP for Hull and remained as MP until his death in 1678. He was a hard-working MP and stood up for freedom of speech and religious toleration, when these came under threat under Charles II, who had returned to England in 1660 to take the crown and restore the monarchy. His published poems in this period (known as the Restoration) were bitterly satirical about the corruption he saw in the royal court, and some were published anonymously so that he did not get into trouble with the authorities. 'To His Coy Mistress' and about another 80 poems were published posthumously: we are not sure when they were written but there is general agreement that they were probably written in the late 1640s when Marvell worked for Fairfax.

Coy – bashful or shy in an affected way.

Mistress – lover. The word in the 17th century did not have its modern connotations of a woman other than a man's wife.

Had we – if we had.

world – space.

Ganges – sacred river in India; only a handful of Englishmen would have actually seen the Ganges when Marvell wrote this poem.

Humber – a river in the north of England which reaches the sea near Hull – near where Marvell was born.

the Flood – he is referring to the story of the Flood in the Bible which took place thousands of years ago.

the conversion of the Jews – an indirect allusion to the Day of Judgment – which may be thousands of years away; according to Christian belief, on the Day of Judgment all Jews will realize they were wrong and be converted to Christianity.

quaint – a pun. It means prim and proper, but was also a 17th century alternative spelling of cunt.

dust – an allusion to the Church of England funeral service – ashes to ashes, dust to dust.

sport us – enjoy ourselves.

slow-chapt – slowly chewed.

Who? The poem is written in the first person and addressed to Marvell's mistress. It starts in the future conditional tense (*I would love you...*) and then changes to the present in the second and third verse paragraphs.

When? The present. The poem is generally thought to have been written around 1649, when Marvell was tutor to Maria Fairfax.

Where? Specific places are mentioned, but the poem itself has no particular setting.

What? Marvell uses the first verse paragraph to describe how he would love his mistress if they had all the time in the world; he then points out that death is inevitable; in the third and final verse paragraph he urges her to make love with him now.

Commentary

'Carpe diem' is a Latin phrase which means 'Seize the day'; in other words, live life to the full now, because life is short and tomorrow we may be dead. It was a very common theme for poets to write about in the 16th and 17th centuries, perhaps because life and death were more unpredictable, life expectancy was shorter and medical knowledge very primitive. It is also possible to relate the idea to the Civil War: in times of warfare you may feel even more at risk and that life is precarious and death just that little bit closer. We do not place much emphasis in schools on the English Civil War, but some historians have calculated that it was the bloodiest civil war ever: not in terms of the total number of deaths, but in terms of the number of deaths as a proportion of the population. So for those who lived through it, it must have been a traumatic, disturbing event. All the more reason then, to seize the day.

Another notable feature of this poem is its syllogistic structure: it is a carefully constructed argument. The first verse paragraph presents one possible scenario; the second proves it cannot happen like that: the third verse paragraph reaches a conclusion. This sort of logical progression is very typical of Metaphysical poetry.

The opening verse paragraph is full of hyperbole. Marvell tells his mistress how he would love her, if they had enough space and time. The rhythm is slow and sensual. If they had all the time in the world then they could sit and think how to

pass our long love's day.

Note how those three words at the end of the line are all stressed and the way *long* and *love* alliterate and assonate. Even physical separation would not be a problem: the poet could be complaining on the banks of the Humber, while his lover could be finding rubies by the side of the Ganges. What would he be complaining about? Well, the fact that they are apart. I find this image very funny because it juxtaposes the very exotic (Ganges and rubies) with the very ordinary English river – the Humber. Marvell then uses hyperbole to suggest how long he would love her: from thousands of years ago (the Flood) to thousands of years in the future (Doomsday). The next couplet is wonderfully suggestive in its imagery:

My vegetable love should grow

Vaster than empires, and more slow.

The poet seems to be boasting that if he loved her for that length of time his erection would become enormous. He then tells her how long he would praise and adore her: two hundred years

to adore each breast.

This is richly comic hyperbole – foreplay that would last for several millennia.

The second verse paragraph begins with the word *but* and Marvell reveals why they cannot spend so long building up to sex – because they will die. He says he is always aware of

Time's winged chariot hurrying near.

What awaits them are

Deserts of vast eternity.

Death will destroy her beauty and his *echoing song* (his poetry). The poet then gives a detailed picture of what will happen to her body when she is dead:

then worms shall try

That long-preserved virginity,

And your quaint honour turn to dust.

This is a gruesome image – the worms burrowing into his mistress's vagina instead of him burrowing into her. The phrase *quaint honour* could be argued to be the rudest, funniest pun in the whole of English poetry. Marvell is saying that her honour is old-fashioned and silly, but also it is honour to do with her quaint – her cunt. I find this hilarious and deliberately shocking. The word *dust* (from the funeral service) deliberately rhymes with *lust* to underline the fact that they must seize the moment. The verse paragraph ends with this couplet:

The grave's a fine and private place

But none, I think, do there embrace.

Of course, the idea of two skeletons embracing each other in the grave is gruesome and impossible, but what makes me laugh in this couplet is Marvell's *I think* – as though there were any doubt whatsoever about it!!

The final verse paragraph begins with the word *Now* – and Marvell reaches his conclusion: because they are going to die, they must make love immediately. The word *now* is repeated twice more before the end of the poem – an indication of the poet's urgency and impatience. The word *therefore* reminds us that this is an argument. Marvell wants to make love while his mistress is still young: while the *youthful hue* colours her skin and while she is full of *instant fires* and capable of passion. The imagery Marvell uses to describe their love-making is full of oxymoron: the simile *like amorous birds of prey* is especially striking. *Amorous* means loving, but birds of prey tear the flesh from other creatures – this is love which is energetic, loving, but also wild and rough. He imagines that they will devour time rather than be slowly chewed up by time itself. This imagines time as a monster who chews us up by ageing us and eventually killing us. Lines 41 and 42 are especially interesting:

Let us roll all our strength and all

Our sweetness up into one ball.

Try reading this aloud. The mainly monosyllabic words and the words beginning with vowels and ending in *l* are difficult to enunciate without slurring the words together – to say them properly makes you slow down and also takes some effort – but then he is describing the sexual act which also takes some effort. As for the ball – some readers suggest this a cannon-ball and make much of the fact that Marvell lived through the Civil War; others suggest it is a sexual position. I am undecided. It is probably both.

As the poem proceeds, the act of love is seen as pleasurable, but also painful in an enjoyable way. He promises her that they will

tear our pleasures with rough strife

Through the iron gates of life.

The word *pleasures* is juxtaposed with *tear* and *rough strife* – an act of love which gives pleasure and pain. The *gates of life* are the entrance to his lover's vagina.

The final couplet means that by having sex, they will not be able to make time (here symbolized by the sun) stop (*stand still*) but they will make time go quickly (*run*). It also begins with *thus* and presents the final conclusion to the poet's argument.

The rhythm of this poem is particularly effective. To put it briefly, it mirrors what it describes: the first verse paragraph is slow and leisurely; the second starts to speed up; and the final verse paragraph is very quick. Why? It is partly because the situation is urgent and pressing – they might die at any moment. Marvell is in a hurry and the rhythm of the poem reflects this. The rhythm also mirrors the sexual act to reach a climax in the final couplet: sex starts slowly and then gets quicker and quicker.

How does Marvell achieve this speeding up of the rhythm in the final third of the poem? And how does he create the slow rhythm of the opening section? The first verse paragraph has a lot of sentences or uses colons to create heavy pauses; there is some enjambment but there are heavy caesuras which then slow the poem down. By contrast, the third verse paragraph consists of only three sentences, there are very few caesuras and extensive use of enjambment – so when it is read aloud it has to be read more quickly and the words are largely monosyllabic so that there is a pounding, regular rhythm – like that of the sexual act.

Let's look in detail at the final couplet:

Thus, though we cannot make our sun

Stand still, yet we will make him run.

The first line flows into the second through enjambment; alliteration then foregrounds *sun stands still* which is followed by perhaps the best-placed caesura in English poetry – if you read it aloud your voice has to stop and stand still so it reflects the sense superbly. Also, given what Marvell is writing` about here – the sexual act – it is not hard to see that pause in the line as the moment of climax. You may feel I am reading too much into one comma, BUT this is a poem that has boasted of his vegetable love, imagined worms burrowing into his lover's vagina and punned on the word *quaint* – so it is more than likely that Marvell places that comma and the alliteration and enjambment that precede it with precise care.

Why?

This very famous and much-anthologized poem

- presents the inevitability of death in frightening images.

- celebrates the physicality of sex.

- uses outrageous humour and frankness to write originally on a stereotypical theme (carpe diem).

- matches its rhythm perfectly to its subject matter.

- manages to be very funny and very serious at the same time.

The Farmer's Bride – Charlotte Mew

Context

Charlotte Mew was born in London in 1869. Her father died in 1898, leaving his family in poverty. Three of her siblings died in childhood and another two suffered from mental illness and were put in hospital permanently. Charlotte and her remaining sister, Anne, made a pact never to marry for fear of passing on insanity to their children. She started publishing short stories in 1896, but her first collection of poetry (for which this poem provided the title) was not published until 1916. After the death of Anne, she descended into a deep depression and eventually committed suicide in 1928.

maid – young girl – the implication is also that she is a virgin.

bide – wait.

woo – a slightly old-fashioned word now, it means to court or win the affections of someone.

fay – a fairy.

fall – autumn. We associate this word with American English, but there is evidence that it survived as a term for *autumn* in some regions of the UK until at least 1900.

abed – in bed.

fast – tightly locked.

beseech – to ask or pray earnestly.

leveret – a young hare; more technically, a hare that is less than a year old.

betwixt – between.

Who? The poet speaks as a farmer who has married a young girl who is scared of men and sex. He tells us a lot about his wife. He also has neighbours who help catch his wife when she runs off.

When? The farmer speaks in the past tense before switching to the present in the third stanza.

Where? It is set in a rural community on a farm and there is a closeness to the natural world and the rhythms and seasons of nature expressed through the imagery.

What? The farmer describes what has happened in his life since he got married just over a year before the poem starts.

Commentary

This poem's narrator is a farmer who tells the story of his courtship of his wife and the progress of their three year marriage.

In the first stanza we are told that on reflection he thinks that perhaps she was too young. He married her quickly in the summer of one year because it was harvest time and he had more pressing things to attend to – bringing in the harvest. The marriage has not gone well. We are not told exactly why, but husband and wife do not sleep together and the final line of the opening stanza tells us that the wife tried to run away, because she was so repulsed by her husband and, it is suggested, having sex with her husband. As soon as they were married we are told:

she turned afraid

Of love and me and all things human.

And then *her smile went out* and one night in the autumn she simply ran away.

In the second stanza the husband recounts how he and others from the community chased her in the dark, found her, brought her home and locked her up. She was among the sheep, he was told, but she wasn't and so *we chased her*. It is not clear who *we* are – the farmer and his friends or his neighbours or other members of the community perhaps; what is important, I think is that it was a group of people chasing after one frightened young woman. They finally caught up with her at Church-town. She was:

All in a shiver and a scare

but they ignore her fear, take her home and lock her in the farmer's house. Line 13 is an interesting line. The farmer says she should have been in bed:

Lying awake with her wide brown stare.

We go to bed to sleep, but this line suggests that normally she does not sleep: this suggests that she deliberately stays awake in order not to be taken sexually in her sleep.

In the third stanza the tense changes to describe the present state of affairs. She performs the work about the house and is happy in the company of small creatures:

With birds and rabbits and such as they,

but she becomes disturbed whenever any man comes near her. She doesn't say anything but her eyes beseech them not to come near her. The women around the farm have noticed that she seems to have an especial affinity with animals when she speaks to them. The farmer ruefully comments in the final line of the stanza that

I've never heard her speak at all.

The speaker changes tone in the fifth stanza which runs from line 30 to line 41. The first four lines describe his wife in a sympathetic way and in a series of similes all drawn from nature. The sibilance creates a wistful sense of longing - the narrator is clearly attracted to his wife. Line 34 switches to describe the autumn in loving yet elegiac tones: the year is ending, the days are getting shorter, the leaves are falling – there is a sense of nature dying off, all the more beautiful because Mew uses almost wholly monosyllabic words for the rest of the stanza. But in line 39 the narrator mentions the berries on the holly trees getting redder and this reminds him that it will soon be Christmas. The red berries have a symbolic function: red is associated with passion: when a woman's virginity is taken and her hymen broken she often sheds blood: here though the symbol is ironic because sex has not occurred between the farmer and his bride. The stanza ends with the farmer wishing that he had children so that Christmas would be more fulfilling:

What's Christmas-time without there be

Some other in the house than we!

It is one of the central ironies of this poem that farmers produce food which keeps us alive, but this farmer cannot produce children because his wife will not sleep with him.

In the final stanza stanza the voice of the farmer breaks down and, to reflect this, the pattern of the stanza changes and is much shorter and, therefore, more intense. The famer seems wracked with sexual frustration. His wife sleeps on the floor above him in the attic.

So she is physically quite close to him, but not in the same bed. He could reach her very easily, but knows he would frighten her and that she does not want him. Are we to imagine that the attic door is locked? I think we are – or she would run away as she has done before. As he thinks of her he is overwhelmed with physical desire for her youthful skin and the beauty of her eyes and hair. The final sentence begins with an exclamation and then becomes very repetitive as the farmer expresses his almost uncontrolled longing for her:

Oh! My God! The down,

The soft young down of her, the brown,

The brown of her – her eyes, her hair, her hair!

Down is an interesting word to use because it is associated with animals. Throughout the poem the wife has been associated with nature or with things that are not human: *fay, like a hare, like a mouse, a leveret, a young larch tree, the first wild violets*. Furthermore, she has an affinity with animals. Farmers control nature, but the wife is compared or associated with things that we cannot control.

Mew is very successful in creating the voice of the farmer. The vocabulary she uses is very simple and the imagery is drawn from the natural world – the world which the farmer would know so well. There are phrases which suggest a man of little formal education and a slightly old-fashioned or ungrammatical way of expressing himself all through the poem, such as *more's to do, the shut of a winter's day, 'twasn't a woman, runned, her be, fetched her home, men-folk, betwixt*. It is a remarkable feat of ventriloquism. Like other dramatic monologues the speaker reveals more and more of himself as the poem proceeds.

This poem could be read as a simple story of male oppression. After all, the wife tries to run away and now cannot because she is locked in the attic. Her imprisonment here recalls the fate of other fictional heroines such as Mr Rochester's wife in *Jane Eyre* and the central character in *The Yellow Wallpaper* by Charlotte Perkins Gilman. Her association with animals and other natural things might suggest that the farmer is trying to control something natural and force it to do his will; but this imagery is paradoxically the very reason why he finds her so attractive – because she reminds him of the animals he is surrounded by in nature.

However, Mew presents the farmer as essentially sympathetic. He uses his power over her, but he controls his sexual desire for his wife and recognizes that she does not want him. Marital rape was not recognized as a crime in the UK until 1991. In the period that Mew was writing in, it would have been considered normal for the husband to have forced himself onto his wife – it would certainly not have been illegal. But the farmer is perceptive enough to know that she fears him and a sexual relationship. And, although he locks her up, he is, in the context of the times, in control of his urges and sympathetic to her lack of desire for him. His descriptions of her – especially those which compare her to small animals – could be said to display a certain amount of patience towards her. Equally you could say that these descriptions are slightly condescending and patronizing, because they do not individualize her or see her humanity. We are never told her name and the title of the poem could be said to sum her up: from the farmer's point of view, her only role in life is to be his bride and give him sex and children.

He is not especially cruel to her, but he is rather conventional. He has married in order to have children, perhaps so that they can inherit the farm. He expects her to have sex with him and is filled with frustration that she does not want to. She seems to like animals because, you could argue, she is treated like one: the beasts are kept in their stalls; she is kept in her attic. In addition, we might note that she has a natural affinity, which the women have noticed, with small frightened creatures like herself.

Why?

This dramatic monologue

- presents two people trapped in a marriage.

- the wife is literally held prisoner in her husband's house.

- the husband is full of desire for his wife, but sensitive enough to ignore his physical desires.

- examines the imprisoning role that women had to fulfil in the past.

- describes nature in beautiful colloquial language especially in lines 34 to 39.

- show two people who are both in different ways in tune with nature.

- is full of the wife's fear and the husband's unrequited desires.

Sister Maude – **Christina Georgina Rossetti**

Context

Christina Rossetti was born in 1830 into a highly talented family – all of whom wrote or painted – and Rossetti was encouraged by her family to pursue her artistic talents from an early age. Her father, a poet and translator, lived in exile and the family were held together by the mother who had a very strong Christian faith. Rossetti's poetry revolves around the themes of love and death, and there is often a strong religious dimension to her work. Her own life was increasingly unhappy: she was engaged to be married twice, but broke off both engagements. She suffered terrible ill-health, although she continued to write, and her final years were darkened by the deaths of most of her family and her two previous lovers. She died in 1894, having achieved much acclaim for her writing.

clotted curls – densely knotted curls of hair.

comeliest – most beautiful.

bide – wait.

Who? The poem is narrated by a woman who has a sister called Maude; her lover and the sisters' parents are also important characters in the poem.

When? The time is not specified, but the archaic word *comeliest* suggests the past – the past even when Rossetti was writing.

Where? The location is not specified, because it is not important, as we shall see.

What? The actual course of events is unclear – which adds to the poem's mystery. I examine this in detail in the commentary.

Commentary

This poem is written in a conventional ballad stanza of rhyming quatrains until the final stanza, which has six lines instead of four. The speaker addresses her sister, Maude, throughout the poem.

The first stanza of the poem accuses Maude of telling their parents of the narrator's shame. The first two lines ask a question which the second half of the quatrain answers. Maude discovered the narrator's shame because she

lurked to spy and peer.

The second stanza changes direction as the speaker tells us about a dead man who even in death is the *comeliest corpse in all the world.* The reader may assume that this dead man was the speaker's lover and, therefore, part of her shame and that Maude somehow found out about their relationship and told their parents.

The speaker goes on in the third stanza to accuse her sister of some part in his death:

You might have spared his soul, sister.

The notion of souls being saved introduces religious ideas – the Christian framework of redemption and damnation. The speaker claims that for what Maude has done, her soul will not be spared. The quatrain asserts that, even if the speaker had not existed, the man, the speaker's lover, would

never have looked at you.

This hints at Maude's possible motives – jealousy and unrequited love – for informing the parents of the speaker's shame. Maude, it would appear, was in love with the same man.

The fourth quatrain imagines the speakers' parents sleeping in heaven, but asserts that Maude will never sleep again.

The final stanza is two lines longer than all the others – it is as if the speaker has such powerful emotions that she has to break out of the pattern of the quatrain to make room for her intense emotions. She repeats the idea that her parents are not to blame and imagines them in heaven with the appearance of angels: *golden gown, crown.* She even thinks she and her lover have a chance of getting into heaven, but Maude is doomed to Hell:

But sister Maude, oh sister Maude,

Bide you with death and sin.

Death and sin (in Christian thought) live in hell.

This is like a traditional ballad because it tells a story, but so many details are missed out or not given to the reader. We are told nothing about where these people live or anything about their social background. Here is a list of things we do not know – it probably isn't exhaustive:

- What did the speaker's shame consist of?
- Why did the man die?
- Was the man killed?
- If he was killed, who killed him?
- Is her father dead? Line 13 suggests he is.
- Is the mother dead or about to die? Line 15 suggests she is.
- Are the deaths of the parents connected to the death of the lover? Or to the speaker's shame?
- Was the shock of the shame so great that the parents are dying of shock?
- In the final stanza we wonder what the shame was? It wasn't bad enough to send them to hell, because the speaker says that she and her lover might be allowed to enter heaven.

There are no answers to these questions. We can say that these details make the poem more compelling because they are not there and also because the main point of the poem is to convey the speaker's sense of betrayal at the hands of her sister and her overwhelming desire for revenge. The speaker, her lover and her parents will be forgiven in the final stanza, but Maude's betrayal of the lovers is unforgivable. The speaker has been hurt by one of her own family and this is seen in the poem as impossible to forgive.

Why?

This simple, intriguing poem conveys

- a deep sense of betrayal.
- a deep and intense desire for revenge.
- a strong implicit belief in Christian ideas of forgiveness and damnation.
- a sense of mystery by leaving out so many details.

Another Context

Another much less personal context of this poem is the fact that Rossetti was writing her version, her variation, of a poem that has its origins in anonymous ballads. Unusually I have saved this until after you have read the commentary on the poem.

Look carefully at the following two poems. The first is anonymous and was first written down in 1656, but may well date from centuries before, handed down from generation to generation. Lines 2 and 4 of the opening stanza are repeated in every stanza which also suggests that this ballad had originally been sung, with lines 2 and 4 acting as a refrain or chorus.

Two Sisters

There were two sisters, they went playing,
With a hie downe downe a downe-a
To see their father's ships come sayling in.
With a hy downe downe a downe-a

And when they came unto the sea-brynn,
The elder did push the younger in.

'0 sister, 0 sister, take me by the gowne,
And drawe me up upon the dry ground.'

'0 sister, 0 sister, that may not bee,
Till salt and oatmeale grow both of a tree.'

Somtymes she sanke, somtymes she swam,
Until she came unto the mill-dam.

The miller runne hastily downe the cliffe,
And up he betook her withouten her life.

What did he doe with her brest-bone?
He made him a violl to play thereupon.

What did he doe with her fingers so small?
He made him peggs to his violl withall.

What did he doe with her nose-ridge?
Unto his violl he made him a bridge.

What did he doe with her veynes so blew?

He made him strings to his violl thereto.

What did he doe with her eyes so bright?
Upon his violl he played at first sight.

What did he doe with her tongue so rough?
Unto the violl it spake enough.

What did he doe with her two shinnes?
Unto the violl they danc'd Moll Syms.

Then bespake the treble string,
' 0 yonder is my father the king.'

Then bespake the second string,
' 0 yonder sitts my mother the queen.'

And then bespake the strings all three,
' 0 yonder is my sister that drowned mee.'

' Now pay the miller for his payne,
And let him bee gone in the divel's name.'

The second poem is by Alfred Tennyson, a contemporary of Rossetti's.

The Sisters' Shame

We were two daughters of one race;
She was the fairest in the face.
    The wind is blowing in turret and tree.
They were together, and she fell;
Therefore revenge became me well.
    O, the earl was fair to see!

She died; she went to burning flame;
She mix'd her ancient blood with shame.
    The wind is howling in turret and tree.
Whole weeks and months, and early and late,
To win his love I lay in wait.
    O, the earl was fair to see!

I made a feast; I bade him come;
I won his love, I brought him home,
   The wind is roaring in turret and tree.
And after supper on a bed,
Upon my lap he laid his head.
   O, the earl was fair to see!

I kiss'd his eyelids into rest,
His ruddy cheeks upon my breast.
   The wind is raging in turret and tree.
I hated him with the hate of hell,
But I loved his beauty passing well.
   O, the earl was fair to see!

I rose up in the silent night;
I made my dagger sharp and bright.
   The wind is raving in turret and tree.
As half-asleep his breath he drew,
Three time I stabb'd him thro' and thro'.
   O, the earl was fair to see!

I curl'd and comb'd his comely head,
He looked so grand when he was dead.
   The wind is blowing in turret and tree.
I wrapt his body in the sheet,
And laid him at his mother's feet.
   O, the earl was fair to see!

'Sister Maude' is not autobiographical. By reading the original ballad and Tennyson's version of it, we can fill in the missing pieces of Rossetti's poem, although all three versions have slight variations. In the original ballad the jealous older sister kills her prettier younger sister by drowning her in a river; in Tennyson's version the sister not only kills her sister, but also the man they both loved.

Nettles – **Vernon Scannell**

Context

Vernon Scannell (1922 – 2007) was born in Spilsby in Lincolnshire and lead a very interesting life, working as both a teacher and a boxer before becoming a full-time writer. The defining experience of his life was being a soldier in the British Army in the Second World War. He fought in North Africa and took part in the 1944 invasion of Normandy, during which he was wounded. Time and time again in his poetry he returns to the war and his memories of it and how they have altered his life.

nettle bed – an area of neglected land on which lots of nettles grow.

hook – scythe, for chopping down tall plants.

Who? Scannell, his son and the mother (*us* in line 8).

When? When Scannell's son was three.

Where? In the back garden, behind the shed where the nettles grow.

What? The poet's son has fallen in the nettle bed and runs to his parents for comfort. His parents soothe him and then Scannell takes his scythe and cuts the nettles down, before burning them. In two weeks they have grown again.

Commentary

In this poem Scannell explores his feelings of care, gentleness and compassion for his son, taking an incident from his son's childhood as a starting point, it reflects on the relationship between father and son. It is tightly structured in rhyming quatrains, but Scannell uses enjambment extensively to make the poem sound almost like real speech and to draw attention away from the rhyme scheme – except at the very start and end of the poem.

The blunt opening line, expressed in very simple language, tells us all we need to know about the situation:

My son aged three fell in the nettle bed.

This simple statement of fact is then followed by a detailed description of the incident. Scannell then reflects on how inappropriate that word *bed* is for something which causes so much pain. Bed is a place where we rest, but his son is clearly very distressed – he rushes to his parents in sobs and tears and Scannell sees *blisters beaded* on his son's skin. His pain is raw and after a while he has *a watery grin* – he is grinning through the tears. Scannell's reaction then is one of rage and protective anger. He hacks the nettles down – *slashed in fury* – and then burns the nettles in order that his son will not be hurt again. Scannell makes extensive use of alliteration, especially sibilance, to emphasise the strong feelings which this incident provoked as well as strong and vivid verbs like *slashed* and words like *fury* and *fierce*.

Scannell uses an extended metaphor to describe the nettles in military terms, suggesting he has had first-hand experience of warfare and that the nettles are violent and aggressive and opposed to human life: *spears, regiment, parade, the fallen dead, recruits*. This metaphor also personifies the nettles (even the word *pyre* is normally associated with humans), but Scannell also personifies *the busy sun and rain* who in two weeks had *called up tall recruits behind the shed* – more nettles which may hurt his son. The final line is full of foreboding and, like the opening line, makes complete sense on its own:

My son would often feel sharp wounds again.

It is tempting, isn't it, to see in this line not just a warning about the nettles behind the shed which have grown back so quickly, but a warning about the future in general. Then the poem becomes something else: it is grounded in a clearly remembered event from his son's childhood, but it is a lament for the human condition – just by being alive Scannell's son will feel sharp wounds again. You might be tempted to go even further and see the military imagery used about the nettles as a warning of what happens to young men in wars – they die – and Scannell knew this from his own experience in the Second World War. Nature too is very hostile in this poem (it isn't in all the poems in the Anthology): the nettles are obviously dangerous and cause pain, but they are helped to grow by the sun and the rain. And what about the bed? Bed is a place of rest, but it can also be the place where you die.

Why?

This poem, based on an everyday incident:

- is a moving poem about a father's love for his son.

- is a warning about his son's future suffering and regrets that the father will not be able to protect his son forever.

- nature is seen as hostile and threatening to human welfare.

- suffering is an inevitable part of being human.

- future wars will also cause pain and suffering.

Born Yesterday – **Philip Larkin**

Context

Larkin (1922 – 1985) was born in Coventry and went to Oxford during the war where he became close friends with Kingsley Amis (1922 – 1995) – himself a famous novelist and poet. It is Amis's daughter, Sally, to whom this poem is dedicated. She was born on January 17th 1954.

After university Larkin became a university librarian. He never married, had no children, never left England and his poems are very often quite melancholic and cynical and world-weary. 'Born Yesterday' is an exception, I would suggest – although it does celebrate the virtues of being 'dull' – a word that many might be tempted to use of Larkin's own life.

'Born Yesterday' – in the title Larkin may be referring to the idiomatic expression 'Do you think I was born yesterday?' – which means 'Do you think I am stupid?' This could be said to fit with what he says in the poem because part of what he wishes for Sally Amis is being alert and happy.

vigilant – alert, watchful.

enthralled – spellbound.

Who? Larkin and Sally Amis to whom the poem is addressed and dedicated; also the *others* in line 3 and *they* in line 8 which are discussed below.

When? January 18th 1954, the day after Sally's birth because the poem is called *Born Yesterday* – although we know that Larkin did not actually complete the poem until January 20th 1954.

Where? Not specified, but the gentle, kindly tone suggests almost that these words are being spoken aloud to the baby in its crib.

What? Larkin makes a wish for the baby – that she be ordinary; in the second stanza he explores what he means by this rather unusual wish.

Commentary

The arresting opening line:

Tightly-folded bud

with its metaphor suggesting something beautiful and full of life that is about to burst into blossom like a bud, is followed by some very ordinary language in a conversational tone – *stuff, running off, you're a lucky girl* – which is appropriate because the poem is all about being ordinary. You might note that each stanza is one complete sentence. The first stanza refers to what other people would have wished Sally on her birth – which, therefore, makes what Larkin has to offer seem special: other people are referred to rather dismissively as the *others* and *they* and their wishes are stereotypical – *they will all wish you that*.

The second stanza then changes to the present tense and reveals Larkin's wish – that Sally Amis should be ordinary. This is immediately a paradox because we do not associate being ordinary with being happy and fulfilled. The stanza proceeds in a fairly negative tone as Larkin lists the things he does want her to be, largely expressed negatively – *not ugly, not good-looking*. The lines suggest that having some unusual talent or gift will upset your balance and lead to unhappiness. Line 20 concludes that Larkin wishes Sally to be *dull* – a word even more negative than *ordinary*, but it is followed by a dash and Larkin then proceeds to convince us through the words and sound of the poem that being *dull* (as he defines it) is something good, something to aspire to.

How does Larkin achieve this? Well, the dash at the end of line 20 marks a distinct break in the poem and it is followed by a list of five adjectives which are polysyllabic and which produce consonance and, therefore, euphony: look at the repeated *l* sounds in *dull, skilled, vigilant, flexible, enthralled*. It helps, of course, that many of the adjectives have very positive connotations. This long list of adjectives – which speed up the tempo of the poem and which are also such a contrast to the colloquial language Larkin uses earlier in the poem - reach a climax in the final line. The final line is bound together by assonance – *catching, happiness, called* – and the fact that *called* rhymes with *enthralled* ends the poem with a neatness that suggests Larkin has proved his point: being dull can be an extraordinary thing – because the language he uses to describe it is extraordinary. You might note too the metaphor in the final line which combines a very physical image – *catching* – with the abstract noun *happiness*.

So – word choice, rhythm, consonance, assonance and rhyme all play their part in making the last four lines of the poem memorable and in explaining the paradox on which the poem is based – how being ordinary and dull can be a wonderful thing.

Why?

This very personal poem suggests:

- friendship is important. Although the poem could be addressed to any new born baby, Sally's father was Larkin's best friend, so this poem is partly a tribute to their friendship.

- finding happiness can be hard but can be achieved in a quiet, un-dramatic way.

- the usual wishes that people make for a new born child are unrealistic and fanciful.

Final Note

You should read about Sally Amis's life on Wikipedia. She had an unusually unhappy life. She suffered from alcoholism and depression; she gave birth to a child which she gave up for adoption; she was devastated by the death of her father; she died at the age of forty-six.

Does this knowledge of what actually happened to Sally Amis affect your reaction to the poem? It did for me: having read about her life, the next time I read the poem made it seem very sad, because I was painfully aware that the very opposite of Larkin's wish had come true.

Relationships: Connecting the Poems

In this section I will be examining the specimen questions provided by AQA and going on to discuss other ways to connect the poems in this section. The difference between questions on Foundation Tier papers and Higher Tier papers is simple: the Foundation questions use bullet points to guide you in your response to the question.

These questions are for English Literature, Unit 2 entitled *Poetry across time*. You have one hour and 15 minutes to answer the paper. There are two questions on each section of the Anthology; you only answer one. There is also a question on an unseen poem. However, the question on the Anthology carries 36 marks and the advice on the paper is to spend 45 minutes on it. The unseen poem carries only 18 marks and you are advised to spend 30 minutes on it. I deal with the unseen poem at the end of this book. There is also general advice on answering questions in the examination at the end of the book. The questions that follow have been produced by AQA as specimen questions. My answers are simply suggestions.

Compare how feelings towards another person are presented in 'In Paris with You' and one other poem from 'Relationships'.

Remember to compare:

- **what the feelings in the poems are.**

- **how the feelings are presented.**

'In Paris with You' by James Fenton presents his feelings towards his new lover in a light-hearted and comical way; Mimi Klavati's 'Ghazal' is also addressed to a potential lover, but her use of imagery and the traditional form of the ghazal produces a completely different effect.

Fenton's poem begins – *Don't talk to me of love* – and it emerges that he is *on the rebound*, seeking solace after the end of a relationship.

Fenton's language is colloquial, everyday and the comic tone is established by invented words like *maroonded* and outrageous rhymes like *Elysées* with *sleazy*. By contrast, Khalvati idealizes herself and her future lover through a series of metaphors drawn from the natural world: in the opening couplet she is the *grass* and he is the *breeze* and she invites him to *blow through me*; she is the *rose* and he is the *bird* and she asks him to *woo me*. In one sense the feelings in both poems are very similar: both poets want a sexual relationship with the person to whom the poem is addressed, but there the similarities end.

Fenton's poem is also comical because he is grouchy and irritated at the thought of having to visit the traditional tourist sites of Paris: his use of taboo words – *sodding* – reveals his casual attitude. The British image of Paris as a place for romance and love is undercut by Fenton's desire to stay in the hotel room:

Doing this and that

To what and whom

Learning who you are

Learning who I am.

He wants to explore his new lover physically, but has already rejected the idea that this might be love. Fenton seems to want intimate but casual sex, as the reference to *all points south* makes clear.

Khalvati also imagines a sexual relationship with her lover as certain lines make clear. She invites her lover to

come and I'll come too when you cue me

and begs him to

die for my sake, my love, every night bedew me.

The difference lies in Khalvati's use of romantic and idealistic metaphors which make her physical need for her lover sound more magical, more intense than Fenton's and this formal structure of the ghazal gives her feelings a certain harmony. Khalvati can look forward to a time when they are just good friends; Fenton can only see *the little bit of Paris in our view* – the hotel room they are in. Nonetheless, Fenton is clearly obsessed with his new acquaintance – he uses *you* or *your* six times in the final stanza and he seems to be delighted to be in Paris with her.

Both poems explore the excitement of a new relationship – one in a cynical, comic way, the other in a romantic, idealized way.

Compare how family relationships are shown in 'Nettles' and one other poem from 'Relationships'.

Remember to compare:

- **what the relationships in the poem are.**
- **how the relationships are presented.**

Vernon Scannell in 'Nettles' and Grace Nichols in 'Praise Song for My Mother' both show family relationships. 'Nettles' deals with the father/son relationship from the father's point of view, while 'Praise Song for My Mother' shows the mother/daughter relationship from the point of view of the daughter.

In both poems the relationship between parent and child is strong, secure and full of love and protection. In 'Nettles' Scannell's son falls in the nettle bed and seeks his parents for comfort:

We soothed him till his pain was not so raw.

The poet then takes revenge on the nettles by chopping them down and burning them. He will do anything to protect his son.

'Nettles' deals with one incident in Scannell's son's childhood; 'Praise Song for My Mother' describes in a more general way the role that Nichols' mother played in her life. Nichols expresses her mother's role through a series of metaphors drawn from nature: her mother was *water*, *moon's eye* and *sunrise to me* – which suggests that a mother's love is natural and inevitable. Line 12 in particular describes her mother as

the flame tree's spread to me,

which suggests that she protected her, just as Scannell tries to do in 'Nettles'.

Although both poems show the parent/child relationship as full of love and protection, they present the world in different ways. Nichols's poem only mentions very good things about her mother: the language she uses is positive and closely associated with her Caribbean background – *the crab's leg/the fried plantain smell*. The metaphors she uses to describe her mother are all drawn from nature. Scannell sees the world as far more hostile: he uses an extended military metaphor which presents the nettles as enemy soldiers: the nettles are a *regiment of spite behind the shed.*

They form a *fierce parade* and have *green spears* – they seem only to exist to harm his son and, despite his burning them, in two weeks they have grown again.

The last lines of both poems are strikingly similar because they both look to the future. In 'Praise Song for My Mother' Nichols' mother says

Go to your wide futures,

an instruction which is full of optimism and a sense of the vast opportunities of life. By contrast, Scannell observes

My son would often feel sharp wounds again

which foresees all the future suffering that his son will have to endure as he goes through life and suggests too that Scannell will be unable to protect him forever.

These two poems show parent/child relationships in a remarkably similar way, but have completely different tones because they present life in completely different ways. Nichols associates her mother with Guyana and is very nostalgic for home; Scannell uses the nettles to symbolize all the things in life that might harm our children.

Compare how feelings towards another person are presented in 'Hour' and one other poem from 'Relationships'.

'Hour' by Carol Ann Duffy and 'Sonnet 43' by Elizabeth Barrett Browning are both sonnets addressed to a person with whom the poet is deeply in love. However, while the feelings in each poem are broadly similar – both poets seem completely devoted to the one they love – the feelings are presented in radically different ways.

Duffy describes one hour spent with her lover; in contrast Barrett Browning sets out to define the ways in which she loves her future husband. So 'Hour' is descriptive, while 'Sonnet 43' is analytical. Both poems are written in the present tense, although Barrett Browning does use the future tense at the very end of the poem.

'Hour' differs from 'Sonnet 43' because Duffy uses rich imagery to present her feelings. In Duffy's poem, love transforms her lover in magical and miraculous ways. Duffy's sonnet says that her lover is transformed by the *Midas light* of the sun which turns her limbs to gold; she uses a simile – *like treasure on the ground* – to describe her lover's hair; they kiss near a *grass ditch*. In Duffy's poem there is a greater sense of the physical world – because the lovers actually kiss and because we are told of their surroundings. Duffy even has a turn in line 9 where she rejects the stereotyped 'props' of romantic love – jewels, candles, chandeliers.

In contrast Barrett Browning uses hardly any figurative language. Her tone is confident and assertive, and the sonnet revolves around the repetition of *I love thee* – which is followed by several different ways in which she loves her future husband. Unlike Duffy's poem, Barrett Browning's does not seem to have a particular setting and there are hardly any details of the physical world of the lovers. Her love is defined in terms of abstract concepts: Grace, Right, Praise.

Although superficially similar in their strong feelings of love, these poems present their feelings very differently. Duffy's poem is far more rooted in reality, whereas Barrett Browning's is full of abstract concepts with a strongly Christian ethos. Both poets could be said to present the feelings towards the other person as overwhelmingly positive and all-consuming: both poems focus solely on the poet's lover.

I think there is another key difference: Barrett Browning ends her poem by asserting that she will love her husband even better after death – she looks to the distant future and is confident that her love will remain unchanged. Is Duffy's love more temporary? We cannot be sure, but perhaps the title – 'Hour' – which focuses on sixty minutes in the lovers' lives, hints at the possibility that this hour is a magical one, but there will be other hours which are less fulfilling and harmonious.

Compare how poets use language to present feelings in 'Quickdraw' and one other poem from 'Relationships'.

Carol Ann Duffy in 'Quickdraw' and Andrew Marvell in 'To His Coy Mistress' both use language to present feelings – but with very different effects. Duffy is describing a relationship which is breaking down, but Marvell is urging his lover to have sex with him. Both poems use imagery which is striking and unusual, and both reflect their meaning through rhythm.

The breakdown of the relationship in 'Quickdraw' is mirrored in the movement of the poem. There are strong caesuras in the middle of lines, enjambment and many short statements which reflect the messages that the lovers are exchanging. The poem has a disjointed feel which appropriately reflects the relationship breaking down. In

'To His Coy Mistress' the rhythm gradually gets faster and faster as the poem proceeds, which reflects the urgency Marvell feels and mirrors the rhythms of sex. In the first section of the poem the rhythm is slow and leisurely as Marvell describes how he might love her if he had enough time. He introduces the idea of death in the second section and then imagines the sexual act in the final, climactic section.

Both poets use imagery to present their feelings. Duffy uses an extended metaphor based on Western gun-fighters: this works in two ways. Firstly, it adds an element of violence to the exchange: Duffy's lover's words are *pellets*, her kisses *silver bullets*; the speaker groans, reels and is blasted through the heart. Secondly, these images are such clichés that they also add an element of humour: an argument with a lover may be painful but you don't end up riddled with bullets. Marvell's imagery is more varied because his poem is longer and because in it he writes as a three-part argument. The first section is full of exotic, hyperbolic imagery: Ganges and rubies, and imagery which is full of sexual suggestion like his *vegetable love* which will grow *vaster than empires*. Marvell continues to use language in this way in the second section with the image of worms trying *that long preserved virginity* and the crude pun of *quaint honour*. In the third section his imagery contains violence, just as 'Quickdraw' does, but he uses it to present sex as involving pain mingled with great pleasure: he and his lover will be *like amorous birds of prey* and they will *tear* their pleasures *with rough strife through the iron gates of life*.

Both poems end memorably. The repetition in Duffy's represents the text message that she sends and re-sends and, with the extended metaphor in mind, the bullets that she is firing at her lover; Marvell's ends with the couple, in the poem and in his imagination, reaching the climax of orgasm.

Both poems use language to present different aspects of love, but the language in both poems adds humour: Duffy through her adoption of the clichés of Western movies and Marvell through his sexual suggestiveness which even extends to the rhythm of the poem.

Other thoughts

Of course, you cannot predict what questions will come up in the examination, but you can do some thinking before the exam and select poems that work well together for various reasons. You will still need to do some quick thinking in the exam AND you must answer the question that has been asked: you cannot simply write about two poems that in your preparation you have decided go well together. What follows now are some brief notes which give some examples of poems that work well together, depending on the question. These are not exclusive – I am sure you can make connections which I have not spotted or thought of.

'Praise Song for My Mother' and 'Ghazal' would work well together because, although the subject matter is very different, both poets are writing in a non-European tradition and using a form of poem from a different culture.

'Quickdraw' and 'In Paris with You' might go well together because they both contain different types of humour and are also based on cultural allusions – the clichés of Western films in Duffy's poem and our notions of Paris as a tourist destination in Fenton's. If you accept my reading of 'To His Coy Mistress' then this too would work well.

Some of the poems in the section deal with children and any two of the following might go well together if childhood is the basis of the question: 'Brothers', 'Praise Song for My Mother', 'Nettles', 'Born Yesterday'.

'Harmonium' and 'Praise Song for My Mother' specifically deal with the parent/child relationship when the child is an adult and, therefore, might make a good pairing.

'Manhunt' and 'Nettles' might be linked by the fact that one is about the aftermath of war and its effect on a relationship, while Scannell's poem uses imagery and metaphors from war to present the nettles.

'Harmonium' and 'To His Coy Mistress' – while being strikingly different poems – both have a strong sense of impending death – although they deal with it in very different ways.

'Sister Maude' (which, of course, presents relationships within a family) could be usefully linked to 'The Farmer's Bride' because both use a narrator who is not the poet; in a sense, both poems are dramatic monologues. And both present a love which has gone wrong.

'Ghazal', 'To His Coy Mistress' and 'In Paris with You' all deal with sex and any two of these three would work well together in any answer about physical love.

'Hour', 'Sonnet 43' and 'Sonnet 116' all show love which is going well (I am referring here to the conventional reading of the Shakespeare sonnet.)

By contrast, 'Quickdraw', 'Sister Maude' and 'The Farmer's Bride' all show romantic love which, in different ways and for different reasons, is not going well.

Finally, within the section, there is a group of poems which deal with family: 'Brothers', 'Harmonium. 'Nettles', 'Sister Maude' and 'Praise Song for My Mother'. Any pairing of any of these might work, if the question focuses on the presentation of family.

The Examination

- Always use the surname of the poet. Don't write *in the poem the punk is a marginalized outsider*; instead write *in the poem Armitage presents the punk as a marginalized outsider.* This shows the examiner that you are aware that the poet has deliberately shaped and crafted the poem in order to achieve a certain effect.

- Make as many intelligent points as you can about the poet's use of language and poetic techniques. Try to ensure that you communicate to the examiner your clear understanding that you are writing about poetry – use the vocabulary this book uses to describe the way a poem is written. When a question asks you how something is presented, the answer will always involve the words that the poet uses – the only way anything is presented in literature is through words and their patterning.

- You are being assessed on your understanding of the poems and your ability to appreciate the poets' use of language BUT ALSO on your ability to COMPARE the poems.

- You are asked to compare two poems in some way and that implies that the poems are linked. BUT they are already linked by being in the same section of the Anthology, so write about points of comparison, but remember that it is where the poems differ that they become really interesting and that will allow you to demonstrate your understanding of their differences. For example, in the section 'Character and Voice', 'Medusa' and 'The River God' are astonishingly similar: they both deal with mythical figures and they both reveal attitudes towards women and love, but the tone of each poem is very different. How is the tone created? Through words and the pattern of the poem.

- The question will name one poem and ask you to choose another to write about. Give yourself some quick thinking time to think of the best poem to choose to go with the one they have asked you to write on. You have to think quickly, but the choice is vital. If you have revised really thoroughly and feel confident about all the poems, you will quickly make a decision about which poem to choose. You need one that fits the question and goes well with the poem named, but has enough differences too, to allow you to say interesting things about how they differ.

- Use short quotations to support your points as often as you can. You can read the commentaries again: I have tried wherever possible to write using short quotations, so that you can use my writing as a model for your own.

- A weak essay structure – if you are writing about two poems – is to write the first half of the essay on one poem and the use the second half of the essay to write about the second poem. In every paragraph try to compare some aspect of both poems: this is important because the task asks you to compare – and you are more likely to fulfil that task if you write about both poems in the same paragraph. In the way I have dealt with the specimen questions, I have tried to model this for you.

- Finally, and perhaps, most importantly, always be aware in what you write that the two poems may have been written in very different circumstances. The context of each poem is different. For example, in 'Characters and Voices' Hardy's 'The Ruined Maid' is a reflection of its time and Victorian attitudes to the rural working class; by contrast, 'Singh Song' is a product of a very modern, multi-cultural society; in 'Place' Wordsworth is heavily influenced by ideas of pantheism, whereas 'Neighbours' could only have been written in the nuclear era and 'The Moment' is an expression of our growing concern with Green issues and the environment – which is a very modern phenomenon. In 'Conflict' Tennyson's 'The Charge of the Light Brigade' reflects the attitudes to war shared by many people in mid-Victorian society, whereas many of the poets in the section deal with the new realities of terrorism – and so what they write and the way they write it will inevitably differ. In 'Relationships' 'Quickdraw' uses modern technology, whereas Marvell's 'To His Coy Mistress' is a carpe diem poem written against the background of the English Civil War. This does not mean that the examiner should be treated to vast amounts of background information at all – that is a waste of words – but your answer should communicate your awareness that the poems' contexts might be very different. Even the gender of the poet can be significant.

The Unseen Poem

In the English Literature examination you will also be asked a question on a poem you have never seen or studied before – it's usually known as the 'unseen'. Your teacher will have given you lots of practice and may have even used some of the poems in the Anthology as if they were unseen poems. In a sense, the way you approach the unseen poem should be the same as you approach any poem – after all, they are all 'unseen' when you encounter them for the first time. This poem is by Vernon Scannell whom some of you will know from the 'Relationships' section of the Anthology. Read it carefully and try, as a starting point, to apply the first four Ws. You will find a commentary on the poem at the very end of the book, after the glossary.

Gunpowder Plot

For days these curious cardboard buds have lain
In brightly coloured boxes. Soon the night
Will come. We pray there'll be no sullen rain
To make these solid orchids flame less bright.

Now in the garden's darkness they begin   5
To flower; the frenzied whizz of Catherine-wheel
Puts forth its fiery petals and the thin
Rocket soars to burst upon the the steel

Bulwark of a cloud. And then the guy,
Absurdly human phoenix, is again   10
Gulped by greedy flames: the harvest sky
Is flecked with threshed and glittering golden grain.

'Uncle! A cannon! Watch me as I light it!'
The women, helter-skelter, squealing high,
Retreat; the paper fuse is quickly lit,   15
A cat-like hiss and spit of fire, a sly

Falter, then the air is shocked with blast.
The cannon bangs, and in my nostrils drifts
A bitter scent that brings the lurking past

Lurching to my side. The present shifts,   20

Allows a ten-year memory to walk
Unhindered now; and so I'm forced to hear
The banshee howl of mortar and the talk
Of men who died; am forced to face my fear.

I listen for a moment to the guns,   25
The torn earth's grunts, recalling how I prayed.
The past retreats. I hear a corpse's sons:
'Who's scared of bangers?' 'Uncle! John's afraid!'
VERNON SCANNELL

----

phoenix – a mythical bird that dies by fire, but is then re-born from its ashes.

helter-skelter – in a confused hurry.

banshee – a fairy who loudly wails and shrieks before there is a death in the human family to which she is attached.

mortar – a short piece of army artillery for throwing a bomb.

Glossary

The Oxford Concise Dictionary of Literary Terms has been invaluable in writing this section of the book. I would again remind the reader that knowledge of these terms is only the start – do NOT define a word you find here in the examination. You can take it for granted that the examiner knows the term: it is up to you to try to use it confidently and with precision and to·explain why the poet uses it or what effect it has on the reader.

ALLITERATION	the repetition of the same sounds – usually initial consonants or stressed syllables – in any sequence of closely adjacent words.
ALLUSION	an indirect or passing reference to some event, person, place or artistic work which is not explained by the writer, but which relies on the reader's familiarity with it.
AMBIGUITY	openness to different interpretations.
ASSONANCE	the repetition of similar vowel sounds in neighbouring words.
ASYNDETIC	an asyndetic list is a list of words not separated by any intervening words.
BALLAD	a folk song or orally transmitted poem telling in a simple and direct way a story with a tragic ending. Ballads are normally composed in quatrains with the second and fourth lines rhyming. Such quatrains are known as the ballad stanza because of its frequent use in what we call ballads.
BLANK VERSE	unrhymed lines of ten syllable length. This is a widely used form by Shakespeare in his plays, by Milton and by Wordsworth.

CAESURA

any pause in a line of verse caused by punctuation. This can draw attention to what precedes or follows the caesura and also, by breaking up the rhythm of the line, can slow the poem down and make it more like ordinary speech.

CANON

a body of writings recognized by authority. The canon of a national literature is a body of writings especially approved by critics or anthologists and deemed suitable for academic study. Towards the end of the 20th century there was a general feeling that the canon of English Literature was dominated by dead, white men and since then there has been a deliberate and fruitful attempt made to give more prominence to writing by women and by writers from non-white backgrounds. Even your Anthology is a contribution to the canon, because someone sat down and decided that the poems included in it were worthy of study by students taking GCSE.

CARPE DIEM

a Latin phrase from the Roman poet Horace which means 'seize the day' – 'make the best of the present moment'. It is a very common theme of European lyric poetry, in which the speaker of a poem argues that since time is short and death is inevitable, pleasure should be enjoyed while there is still time.

COLLOCATION

the act of putting two words together. What this means in practice is that certain words have very common collocations – in other words they are usually found in written or spoken English in collocation with other words. For example, the word *Christmas* is often collocated with words such as *cards*, *presents*, *carols*, *holidays*, but you won't often find it collocated with *sadness*. This can be an important term because poets, who are seeking to use words in original ways, will often put two words together which are not often collocated.

COLLOQUIALISM   the use of informal expressions or vocabulary appropriate to everyday speech rather than the formality of writing. When used in poetry it can make the poem seem more down-to-earth and real, more honest and intimate.

CONCEIT   an unusually far-fetched metaphor presenting a surprising and witty parallel between two apparently dissimilar things or feelings.

CONSONANCE   the repetition of identical or similar consonants in neighbouring words whose vowel sounds are different.

CONTEXT   the biographical, social, cultural and historical circumstances in which a text is produced and read and understood – you might like to think of it as its background. However, it is important sometimes to consider the reader's own context – especially when we look back at poems from the Literary Heritage. To interpret a poem with full regard to its background is to contextualize it.

COUPLET   a pair of rhyming verse lines, usually of the same length.

CROSSED RHYME   the rhyming of one word in the middle of a long line of poetry with a word in a similar position in the next line.

DIALECT   a distinctive variety of language, spoken by members of an identifiable regional group, nation or social class. Dialects differ from one another in pronunciation, vocabulary and grammar. Traditionally they have been looked down on and viewed as variations from an educated 'standard' form of the language, but linguists point out that standard forms themselves are merely dialects which have come to dominate for social and political reasons. In English this notion of dialect is especially important because English is spoken all over the world and there are variations between the English spoken in, say, Yorkshire, Delhi and Australia. Dialects now are increasingly celebrated as a distinct way of speaking and writing which are integral to our identity.

DICTION — the choice of words used in any literary work.

DISSONANCE — harshness of sound.

DRAMATIC MONOLOGUE — a kind of poem in which a single fictional or historical character (not the poet) speaks to a silent audience and unwittingly reveals the truth about their character.

ELEGY — a lyric poem lamenting the death of a friend or public figure or reflecting seriously on a serious subject. The word *elegiac* has come to refer to the mournful mood of such poems.

ELLIPSIS — the omission from a sentence of a word or words which would be required for complete clarity. It is used all the time in everyday speech, but is often used in poetry to promote compression and/or ambiguity. The adjective is elliptical.

END-RHYME — rhyme occurring at the end of a line of poetry. The most common form of rhyme.

END-STOPPED — a line of poetry brought to a pause by the use of punctuation. The opposite of enjambment.

ENJAMBMENT	caused by the lack of punctuation at the end of a line of poetry, this causes the sense (and the voice when the poem is read aloud) to 'run over' into the next line. In general, this can impart to poems the feel of ordinary speech, but there are examples in the Anthology of more precise reasons for the poet to use enjambment.
EPIPHANY	a sudden moment of insight or revelation, usually at the end of a poem.
EPIZEUXIS	the technique by which a word is repeated for emphasis with no other words intervening.
EUPHONY	a pleasing smoothness of sound.
FIGURATIVE	Not literal. Obviously 'figurative' language covers metaphor and simile and personification.
FIGURE OF SPEECH	any expression which departs from the ordinary literal sense or normal order of words. Figurative language (the opposite of literal language) includes metaphor, simile and personification. Some figures of speech – such as alliteration and assonance achieve their effects through the repetition of sounds.
FOREGROUNDING	giving unusual prominence to one part of a text. Poetry differs from everyday speech and prose by its use of regular rhythm, metaphors, alliteration and other devices by which its language draws attention to itself.
FREE VERSE	a kind of poetry that does not conform to any regular pattern of line length or rhyme. The length of its lines are irregular as is its use of rhyme – if any.
HALF-RHYME	an imperfect rhyme – also known as para-rhyme, near rhyme and slant rhyme – in which the final consonants but the vowel

sounds do not match. Pioneered in the 19th century by Emily Dickinson and Gerard Manley Hopkins, and made even more popular by Wilfred Owen and T S Eliot in the early 20th century,

HOMONYM   a word that is identical to another word either in sound or in spelling.

HOMOPHONE   a word that is pronounced in the same way as another word but which differs in meaning and/or spelling.

HYPERBOLE   exaggeration for the sake of emphasis.

IDIOM   an everyday phrase that cannot be translated literally because its meaning does not correspond to the specific words in the phrase. There are thousands in English like – *you get up my nose, when pigs fly, she was all ears*.

IMAGERY   a rather vague critical term covering literal and metaphorical language which evoke sense impressions with reference to concrete objects – the things the writer describes.

INTERNAL RHYME   a poetic device in which two or more words in the same line rhyme.

INTERTEXTUALITY   the relationship that a text may have with another preceding and usually well-known text.

INVERSION   the reversal of the normally expected order or words. 'Normally expected' means how we might say the words in the order of normal speech; to invert the normal word order usually draws attention to or foregrounds the words.

JUXTAPOSITION   two things that are placed alongside each other.

LAMENT   any poem expressing profound grief usually in the face of death.

LATINATE	Latinate diction in English means the use of words derived from Latin rather than those derived from Old English.
LITOTES	understatement – the opposite of hyperbole.
LYRIC	any fairly short poem expressing the personal mood of the speaker.
METAPHOR	the most important figure of speech in which one thing is referred to by a word normally associated with another thing, so as to suggest some common quality shared by both things. In metaphor, this similarity is directly stated, unlike in a simile where the resemblance is indirect and introduced by the words *like* or *as*. Much of our everyday language is made up of metaphor too – to say *someone is as greedy as a pig* is a simile; to say *he is a pig* is a metaphor.
METAPHYSICAL POETS	the name given to a group of 17th century poets whose work is characterized by intellectual concepts, surprising conceits, strange paradoxes and far-fetched imagery.
MNEMONIC	a form of words or letters that helps people remember things. It is common in everyday sayings and uses some of the features of language that we associate with poetry. For example, the weather saying 'Red sky at night, shepherd's delight' uses rhyme.
MONOLOGUE`	an extended speech uttered by one speaker.
NARRATOR	the one who tells or is assumed to be the voice of the poem.
OCTAVE or OCTET	a group of eight lines forming the first part of a sonnet.
ONOMATOPOEIA	the use of words that seem to imitate the sounds they refer to (*bang, whizz, crackle, fizz*) or any combination or words in which

the sound echoes or seems to echo the sense. The adjective is onomatopoeic, so you can say that *blast* is an onomatopoeic word.

ORAL TRADITION   the passing on from one generation to another of songs, chants, poems, proverbs by word of mouth and memory.

OXYMORON   a figure of speech that combines two seemingly contradictory terms as in the everyday terms bitter-sweet and living death.

PARALLELISM   the arrangement of similarly constructed clauses, phrases, sentences or lines of poetry.

PARADOX   a statement which is self-contradictory.

PATHETIC FALLACY   this is the convention that natural phenomena (usually the weather) are a reflection of the poet's or the narrator's mood. It may well involve the personification of things in nature, but does not have to. At its simplest, a writer might choose to associate very bad weather with a mood of depression and sadness.

PERSONA   the assumed identity or fictional narrator assumed by a writer.

PERSONIFICATION   a figure of speech in which animals, abstract ideas or lifeless things are referred to as if they were human. Sometimes known as personal metaphor.

PETRARCHAN   characteristic of the Italian poet Petrarch (1304–1374). Mainly applied to the Petrarchan sonnet which is different in its form from the Shakespearean sonnet.

PHONETIC SPELLING   a technique writers use which involves misspelling a word in order to imitate the accent in which the word is said.

PLOSIVE	explosive. Used to describe sounds that we form by putting our lips together such as *b* and *p*.
POSTCOLONIAL LITERATURE	a term devised to describe what used to be called Commonwealth Literature (and before that Empire Writing!), the term covers a very wide range of writing from countries that were once colonies of European countries. It has come to include some writing by writers of non-white racial backgrounds whose roots or family originated in former colonies – no matter where they live now.
PUN	an expression that derives humour either through using a word that has two distinct meanings or two similar sounding words (homophones).
QUATRAIN	a verse stanza of four lines – usually rhymed.
REFRAIN	a line, or a group of lines, repeated at intervals throughout a poem – usually at regular intervals and at the end of a stanza.
RHYME	the identity of sound between syllables or paired groups of syllables usually at the end of a line of poetry.
RHYME SCHEME	the pattern in which the rhymed line endings are arranged in any poem or stanza. This is normally written as a sequence of letters where each line ending in the same rhyme is given the same alphabetical letter. So a Shakespearean sonnet's rhyme scheme is ababcdcdefefgg, but the rhyme scheme of a Petrarchan sonnet is abbaabbacdecde. In other poems the rhyme scheme might be arranged to suit the poet's convenience or intentions. For example, in Blake's 'London' the first stanza rhymes abab, the

second cdcd and so on.

RHYTHM	a pattern of sounds which is repeated with the stress falling on the same syllables (more or less) in each line. However, variations to the pattern, especially towards the end of the poem, often stand out and are foregrounded because they break the pattern the poet has built up through the course of the poem.
ROMANTICISM	the name given to the artistic movement that emerged in England and Germany in the 1790s and in the rest of Europe in the 1820s and beyond. It was a movement that saw great changes in literature, painting, sculpture, architecture and music and found its catalyst in the new philosophical ideas of Jean Jacques Rousseau and Thomas Paine, and in response to the French and Industrial Revolutions. Its chief emphasis was on freedom of individual self-expression, sincerity, spontaneity and originality, but it also looked to the distant past of the Middle Ages for some of its inspiration.
SATIRE	any type of writing which exposes and mocks the foolishness or evil of individuals, institutions or societies. A poem can be satiric (adjective) or you can say a poet satirizes something or somebody.
SESTET	a group of six lines forming the second half of a sonnet, following the octet.
SIBILANCE	the noticeable recurrence of *s* sounds.
SIMILE	an explicit comparison between two different things, actions or feelings, usually introduced by *like* or *as*.
SONNET	a lyric poem of 14 lines of equal length. The form originated in Italy and was made famous as a vehicle for love poetry by

Petrarch and came to be adopted throughout Europe. The standard subject matter of early sonnets was romantic love, but in the 17th century John Donne used it to write religious poetry and John Milton wrote political sonnets, so it came to be used for any subject matter. The sonnet form enjoyed a revival in the Romantic period (Wordsworth, Keats and Shelley all wrote them) and continues to be widely used today. Some poets have written connected series of sonnets and these are known as sonnet cycles. Petrarchan sonnets differ slightly in their rhyme scheme from Shakespearean sonnets (see the entry above on rhyme scheme). A Petrarchan sonnet consists of two quatrains (the octet) followed by two tercets (the sestet). A Shakespearean sonnet consists of two quatrains (the octet) followed by another quatrain and a final couplet (the sestet).

STANZA

a group of verse lines forming a section of a poem and sharing the same structure in terms of the length of the lines, the rhyme scheme and the rhythm.

STYLE

any specific way of using language, which is characteristic of an author, a period, a type of poetry or a group of writers.

SYLLOGISM

a form of logical argument that draws a conclusion from two propositions. It is very characteristic of Metaphysical poetry and is exemplified in the anthology by Marvell's 'To His Coy Mistress'.

SYMBOL

anything that represents something else. A national flag symbolizes the country that uses it; symbols are heavily used in road signs. In poetry symbols can represent almost anything. Blake's 'The Sick Rose' and Armitage's 'Harmonium' are two good examples of symbols dealt with in this book.

SYNECDOCHE   a figure of speech in which a thing or person is referred to indirectly, either by naming some part of it (*hands* for manual labourers) or by naming some big thing of which it is a part (*the law* for police officers). As you can see from these examples, it is a common practice in speech.

TONE   a critical term meaning the mood or atmosphere of a piece of writing. It may also include the sense of the writer's attitude to the reader of the subject matter.

TURN   the English term for a sudden change in mood or line of argument, especially in line 9 of a sonnet.

VERSE   another word for poetry as opposed to prose. The use of the word 'verse' sometimes implies writing that rhymes and has a rhythm, but perhaps lacks the merit of real poetry.

VERSE PARAGRAPH   a group of lines of poetry forming a section of a poem, the length of the unit being determined by the sense rather than a particular stanza pattern. Marvell's 'To His Coy Mistress' consists of verse paragraphs.

VOLTA   the Italian term for the 'turn' in the argument or mood of a sonnet which normally occurs in the ninth line at the start of the sestet, but sometimes in Shakespearean sonnets is delayed until the final couplet.

WIT   a general term which covers the idea of intelligence, but refers in poetry more specifically to verbal ingenuity and cleverness.

Analysis of 'Gunpowder Plot'

Who? The narrator of the poem, women (wives and mothers, we might assume), children.

When? November 5th, 1954 or 1955. If we assume Scannell is thinking about his experiences in the Second World War, then the poem must be set in the mid-fifties because he refers to a *ten year old memory*. Scannell uses the present tense for much of the poem to give it added immediacy and impact. After the Second World War British soldiers fought in the Korean War, were fighting Communist guerrillas in the Malayan Emergency and, because of the Cold War, Scannell was writing at a time when war against the Soviet Union was a constant fear. Remember this contextual information when we reach the end of the analysis.

Where? A back garden in England.

What? There is a Bonfire Night party which has been eagerly looked forward to. The explosions and sounds are beautiful, but they remind the narrator of his wartime experiences and he remembers the fear he felt ten years ago. Towards the end of the poem it is revealed that some of the boys have lost their father in a war – the poet hears a corpse's sons talking.

This poem is similar in many ways to 'Nettles', also by Vernon Scannell, because it takes a very ordinary incident – Bonfire Night parties and firework displays are part of English culture - and then towards the end it becomes a very different poem, before ending with an ironic last line.

Scannell also uses a very highly structured form – quatrains with a strict rhyme scheme, but then also uses enjambment to take emphasis away from the rhyme scheme and make parts of the poem sound more like ordinary speech: this suits the ordinariness of the subject matter. It is also similar to 'Nettles' in the way Scannell returns to his memories of war. The difference is that 'Nettles' began with his son's suffering and introduced the extended military metaphor in the second line of the poem. Here, however, the memories of war do not begin until the final two stanzas.

What is extraordinary is the <u>sound</u> of the poem; Scannell makes extensive use of onomatopoeia – sometimes combined with alliteration. Examples of alliteration are: *whizz, burst, squealing, hiss, spit, shocked, blast, bangs, banshee howl, grunts*. Even the word used to describe the women rushing away as a firework is lit – *helter-skelter* – has an onomatopoeic quality to it. Of course, writing about a firework party gives the poet many opportunities to imitate the sounds he hears.

The first four stanzas are full of the excitement and sounds of a firework party. There is an extended metaphor which compares the fireworks to flowers or grain – flowers are attractive and grain is useful, so this very positive opening gives no hint about the development of the poem. These are the words that Scannell uses to develop this metaphor: *buds, orchids, flower, petals, grain, harvest sky.*

Scannell uses assonance brilliantly to give the poem extra aural coherence: *s<u>o</u>lid <u>o</u>rchids, m<u>a</u>ke/fl<u>a</u>me, g<u>a</u>rden's/d<u>a</u>rkness, fl<u>e</u>cked/thr<u>e</u>shed, h<u>i</u>ss/sp<u>i</u>t, l<u>u</u>rking/l<u>u</u>rching.* There is also widespread use of alliteration: *curious/cardboard/coloured; buds, brightly, boxes; flower, frenzied, forth, fiery; soars, steel; burst, bulwark; guy, gulped, greedy; glittering golden grain; blast, bangs, bitter; forced, face, fear.* So with these three features – onomatopoeia, assonance and alliteration – Scannell uses sound to bring the firework party alive to our ears and to make the poem more memorable.

But then in stanza 5 when the *cannon bangs*, Scannell's memories of war return: there is a sense that he cannot control his own memories. The *lurching past* and the *ten-year memory* are personified and, because of this, seem to have a life of their own which the poet cannot control. Instead of fireworks he now hears the *banshee howl of mortar, the talk of men who died*, the grunts of the *torn earth* – and he revisits his fear of battle and warfare.

Then in the last two lines the poet returns to the present. Two of the children are talking. The children are the poet's nephews – one calls him *uncle*. Their father, Scannell's brother, has died in the war: they are a corpse's sons. One is teasing the other about being scared of bangers and the other says, in the poem's final words: *'Uncle! John's afraid.'* This is a poignant sentence, said in childish innocence and perhaps typical of the way small boys might tease each other. However, given Scannell's own fear, there is a sense in which John is right to be afraid – war is a frightening thing and the poem ends on the innocent words of a child – who may, in a future war, come to realize that it is natural to be frightened in this way.

Now when we look back at the poem as a whole, the title seems deliberately ambiguous: clearly it refers to the original plot of Guy Fawkes to blow up parliament, but it takes on an added paranoia as if the Bonfire Night party is a 'plot' to force Scannell to remember his terrible experiences in the war.

There are all sorts of clever things going on in this poem to do with words: note that in the first stanza the people in the poem *pray* there will be no rain to spoil the Firework Party – here the prayer is casual, everyday. In the final stanza, as Scannell recalls his experiences in the war, he remembers *how I prayed* – the desperate, frightened prayers of a man in combat. In the final stanza note too how as Scannell forces himself back to the present and the memories fade – *the past retreats* – just as an army might do in battle. Although this is, finally, an intensely personal poem, the word *I* (referring to the poet) is delayed until the penultimate stanza: this suggests that before that the poet had been part of the communal celebration.

Why?

Readers in the UK will be very familiar with the rituals of Bonfire Night, including the burning of the guy. This poem based on an annual event shows:

- that memory and the past are very powerful and can come back to haunt us.

- that the loss of your brother in war is a haunting and appalling experience.

- that war is a terrible and traumatic experience. (Is there a warning that war might recur – just as Bonfire Night is celebrated every year?).

- how the poet skilfully uses sound effects, personification and direct speech to create atmosphere and to make his poem memorable.

- that children in their innocence do not understand the terrors of the adult world – the child's teasing of John in the last line demonstrates that they do not understand the horrors of war.